2008 road atlas

UNITED STATES • CANADA • MEX...

T5-AQQ-381

Map Contents

Legend

TRANSPORTATION

CONTROLLED ACCESS HIGHWAYS
Freeway
Tollway; Toll Booth
Under Construction
Interchange and Exit Number
Rest Area; Service Area
Yellow with facilities; City maps only

OTHER HIGHWAYS
Primary Highway
Secondary Highway
Multilane Divided Highway
Primary and Secondary highways only; City maps only
Multilane Divided Highway
State and province maps only
Other Paved Road
State and province maps only
Other Paved Road
City maps only
Unpaved Road
State and province maps only; Check conditions locally
Unpaved Road
City maps only; Check conditions locally

HIGHWAY MARKERS
Interstate Route
U.S. Route
State or Provincial Route
County or Other Route
Business Route
Trans-Canada Highway
Canadian Provincial Autoroute
Mexican Federal Route

OTHER SYMBOLS
Distances along Major Highways
Miles in U.S.; kilometers in Canada and Mexico
Tunnel; Pass
Wayside Stop
City maps only
One-way Street
City maps only
Port of Entry
City maps only
Airport
City maps only; Official airport codes in parentheses
Auto Ferry; Passenger Ferry

RECREATION AND FEATURES OF INTEREST

National Park
National Forest; National Grassland
Other Large Park or Recreation Area
Military Lands
Indian Reservation
Small State Park with
and without Camping
City maps only
Public Campsite
City maps only
Trail
Point of Interest
Visitor Information Center
City maps only
Public Golf Course; Private Golf Course
Professional tournament location; City maps only
Hospital
City maps only
Ski Area
City maps only

CITIES AND TOWNS

National Capital; State or
Provincial Capital
Cities, Towns, and Populated Places
Type size indicates relative importance
Urban Area
State and province maps only
Large Incorporated Cities
City maps only

OTHER MAP FEATURES

JEFFERSON   County Boundary and Name
City maps only
Time Zone Boundary
Mt. Olympus Mountain Peak
7,965   Elevation in Feet
Perennial; Intermittent River

Copyright © 2008
American Map Corporation
www.americanmap.com

Printed in Canada

Cover photo: Man driving convertible car at sunrise,
rear view Cle Elum, Washington from Getty Images®

Fabulous Drives & Adventures

NORTHWEST

- 101 Miracle Miles, Oregon
- Yellowstone National Park, Wyoming
- Columbia River Gorge and Mount Hood, Oregon

⊘ 101 Miracle Miles

Oregon's coast road, US 101, runs for more than 200 miles along the full length of the state from Astoria to Brookings. It's possible to drive this long and winding road – the Pacific Coast Scenic Byway – in a single day, but this would be pointless, as you would have no time to experience any of the breathtaking sights. It's not for nothing that this road is referred to as the 101 Miracle Miles.

There are over 60 state parks along US 101, including some that preserve vestiges of the state's impressive coniferous forests. Everywhere, the parks beckon tourists to leave the car and actively enjoy the beach, trails and hillsides. Astoria itself is a very pretty place. Hundreds of Victorian-style homes cling to hillsides against a backdrop of misty rainforests and an extensive waterfront.

South of Tillamook, famous for it's Cheese Center, Three Capes Scenic Loop covers three promontories: Cape Meares, Cape Lookout, and Cape Kiwanda – each a state park. Here the tall forests go right down to the pounding surf. The Cape Meares Lighthouse, built in 1890, is definitely one of the highlights here. Viewpoints overlook offshore islets inhabited by Steller sea lions and peregrine falcons, tufted puffins and pelagic cormorants that nest on the cliff walls. Depoe Bay claims to be the "whale-watching capital of the Oregon Coast" due to a resident pod of gray whales that makes its home here 10 months of the year. Higher than those of Africa's Sahara Desert, the Oregon Dunes are the largest expanse of coastal sand dunes in the US and stretch for 50 miles between Florence and Coos Bay. Huge oceanfront dunes cover over 10,000 acres and reach up to 500 feet high forming long banks up to 3 miles deep.

Contacts: By mail: *Oregon Coast Visitor's Association, 137 Northeast First Street, P.O. Box 74, Newport, OR 97365;* ***By phone:*** *888-OCVA-101* ***Website:*** *www.visittheoregoncoast.com*

⊘ Yellowstone National Park

...wstone National Park, ...tte of a more primi-... America, is both ... sanctuary. ... northwest ...g, it was ...ational ...ople ...t

1988. This primitive landscape, forged by fire and water, has been called the greatest concentration of wonders on the face of the earth," its shapes and colors "beyond the reach of human art." It is a hotbed of geothermal activity, with more than 10,000 thermal features, as well as being one of the last remaining habitats of the grizzly bear in the continental United States. All this, and enough canyons, cliffs, and cataracts to please the most jaded eye. Yellowstone encompasses an area of more than 2 million acres. Those who prefer being at one with nature can rest assured that 95 percent of this area is backcountry. For the less intrepid, there are nearly 300 miles of roads. The Grand Loop road provides access to most of the major attractions, from Yellowstone Lake and the Grand Canyon of Yellowstone to Mammoth Hot Springs and Old Faithful. They are simply magnificent. The main road from any entrance will lead you onto the Grand Loop road.

Many visitors view Old Faithful's performance with a sense of obligation. Although not as faithful as it once was, the geyser pleases the crowd regularly – 21 to 23 times daily. This is also a prime location for people watching: a chance to glimpse a real slice of American life frozen in anticipation.

Contacts: By mail: *Yellowstone National Park, P.O. Box 168, Yellowstone National Park, WY 82190-0168;* ***By phone:*** *307-344-7381;* ***Website:*** *www.nps.gov/yell*

⊘ Columbia River Gorge and Mount Hood

A river canyon that straddles both Northwest states and the highest mountain in Oregon are two of the spectacular sights just a short drive away from Portland. Originating as melt water trickling from frozen glaciers in Canada's Rocky Mountains, this legendary river gathers strength while draining an area of 259,000 square miles, amassing a volume of water each year sufficient to cover both Washington and Oregon states – knee deep. Dammed, but never tamed, the river courses through the Columbia Gorge, a river

canyon cutting the only sea-level route through the Cascade Mountains. The 160-mile Mount Hood Loop, from the outskirts of Portland to The Dalles, features viewpoints above the Columbia River and takes in rainforest wildflowers, rustic mountain lodges, gossamer waterfalls, old-growth forests, and abundant orchards. This trip will take one long day, or ideally two, to appreciate its entirety. The drive begins with the Historic Columbia River Highway, or the 24 miles of US 30 that is also referred to as the "scenic route." The highway was an engineering marvel in its day; when it opened in 1916, President Teddy Roosevelt praised its scenic grandeur, and the Illustrated London News called it the "king of the roads." The first grand view of the gorge comes at the Portland Women's Forum State Park, 9 miles east of Troutdale at Chanticleer Point. The road then descends to an area with 11 waterfalls in as many miles before it merges again with I-84. For those wishing to get a closer look at Mount Hood, exit onto Highway 35 just east of Hood River and follow the Mount Hood Loop as it climbs to Barlow Pass, which, at 4,157 feet, is the highest point on the loop road and offers spectacular views of the Mountain.

Contacts: By mail: *Hood River County Chamber of Commerce, 405 Portway Avenue, Hood River, OR 97031;* ***By phone:*** *800-366-3530* ***Website:*** *www.hoodriver.org*

SOUTHWEST

- Red Rock Canyon, Nevada
- Yosemite Valley, California
- Zion National Park, Utah

Red Rock Canyon Loop

A 40-mile loop from the Las Vegas Strip will take you through old mining towns, ranches and to a sacred site of the Paiute tribe. Take I-15 south of town and head west on SR 160 to Blue Diamond, an old gypsum town where SR 159 curves right through Red Rock Canyon. But first comes Bonnie Springs Old Nevada, a faux Old Western town where the motel has themed rooms with décor ranging from covered wagons to Chinese.

More than a million visitors a year travel SR 159 to explore 197,000-acre Red Rock Canyon National Conservation Area. The informative Red Rock Visitor Center is at the end of the 13-mile loop. Red Rock Canyon really ought to be called "red-rock and green-tree canyon," because the far side of the loop is green and fertile compared to the arid beauty of the near side. Along the way are sculpted vistas, hidden waterfalls, and desert vegetation, as well as bighorn sheep, coyotes, antelope, wild horses, and donkeys. Traces of the Paiute tribe have been found at Willow Spring where a well-preserved panel of five red-painted pictographs and petroglyphs survive. Some archeologists say that the paintings "reflect the belief that the rock face was a permeable boundary between the natural and supernatural worlds... the door the shaman entered to visit the spirits." The magnificent colors of the ochre and gray morning landscape come from ferrous minerals in the rocks, and change color as the day progresses. When the evening shadows grow long, the canyon turns deep terracotta red. After heavy winter rains, wildflowers are abundant, and, in late spring, the air is filled with the aroma of blossoming cliff rose, a tall, attractive shrub covered with tiny, cream-colored flowers.

Contacts:
Red Rock Visitor Center **By phone:** 702-363-1921

Yosemite Valley

From the Yosemite National Park's southern entrance Highway 41 climbs 9 miles to Chinquapin junction, where a much less developed 15-mile paved road departs for Glacier Point. From this famed viewpoint, 3,200 feet above the floor of Yosemite Valley, the entire park comes into unforgettable, stomach-clutching focus. No less compelling is the 80-mile vista to the east and south, a panorama of lakes, canyons, waterfalls, and the rugged peaks of Yosemite's High Sierra Mountains. Close at hand are the granite steps of the Giant's Staircase, where Vernal and Nevada falls drop the raging waters of the Merced River, 320 and 594 feet respectively.

From Glacier Point, Half Dome is the most prominent landmark, a great solitary stone thumb thrusting skyward.

At the height of glaciations, 250,000 years ago, Glacier Point itself lay under 700 feet of ice and interpretive markers explain how the 2,000-foot thick Merced and Tenaya glaciers ground down from the high country to merge near Half Dome and hollow out vast Yosemite Valley.

Five miles south of Wawona, just inside the park's southern boundary a short side road leads to the Mariposa Grove of giant sequoias, a preserve containing more than 500 mammoth redwood trees. It was here that John Muir slept under the stars alongside President Theodore Roosevelt, and persuaded the chief executive that the forest should be added to the infant Yosemite National Park. The grove's largest tree, the Grizzly Giant, is at least 3,800 years old, 200 feet high, and with a girth of 94 feet. The best way to experience the trees is on foot, wandering among living things that were already giants when Christ walked the Holy Land.

Contacts:
By mail: Yosemite National Park, P.O. Box 577, Yosemite Nat. Park, CA 95389; **By phone:** 209-372-0200; **Website:** www.nps.gov/yose

Zion National Park

Set in the rocky heart of southern Utah's convoluted canyon country, Zion National Park is nature at its most eloquent: a dramatic juxtaposition of towering sandstone monoliths, narrow set canyons, fast-flowing water, dense greenery, and myriad wildlife. From afar, the park's enormous buttes and domes rise like temples beckoning the faithful. From up close, its sheltering walls seem to offer a protected sanctuary. For the Mormon settlers who came here in the mid-1800s, this seemed to be Zion, "the Heavenly City of God." As a national park since 1919, Zion continues to draw millions of "worshippers" who marvel at the extraordinary geology and natural beauty found in these precipitous canyons. The best way to read the rocks is to drive into Zion from the west, via Hurricane, along Highway 9, following the course of the pretty Virgin River through spick-and-span villages into the park's South Entrance. Many people choose to drive or even cycle through Zion via the Zion-Mount Carmel Highway (Highway 9), which proceeds eastward once in the park, following a tributary of the Virgin river. The road climbs in zigzag fashion through the canyon until it enters the 1-mile long Zion-Mount Carmel Tunnel, built in 1930 to shorten the route between Zion and Bryce Canyon and Grand Canyon national parks. On the other side of the tunnel, the road passes beneath an alcove known as the Great Arch of Zion, then alongside marvelously eroded slick rock formations, which are exactly what they look like: petrified sand dunes. The most distinctive of these is the spectacular Checkerboard Mesa, a huge, creamy giant with crosshatched surfaces. The scenic drive dead-ends beneath the amphitheater of the Temple of Sinawava and the popular Riverside Walk.

Contacts: **By mail:** Zion National Park, Springdale, UT 84767;
By phone: 435-772-3256; **Website:** www.nps.gov/zion

NORTHEAST

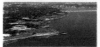  

- Colonial Virginia, Virginia
- Cape Cod, Massachusetts
- Maine's South Coast, Maine

Colonial Virginia

When many Virginia visitors think of the Old Dominion, they think of colonial Williamsburg, which, along with its two stately companions, Jamestown and Yorktown, form Virginia's Historic Triangle, the oldest part of the state and among the oldest places in the US. The three sites, which make up the Colonial National Historical Park, are linked by the lovely 23-mile Colonial Parkway, a road that meanders through forests and fields. Although you could get to Williamsburg from the capital in less than an hour on I-64, the more interesting route from Richmond follows the Plantation Road, Highway 5. In a drive of less than 60 miles, the road between Richmond and Williamsburg winds through more than 300 years of Virginian, and American history. Williamsburg was once the capital of a colony that extended all the way to the present-day state of Minnesota. Its Historical Area contains 88 original structures, 50 major reconstructions, and 40 exhibition buildings. There are also 90 acres of gardens and greens, plus several museums. The town may look and feel something like a stylish, up market theme park minus the cotton candy, but it's a great place to depart from the strains of 21st-century life and become immersed into a slower, and more languorous pace.

Jamestown Settlement, where costumed interpreters portray life at the beginning of the 17th century, recounts the story of the first permanent English settlement in the New World. If Jamestown marks the beginning of English rule, Yorktown, less than 30 miles away, marks its end. Here was the site of the last major battle of the Revolutionary War and in 1781, the surrender of Lord Cornwallis to General George Washington. The visitor center presents a film about the history of the town, and, is the place to begin a Battlefield Tour.

Contacts: By mail: Colonial National Historical Park, P.O. Box 210, Yorktown, VA 23690; By phone: 757-898-3400 ext.3400; Website: www.nps.gov/colo

⊙ Cape Cod

Shaped like a bodybuilder's flexed arm, Cape Cod extends 31 miles eastward into the Atlantic Ocean then another 31 miles to the north. Well forested up to about the "elbow," then increasingly reduced to scrub oak and pitch pine, this sandy peninsula is lined with more than 310 miles of beaches. The crook of the arm forms Cape Cod Bay, where the waters are placid and free of often-treacherous ocean surf. Lighthouses guide mariners plying the cold Atlantic waters. Bostonians consider Cape Cod their own private playground, but its fame has spread so far that it attracts international travelers. In high season (July and August), lodgings are filled to capacity. But even during this packed period, Cape Cod manages to preserve its wild charm and dramatic beauty.

Much of this quality is protected within the boundaries of the Cape Cod National Seashore, a vast 27,000-acre nature reserve established by foresighted legislators in 1961. Precisely because it has not been commercially exploited, this huge expanse of untouched dunes survives as one of the Cape's most alluring features.

Itineraries on the Upper and Mid-Cape offer a choice of speedy, featureless highways or scenic, meandering roads. Those intent on reaching the Outer Cape in a hurry generally opt for US 6, the four-lane, limited-access Mid-Cape Highway; those headed for Falmouth, Woods Hole, and points along Nantucket Sound can take the equally speedy Highway 28. Anyone wishing to get a true sense of the Cape, however, will be well rewarded by taking the prettier non-highway counterparts. Roughly parallel to Mid-Cape Highway, two-lane Route 6A starts in Sagamore and runs eastward along the Bay through old towns full of graceful historic houses, crafts, and antique shops. The same can be said of Route 28A, hugging the shore en route to Falmouth.

Contacts:
By mail: Cape Cod National Seashore, 99 Marconi Site Road, Wellfleet, MA 02667; By phone: 508-349-3785

⊙ Maine's South Coast

The best way to see Maine is to start at the southern tip and head northeast along the old coastal highway, US 1. I-95 is bigger and faster, for those who have a specific destination in mind, but utterly lacking in scenery. The southernmost segment, extending from Kittery to Freeport, attracted the earliest settlers and to this day is the most heavily traveled, blending historic enclaves with built-up beaches. Kittery is home to Portsmouth Naval Yard – the nation's first, founded in 1806. Its Historical and Naval Museum documents the shipyard's history. A few miles to the north is York, one of Maine's first settlements. Its Historical Society maintains seven historic buildings, including the John Hancock Warehouse, the 1750 Jefferds Tavern and the Old Gaol, built in 1719, thought to be the oldest public building in the US. The cliff walk off York Harbor's boardwalk – lined with every imaginable type of fast-seafood shack and family-entertainment facility – affords beautiful views of the coastline, and of Cape Neddick's 1879 Nubble Light off Route 1A.

Watch for the turn-off to the National Estuarine Research Reserve at Laudholm Farm. The 1,600-acre preserve has 7 miles of hiking trails along coastal marsh, uplands, and pristine beach. East of Wells on Route 9 is Kennebunkport, once the shipbuilding center of York County, now the summer home to notaries such as the Bush family.

Eastward, just south of Portland on Cape Elizabeth, is the oldest lighthouse on the eastern seaboard, the Portland Head Lighthouse. The sweeping views are spectacular and largely unchanged since Henry Wadsworth Longfellow's day. The Portland-born poet often walked here from town to chat with the keeper and draw inspiration from the surroundings.

Contacts:
By mail: Maine Office of Tourism, #59 State House Station, Augusta, ME 04333-0059; By phone: 888-624-6345; Website: www.visitmaine.com

CENTRAL REGION

■ Big Bend National Park, Texas
■ Amish Country, Indiana

⊙ Big Bend National Park

Texas's largest national park, Big Bend, where the Rio Grande River lurches to the northeast, has canyons, waterfalls, and enough hiking trails to keep even the most prolific hikers happy. Sandwiched between the Chisos Mountains and the river the park is still a true wilderness with sections still relatively unexplored. Big Bend is one of those places you have to be going to in order to get there. The closest town is Alpine, about 65 miles to the northwest of the northernmost tip. Cattle rustlers exploited this remoteness at the beginning of the 20th century as Texas Rangers were scarce and didn't get to that part of the country very often. The park encompasses a vast area of 801,163 acres and varies in altitude from 1,850 feet all the way up to 7,825 feet. Panther Junction is the park headquarters and home of the visitors' center.

Even from a car the Big Bend visitor can see the wild country. The River Road traverses the 51 miles between the Boquillas-Rio Grande Village road and Castolon. Most high-clearance vehicles can travel the road, but its side roads usually require four-wheel-drive. Old ranches and fishing camps occasionally appear along the road, and it passes the ruins of Mariscal Mine, an old mercury working at the foot of Mariscal Mountain. Though you may be tempted to explore, beware of open, unmarked mine shafts. Further west lie the remains of the Johnson Ranch House, probably the largest adobe ruin in the park. The road ends at Castolon, a 19th-century farming settlement and early 20th-century US Calvary and Texas Rangers post.

Contacts:
By mail: Big Bend National Park, P.O. Box 129, Big Bend National Park, TX 79834; By phone: 432-477-2251; Website: www.nps.gov/bibe

Indiana's Amish Country

US 6 cuts through tiny towns that punctuate a landscape of corn in a region known for the productivity of its land and for its considerable Amish population. The Amish have been in this area for more than a century. These inventive, industrious, and deeply religious people go about their business while shunning worldly things such as buttons, zippers, electricity, and motor vehicles. Cut north up Indiana 5 for a look at their farms, homes, and horse-drawn buggies.

First you pass through Ligonier, a real find of a small town complete with a single main street. Continue north on State 5 and then turn right at a gas station to reach Topeka, a tiny town whose slogan is "Life in the Past Lane." It's the kind of place where Amish buggies line up in parking lots, and hardware and feed stores outnumber banks three-to-one. Amish ride cycles around town, work the counter at restaurants, and just generally

blend into life in this farming community. For a more intimate experience enquire locally about the Amish Bed and Breakfast network, or just drive one of the many other county roads in this area. You'll find plenty of white farmhouses with full clotheslines and empty driveways – usually Amish.

Now retrace your steps back to US 6 and continue west. Amish Acres in Nappanee, a historic farm homestead that interprets the Amish lifestyle for visitors, is fun, though a bit over-commercialized. The round red barn hosts theater performances. Beyond that, it's more lovely country driving through more fields of corn and occasional stands of maple trees. Drift along US 6 like the "Windiana winds" through the last of rural Indiana before Chicago's industrial fringe begins.

Contacts:
By mail: *Indiana Office of Tourism Development, One North Capitol, Suite 100, Indianapolis, IN 46204-2288;* **By phone:** *800-677-9800;* **Website:** *www.in.gov/visitindiana*

SOUTHEAST

- Antebellum Trail, Georgia
- The Everglades, Florida
- Blues Highway, Mississippi

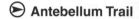

Antebellum Trail

Much of the quintessential – and mythical – Old South romanticized by Gone with the Wind is here to explore; the type of territory foreigners think Atlanta should be, but isn't: old plantation homes and an unconquerable spirit predominate. It even includes Br'er Rabbit, the South's most famous critter. From Atlanta, pick up the Antebellum Trail by driving I-20 for 30 miles east towards Social Circle. Exit onto US 278 to Rutledge and then Madison, renowned as the town so beautiful that even General Sherman couldn't bear to burn it down. There are dozens of palatial Greek revival mansions built in the 1830s that survived the ravages of the Civil War, the Great Depression, and progress. At the Madison County Welcome Center, pick up brochures to the town's historic buildings. Two well-known authors were born in nearby Eatonton south of Madison on US 129/441. Stories from antebellum plantations inspired Joel Chandler Harris to write the folksy Tales of Uncle Remus. Later on, Alice Walker turned her early experiences here into the Pulitzer Prize-winning The Color Purple. Harris's tales of Br'er Rabbit, Br'er Fox, The Tar Baby, and other "critters" are commemorated at the child-friendly Uncle Remus Museum. A walking/driving tour is available at the Chamber of Commerce on the courthouse square and guides visitors past landmarks in the life of Alice Walker. One of Georgia's most cherished historic landmarks is Milledgeville's Old Governors' Mansion (Milledgeville was Georgia's capital until 1868), built in Palladian Greek Revival style. Just south of Eatonton on US 441, Milledgeville is also home to Georgia College and only half an hour's drive on Highway 49 to Macon, the largest city on the Antebellum Trail and birthplace of Ottis Redding, "Little Richard" Penniman, and the Allman Brothers Band, all commemorated at the Georgia Music Hall of Fame.

Contacts:
By mail: *Madison County Welcome Center, 115 East Jefferson Street;*
By phone: *706-342-4454;*
Website: *www.madisonga.org*

The Everglades

The Everglades flow for about 200 miles, bulging up to 70 miles in width and at a mean depth of only 6 inches that rise and fall during the rainy and dry seasons. It oozes down a gradual incline in Florida's surface that drops only 15 feet over hundreds of miles. A drop of water takes more than a year to make the journey. Begin your trip at the main visitor center at the park's main entrance on SR 9336. It provides maps and brochures as well as informative displays. SR 9336 is the main road into Everglades National Park and begins at Florida City. It is about 38 miles from the entrance to its southwest dead end at Flamingo. But even if you are wedded to your car, make sure you detour to at least a few of the other trails and boardwalks along the way. The Royal Palm Visitor Center just 2 miles from the park entrance, has an easy trail through a typical hardwood hammock, named for the gumbo limbo tree, a com-

mon sight along the path. Here you will find ferns, air plants, orchids, and a cool, rainforest-type environment. Yes, the lumps you see in the water are the eyes of alligators. In winter this is one of the best places for wildlife, since there is more water here than in many other parts of the national park. At the end of SR 9336 sits Flamingo. Once an isolated fishing village accessible only by boat (and for that reason a popular hideout for hunters), Flamingo now exists mainly as an isolated colony catering to tourists and offers numerous short and long cruises through the Everglades.

Contacts:
By mail: *Everglades National Park, 40001 State Road 9336, Homestead, FL 33034-6733;* **By phone:** *305-242-7700;* **Website:** *www.nps.gov/ever*

Mississippi Blues Tour

US Highway 61 – the Blue Highway – runs North to South right through the Mississippi Delta, and was immortalized in the title of Bob Dylan's album Highway 61 Revisited. As well as connecting much of Mississippi, the road took players from the Delta to the riches of Memphis. State Highways 61 and 49 were the tracks of trade for Delta musicians in the first half of the 20th century, linking most of the major music venues, and where 61 crosses Highway 49 in Clarksdale is a large crossroads sign, with three blue guitars. Clarksdale is the hub of the delta blues – when the blues was bursting out, it was said, "if you could make it in Clarksdale, you could make it in Memphis or Chicago." Clarksdale's Delta Blues Museum celebrates most of the great Delta bluesmen, and the story of plantation life, so bound up with the evolution of the music, is well described too. North of Vicksburg on Highway 61 where it intersects with Highway 1, a sign may appear at the roadside saying, "Rolling Fork, home of McKinley (Muddy Waters) Morganfield." Or it may not; folks are apt to poach them. A memorial on Courthouse Square remembers the Father of the Chicago electric blues style and each May, the square hosts the Deep Delta Music Festival. Head north on Highway 61, and turn left on Highway 82 to Greenville, the largest city in the Delta. Greenville plays host to the biggest and oldest festival, the Mississippi Delta Blues Festival, each September. The Nelson Street area is probably as close an evocation as there is to the 1920s atmosphere of Memphis's Beale Street. There are bars with bands, singers and records, and people hustling through the night.

Contacts:
By mail: *Delta Blues Museum, 1 Blues Alley;* **By phone:** *662-627-6820;*
Website: *www.deltabluesmuseum.org*

1 inch represents 195 miles
or 314 kilometers
(1:12,350,000)

© GeoNova Publishing, Inc.

BORDER CROSSING

CANADA

U.S. Citizens entering Canada from the U.S. are required to present passports or proof of U.S. citizenship accompanied by photo identification. U.S. citizens entering from a third country must have a valid passport. Visas are not required for U.S. citizens entering from the U.S. for stays of up to 180 days. Naturalized citizens should travel with their naturalization certificates. Alien permanent residents of the U.S. must present their Alien Registration Cards. Individuals under the age of 18 and travelling alone should carry a letter from a parent or legal guardian authorizing their travel in Canada.

U.S. driver's licenses are valid in Canada, and U.S. citizens do not need to obtain an international driver's license. Proof of auto insurence, however, is required.

For additional information, consult http://travel.state.gov/tips_canada.html before you travel.

UNITED STATES (FROM CANADA)

Everyone traveling by air, including U.S. citizens, is required to have a passport, U.S. Permanent Resident card, asylee or refugee document, Merchant Mariner's Document, or NEXUS Air card. Everyone, including U.S. citizens, traveling by land or sea, including ferries, may be required to have a passport or one of the other documents listed above. For additional information, contact http://www.travel.state.gov or http://www.dhs.gov before you travel. Individuals under the age of 18 and travelling alone should also carry notarized documentation, signed by both parents, authorizing their travel.

Canadian driver's licenses are valid in the U.S. for one year, and automobiles may enter free of payment or duty fees. Drivers need only provide customs officials with proof of vehicle registration, ownership, and insurance.

Travel Alert!

Before you travel, find out about any road construction or road closures. You can find this information on individual state transportation websites. A full list of these websites can be found at www.fhwa.dot.gov/webstate.htm.

In addition, 511 is a nationwide telephone number that provides current information about road conditions. A list of active 511 locations can be found at www.fhwa.dot.gov/trafficinfo/511.htm.

Distances in chart are in miles. To convert miles to kilometers, multiply the distance in miles by 1.609. Example: New York, NY to Boston, MA = 215 miles or 346 kilometers (215 x 1.609)	ALBANY, NY	ALBUQUERQUE, NM	AMARILLO, TX	ATLANTA, GA	BALTIMORE, MD	BILLINGS, MT	BIRMINGHAM, AL	BISMARCK, ND	BOISE, ID	BOSTON, MA	BUFFALO, NY	CHARLESTON, SC	CHARLESTON, WV	CHARLOTTE, NC	CHEYENNE, WY	CHICAGO, IL	CINCINNATI, OH	CLEVELAND, OH	COLUMBUS, OH	DALLAS, TX	DENVER, CO	DES MOINES, IA	DETROIT, MI	EL PASO, TX	HARTFORD, CT	HOUSTON, TX	INDIANAPOLIS, IN	JACKSON, MS	JACKSONVILLE, FL	KANSAS CITY, MO	LAS VEGAS, NV
ALBANY, NY		2095	1811	1010	333	2083	1093	1675	2526	172	292	913	634	771	1789	832	730	484	621	1680	1833	1155	571	2326	111	1768	795	1331	1094	1282	2586
ALBUQUERQUE, NM	2095		286	1490	1902	991	1274	1333	966	2240	1808	1793	1568	1649	538	1352	1409	1619	1476	754	438	1091	1608	263	2139	994	1298	1157	1837	894	578
AMARILLO, TX	1811	286		1206	1618	988	991	1398	1266	1957	1524	1510	1285	1365	534	1069	1126	1335	1192	470	434	808	1324	438	1855	711	1014	874	1517	610	864
ATLANTA, GA	1010	1490	1206		679	1889	150	1559	2218	1100	910	317	503	238	1482	717	476	726	577	792	1403	967	735	1437	998	800	531	386	344	801	2067
BALTIMORE, MD	333	1902	1618	679		1959	795	1551	2401	422	370	583	352	441	1665	708	521	377	420	1399	1690	1031	532	2045	321	1470	600	1032	763	1087	2445
BILLINGS, MT	2083	991	988	1889	1959		1839	413	626	2254	1796	2157	1755	2012	455	1246	1552	1597	1608	1433	554	1007	1534	1255	2153	1673	1432	1836	2237	1088	965
BIRMINGHAM, AL	1093	1274	991	150	795	1839		1509	2170	1215	909	466	578	389	1434	667	475	725	576	647	1356	919	734	1292	1114	678	481	241	494	753	1852
BISMARCK, ND	1675	1333	1398	1559	1551	413	1509		1039	1846	1388	1749	1347	1604	594	838	1144	1189	1200	1342	693	675	1126	1597	1745	1582	1024	1548	1906	801	1378
BOISE, ID	2526	966	1266	2218	2401	626	2170	1039		2697	2239	2520	2182	2375	737	1708	1969	2040	2036	1711	833	1369	1977	1206	2595	1952	1852	2115	2566	1376	760
BOSTON, MA	172	2240	1957	1100	422	2254	1215	1846	2697		462	1003	741	861	1961	1003	862	654	760	1819	2004	1326	741	2465	102	1890	940	1453	1184	1427	2757
BUFFALO, NY	292	1808	1524	910	370	1796	909	1388	2239	462		899	431	695	1502	545	442	197	333	1393	1546	868	277	2039	401	1513	508	1134	1080	995	2299
CHARLESTON, SC	913	1793	1510	317	583	2157	466	1749	2520	1003	899		468	204	1783	907	622	724	637	1109	1705	1204	879	1754	901	1110	721	703	238	1102	2371
CHARLESTON, WV	634	1568	1285	503	352	1755	578	1347	2182	741	431	468		265	1445	506	209	255	168	1072	1367	802	410	1718	639	1192	320	816	649	764	2122
CHARLOTTE, NC	771	1649	1365	238	441	2012	389	1604	2375	861	695	204	265		1637	761	476	520	433	1031	1559	1057	675	1677	760	1041	575	625	385	956	2225
CHEYENNE, WY	1789	538	534	1482	1665	455	1434	594	737	1961	1502	1783	1445	1637		972	1233	1304	1300	979	100	633	1241	801	1859	1220	1115	1382	1829	640	843
CHICAGO, IL	832	1352	1069	717	708	1246	667	838	1708	1003	545	907	506	761	972		302	346	359	936	1015	337	283	1543	901	1108	184	750	1065	532	1768
CINCINNATI, OH	730	1409	1126	476	521	1552	475	1144	1969	862	442	622	209	476	1233	302		253	105	958	1200	599	261	1605	760	1079	116	700	803	597	1955
CLEVELAND, OH	484	1619	1335	726	377	1597	725	1189	2040	654	197	724	255	520	1304	346	253		144	1208	1347	669	171	1854	570	1328	319	950	904	806	2100
COLUMBUS, OH	621	1476	1192	577	420	1608	576	1200	2036	760	333	637	168	433	1300	359	105	144		1059	1266	665	192	1706	659	1179	176	801	818	663	2021
DALLAS, TX	1680	754	470	792	1399	1433	647	1342	1711	1819	1393	1109	1072	1031	979	936	958	1208	1059		887	752	1218	647	1717	241	913	406	1049	554	1331
DENVER, CO	1833	438	434	1403	1690	554	1356	693	833	2004	1546	1705	1367	1559	100	1015	1200	1347	1266	887		676	1284	701	1903	1127	1088	1290	1751	603	756
DES MOINES, IA	1155	1091	808	967	1031	1007	919	675	1369	1326	868	1204	802	1057	633	337	599	669	665	752	676		606	1283	1225	992	481	931	1315	194	1429
DETROIT, MI	571	1608	1324	735	532	1534	734	1126	1977	741	277	879	410	675	1241	283	261	171	192	1218	1284	606		1799	679	1338	318	960	1060	795	2037
EL PASO, TX	2326	263	438	1437	2045	1255	1292	1597	1206	2465	2039	1754	1718	1677	801	1543	1605	1854	1706	647	701	1283	1799		2364	758	1489	1051	1642	1085	717
HARTFORD, CT	111	2139	1855	998	321	2153	1114	1745	2595	102	401	901	639	760	1859	901	760	570	659	1717	1903	1225	679	2364		1788	839	1351	1082	1326	2655
HOUSTON, TX	1768	994	711	800	1470	1673	678	1582	1952	1890	1513	1110	1192	1041	1220	1108	1079	1328	1179	241	1127	992	1338	758	1788		1033	445	884	795	1474
INDIANAPOLIS, IN	795	1298	1014	531	600	1432	481	1024	1852	940	508	721	320	575	1115	184	116	319	176	913	1088	481	318	1489	839	1033		675	879	485	1843
JACKSON, MS	1331	1157	874	386	1032	1836	241	1548	2115	1453	1134	703	816	625	1382	750	700	950	801	406	1290	931	960	1051	1351	445	675		598	747	1735
JACKSONVILLE, FL	1094	1837	1517	344	763	2237	494	1906	2566	1184	1080	238	649	385	1829	1065	803	904	818	1049	1751	1315	1060	1642	1082	884	879	598		1148	2415
KANSAS CITY, MO	1282	894	610	801	1087	1088	753	801	1376	1427	995	1102	764	956	640	532	597	806	663	554	603	194	795	1085	1326	795	485	747	1148		1358
LAS VEGAS, NV	2586	578	864	2067	2445	965	1852	1378	760	2757	2299	2371	2122	2225	843	1768	1955	2100	2021	1331	756	1429	2037	717	2655	1474	1843	1735	2415	1358	
LITTLE ROCK, AR	1354	900	617	528	1072	1530	381	1183	1808	1493	1066	900	745	754	1076	662	632	882	733	327	984	567	891	974	1391	447	587	269	873	382	1478
LOS ANGELES, CA	2859	806	1092	2237	2705	1239	2092	1702	1033	3046	2572	2554	2374	2453	1116	2042	2215	2374	2281	1446	1029	1703	2310	801	2944	1558	2104	1851	2441	1632	274
LOUISVILLE, KY	832	1320	1036	419	602	1547	369	1139	1933	964	545	610	251	464	1197	299	106	356	207	852	1118	595	366	1499	862	972	112	594	766	516	1874
MEMPHIS, TN	1214	1033	750	389	933	1625	241	1337	1954	1353	927	760	606	614	1217	539	493	742	594	466	1116	720	752	1112	1251	586	464	211	733	536	1611
MIAMI, FL	1439	2155	1834	661	1109	2554	812	2224	2883	1529	1425	583	994	730	2147	1382	1141	1250	1163	1367	2069	1632	1401	1959	1427	1201	1196	915	345	1466	2733
MILWAUKEE, WI	929	1426	1142	813	805	1175	763	767	1748	1100	642	1003	601	857	1012	89	398	443	454	1010	1055	378	380	1617	999	1193	279	835	1160	573	1808
MINNEAPOLIS, MN	1245	1339	1055	1129	1121	839	1079	431	1465	1417	958	1319	918	1173	881	409	714	760	771	999	924	246	697	1530	1315	1240	596	1151	1477	441	1677
MOBILE, AL	1344	1344	1106	332	1013	2019	258	1765	2302	1433	1165	642	837	572	1570	923	731	981	832	639	1478	1115	991	1231	1332	473	737	187	410	930	1922
MONTPELIER, VT	167	2226	1943	1193	516	2219	1308	1811	2661	178	423	1096	834	954	1925	967	861	615	752	1811	1969	1291	690	2458	195	1983	927	1546	1277	1413	2722
MONTREAL, QC	230	2172	1888	1241	564	2093	1289	1685	2535	313	397	1145	822	1003	1799	841	815	588	725	1772	1843	1165	564	2363	338	1892	872	1514	1325	1359	2596
NASHVILLE, TN	1003	1248	965	242	716	1648	194	1315	1976	1136	716	543	395	397	1240	474	281	531	382	681	1162	725	541	1328	1034	801	287	423	589	559	1826
NEW ORLEANS, LA	1440	1276	993	473	1142	1955	351	1734	2234	1563	1254	783	926	713	1502	935	820	1070	921	525	1409	1117	1079	1118	1461	360	826	185	556	932	1854
NEW YORK, NY	151	2015	1731	869	192	2049	985	1641	2491	215	400	773	515	631	1755	797	636	466	535	1589	1799	1121	622	2235	115	1660	715	1223	953	1202	2552
NORFOLK, VA	570	1970	1686	558	239	2141	708	1733	2584	660	573	437	415	319	1847	890	624	559	604	1350	1782	1213	714	1996	558	1360	735	944	617	1179	2537
OKLAHOMA CITY, OK	1549	546	262	944	1354	1227	729	1136	1506	1694	1262	1248	1022	1102	773	807	863	1073	930	209	681	546	1062	737	1593	449	752	612	1291	348	1124
OMAHA, NE	1292	973	726	989	1168	904	941	616	1234	1463	1005	1290	952	1144	497	474	736	806	802	669	541	136	743	1236	1362	910	618	935	1336	188	1294
ORLANDO, FL	1235	1934	1613	440	904	2333	591	2003	2662	1324	1221	379	790	525	1926	1161	920	1045	958	1146	1847	1411	1180	1738	1223	980	975	694	141	1245	2512
PHILADELPHIA, PA	223	1954	1671	782	104	2019	897	1611	2462	321	414	685	454	543	1725	768	576	437	474	1501	1744	1091	592	2147	219	1572	655	1135	866	1141	2500
PHOENIX, AZ	2561	466	753	1868	2366	1199	1723	1662	993	2706	2274	2184	2035	2107	1004	1819	1876	2085	1942	1077	904	1558	2074	432	2605	1188	1764	1482	2072	1360	285
PITTSBURGH, PA	485	1670	1386	676	246	1719	763	1311	2161	592	217	642	217	438	1425	467	292	136	190	1246	1460	791	292	1893	491	1366	370	988	822	857	2215
PORTLAND, ME	270	2338	2054	1197	520	2352	1313	1944	2795	107	560	1101	839	959	2059	1101	960	751	858	1917	2102	1424	838	2563	199	1988	1038	1550	1281	1525	2855
PORTLAND, OR	2954	1395	1695	2647	2830	889	2599	1301	432	3126	2667	2948	2610	2802	1166	2137	2398	2469	2464	2140	1261	1798	2405	1767	3024	2381	2280	2544	2994	1805	1188
RALEIGH, NC	639	1782	1499	396	309	2110	547	1702	2495	729	642	279	313	158	1758	861	522	568	482	1189	1680	1157	724	1834	627	1198	639	783	460	1077	2360
RAPID CITY, SD	1750	841	837	1511	1626	379	1463	320	930	1921	1463	1824	1422	1678	305	913	1219	1264	1275	1077	404	629	1201	1105	1820	1318	1101	1458	1859	710	1035
RENO, NV	2747	1020	1306	2440	2623	960	2392	1372	430	2919	2460	2741	2403	2595	959	1930	2191	2262	2257	1933	1054	1591	2198	1315	2817	2072	2073	2337	2787	1598	442
RICHMOND, VA	482	1876	1593	527	152	2053	678	1645	2496	572	485	428	322	289	1760	802	530	471	517	1309	1688	1126	627	1955	471	1330	641	914	609	1085	2444
ST. LOUIS, MO	1036	1051	767	549	841	1341	501	1053	1628	1181	749	850	512	704	892	294	350	560	417	635	855	436	549	1242	1080	863	239	505	896	252	1610
SALT LAKE CITY, UT	2224	624	964	1916	2100	548	1868	960	342	2395	1936	2218	1880	2072	436	1406	1667	1738	1734	1410	531	1067	1675	864	2293	1650	1549	1813	2264	1074	417
SAN ANTONIO, TX	1953	818	513	1000	1671	1500	878	1599	1761	2092	1665	1310	1344	1241	1046	1270	1231	1481	1332	271	946	1009	1490	556	1990	200	1186	644	1084	812	1272
SAN DIEGO, CA	2919	825	1111	2166	2724	1302	2021	1765	1096	3065	2632	2483	2393	2405	1179	2105	2234	2437	2300	1375	1092	1766	2373	730	2963	1487	2122	1780	2370	1695	337
SAN FRANCISCO, CA	2964	1111	1397	2618	2840	1176	2472	1749	646	3135	2677	2934	2620	2759	1176	2146	2407	2478	2474	1827	1271	1807	2415	1181	3034	1938	2290	2232	2822	1814	575
SEATTLE, WA	2899	1463	1763	2705	2775	816	2657	1229	500	3070	2612	2973	2571	2827	1234	2062	2368	2413	2424	2208	1329	1822	2350	1944	2969	2449	2249	2612	3052	1872	1256
TAMPA, FL	1290	1949	1628	455	960	2348	606	2018	2677	1380	1276	434	845	581	1941	1176	935	1101	1036	1161	1862	1426	1194	1753	1278	995	990	709	196	1259	2526
TORONTO, ON	400	1841	1557	958	565	1762	958	1354	2204	570	106	1006	537	802	1468	510	484	303	440	1441	1512	834	233	2032	509	1561	541	1183	1187	1028	2265
VANCOUVER, BC	3032	1597	1897	2838	2908	949	2791	1362	633	3204	2745	3106	2705	2960	1368	2196	2501	2547	2558	2342	1463	1956	2483	2087	3102	2583	2383	2746	3186	2007	1390
WASHINGTON, DC	369	1896	1612	636	38	1953	758	1545	2395	458	384	539	346	397	1659	701	517	370	416	1362	1686	1025	526	2008	357	1433	596	996	720	1083	2441
WICHITA, KS	1471	707	423	989	1276	1067	838	934	1346	1616	1184	1291	953	1145	613	728	7856	995	852	367	521	390	984	898	1515	608	674	771	1337	192	1276

LITTLE ROCK, AR	LOS ANGELES, CA	LOUISVILLE, KY	MEMPHIS, TN	MIAMI, FL	MILWAUKEE, WI	MINNEAPOLIS, MN	MOBILE, AL	MONTPELIER, VT	MONTREAL, QC	NASHVILLE, TN	NEW ORLEANS, LA	NEW YORK, NY	NORFOLK, VA	OKLAHOMA CITY, OK	OMAHA, NE	ORLANDO, FL	PHILADELPHIA, PA	PHOENIX, AZ	PITTSBURGH, PA	PORTLAND, ME	PORTLAND, OR	RALEIGH, NC	RAPID CITY, SD	RENO, NV	RICHMOND, VA	ST. LOUIS, MO	SALT LAKE CITY, UT	SAN ANTONIO, TX	SAN DIEGO, CA	SAN FRANCISCO, CA	SEATTLE, WA	TAMPA, FL	TORONTO, ON	VANCOUVER, BC	WASHINGTON, DC	WICHITA, KS
1354	2859	832	1214	1439	929	1245	1344	167	230	1003	1440	151	151	1549	1292	1235	223	2561	485	270	2954	639	1750	2747	482	1036	2224	1953	1919	2964	2899	1290	400	3032	369	1471
900	806	1320	1033	2155	1426	1339	1344	2226	2172	1248	1276	2015	2015	546	973	1934	1954	466	1670	2338	1395	1782	841	1020	1876	1051	624	818	825	1111	1463	1949	1841	1597	1896	707
617	1092	1036	750	1834	1142	1055	1106	1943	1888	965	993	1731	1731	262	726	1613	1671	753	1386	2054	1695	1499	837	1306	1593	767	964	513	1111	1397	1763	1628	1557	1897	1612	423
528	2237	419	389	661	813	1129	332	1193	1241	242	473	869	869	944	989	440	782	1868	676	1197	2647	396	1511	2440	527	549	1916	1000	2166	2618	2705	455	958	2838	636	989
1072	2705	602	933	1109	805	1121	1013	516	564	716	1142	192	192	1354	1168	904	104	2366	246	520	2830	309	1626	2623	152	841	2100	1671	2724	2840	2775	960	565	2908	38	1276
1530	1239	1547	1625	2554	1175	839	2019	2219	2093	1648	1955	2049	2049	1227	904	2333	2019	1199	1719	2352	889	2110	379	960	2053	1341	548	1500	1302	1176	816	2348	1762	949	1953	1067
381	2092	369	241	812	763	1079	258	1308	1289	194	351	985	985	729	941	591	897	1723	763	1313	2599	547	1463	2392	678	501	1868	878	2021	2472	2657	606	958	2791	758	838
1183	1702	1139	1337	2224	767	431	1765	1811	1685	1315	1734	1641	1641	1136	616	2003	1611	1662	1311	1944	1301	1702	320	1372	1645	1053	960	1599	1765	1749	1229	2018	1354	1362	1545	934
1808	1033	1933	1954	2883	1748	1465	2302	2661	2535	1976	2234	2491	2491	1506	1234	2662	2462	993	2161	2795	432	2495	930	430	2496	1628	342	1761	1096	646	500	2677	2204	633	2395	1346
1493	3046	964	1353	1529	1100	1417	1433	178	313	1136	1563	215	215	1694	1463	1324	321	2706	592	107	3126	729	1921	2919	572	1181	2395	2092	3065	3135	3070	1380	570	3204	458	1616
1066	2572	545	927	1425	642	958	1165	423	397	716	1254	400	400	1262	1005	1221	414	2274	217	560	2667	642	1463	2460	485	749	1936	1665	2632	2677	2612	1276	106	2745	384	1184
900	2554	610	760	583	1003	1319	642	1096	1145	543	783	773	773	1248	1290	379	685	2184	642	1101	2948	279	1824	2741	428	850	2218	1310	2483	2934	2973	434	1006	3106	539	1291
745	2374	251	606	994	601	918	837	834	822	395	926	515	515	1022	952	790	454	2035	217	839	2610	313	1422	2403	322	512	1880	1344	2393	2620	2571	845	537	2705	346	953
754	2453	464	614	730	857	1173	572	954	1003	397	713	631	631	1102	1144	525	543	2107	438	959	2802	158	1678	2595	289	704	2072	1241	2405	2759	2827	581	802	2960	397	1145
1076	1116	1197	1217	2147	1012	881	1570	1925	1799	1240	1502	1755	1755	773	497	1926	1725	1004	1425	2059	1166	1758	305	959	1760	892	436	1046	1179	1176	1234	1941	1468	1368	1659	613
662	2042	299	539	1382	89	409	923	967	841	474	935	797	797	807	474	1161	768	1819	467	1101	2137	861	913	1930	802	294	1406	1270	2105	2146	2062	1176	510	2196	701	728
632	2215	106	493	1141	398	714	731	861	815	281	820	636	636	863	736	920	576	1876	292	960	2398	522	1219	2191	530	350	1667	1231	2234	2407	2368	935	484	2501	517	785
882	2374	356	742	1250	443	760	981	615	588	531	1070	466	466	1073	806	1045	437	2085	136	751	2469	568	1264	2262	471	560	1738	1481	2437	2478	2413	1101	303	2547	370	995
733	2281	207	594	1163	454	771	832	752	725	382	921	535	535	930	802	958	474	1942	190	858	2464	482	1275	2257	517	417	1734	1332	2300	2474	2424	1036	440	2558	416	852
327	1446	852	466	1367	1010	999	639	1811	1772	681	525	1589	1589	209	669	1146	1501	1077	1246	1917	2140	1189	1077	1933	1309	635	1410	271	1375	1827	2208	1161	1441	2342	1362	367
984	1029	1118	1116	2069	1055	924	1478	1969	1843	1162	1409	1799	1799	681	541	1847	1744	904	1460	2102	1261	1680	404	1054	1688	855	531	946	1092	1271	1329	1862	1512	1463	1686	521
567	1703	595	720	1632	378	246	1115	1291	1165	725	1117	1121	1121	546	136	1411	1091	1558	791	1424	1798	1157	629	1591	1126	436	1067	1009	1766	1807	1822	1426	834	1956	1025	390
891	2310	366	752	1401	380	697	991	690	564	541	1079	622	622	1062	743	1180	592	2074	292	838	2405	724	1201	2198	627	549	1675	1490	2373	2415	2350	1194	233	2483	526	984
974	801	1499	1112	1959	1617	1530	1231	2458	2363	1328	1118	2235	2235	737	1236	1738	2147	432	1893	2563	1767	1834	1105	1315	1955	1242	864	556	730	1181	1944	1753	2032	2087	2008	898
1391	2944	862	1251	1427	999	1315	1332	195	338	1034	1461	115	115	1593	1362	1223	219	2605	491	199	3024	627	1820	2817	471	1080	2293	1990	2963	3034	2969	1278	509	3102	357	1515
447	1558	972	586	1201	1193	1240	473	1983	1892	801	360	1660	1660	449	910	980	1572	1188	1366	1988	2381	1198	1318	2072	1330	863	1650	200	1487	1938	2449	995	1561	2583	1433	608
587	2104	112	464	1196	279	596	737	927	872	287	826	715	715	752	618	975	655	1764	370	1038	2280	639	1101	2073	641	239	1549	1186	2122	2290	2249	990	541	2383	596	674
269	1851	594	211	915	835	1151	187	1546	1514	423	185	1223	1223	612	935	694	1135	1482	988	1550	2544	783	1458	2337	914	505	1813	644	1780	2232	2612	709	1183	2746	996	771
873	2441	766	733	345	1160	1477	410	1277	1325	589	556	953	953	1291	1336	141	866	2072	822	1281	2994	460	1859	2787	609	896	2264	1084	2370	2822	3052	196	1187	3186	720	1337
382	1632	516	536	1466	573	441	930	1413	1359	559	932	1202	1202	348	188	1245	1141	1360	857	1525	1805	1077	710	1598	1085	252	1074	812	1695	1814	1872	1259	1028	2007	1083	192
1478	274	1874	1611	2733	1808	1677	1922	2722	2596	1826	1854	2552	2552	1124	1294	2512	2500	285	2215	2855	1188	2360	1035	442	2444	1610	417	1272	337	575	1256	2526	2265	1390	2441	1276
	1706	526	140	1190	747	814	457	1485	1446	355	455	1262	1262	355	570	969	1175	1367	920	1590	2237	889	1093	2030	983	416	1507	600	1703	2012	2305	984	1115	2439	1036	464
1706		2126	1839	2759	2082	1951	2031	2995	2869	2054	1917	2820	2820	1352	1567	2538	2760	369	2476	3144	971	2588	1309	519	2682	1856	691	1356	124	385	1148	2553	2538	1291	2702	1513
526	2126		386	1084	394	711	625	963	920	175	714	739	739	774	704	863	678	1786	394	1062	2362	564	1215	2155	572	264	1631	1125	2144	2372	2364	878	589	2497	596	705
140	1839	386		1051	624	940	395	1345	1306	215	396	1123	1123	487	724	830	1035	1500	780	1451	2382	749	1247	2175	843	294	1652	739	1841	2144	2440	845	975	2574	896	597
1190	2759	1084	1051		1478	1794	727	1622	1671	907	874	1299	1299	1609	1654	232	1211	2390	1167	1627	3312	805	2176	3105	954	1214	2581	1401	2688	3140	3370	274	1532	3504	1065	1655
747	2082	394	624	1478		337	1019	1064	939	569	1020	894	894	880	514	1257	865	1892	564	1198	2063	956	842	1970	899	367	1446	1343	2145	2186	1991	1272	607	2124	799	769
814	1951	711	940	1794	337		1335	1381	1255	886	1337	1211	1211	793	383	1573	1181	1805	881	1515	1727	1273	606	1839	1216	621	1315	1257	2014	2055	1654	1588	924	1788	1115	637
457	2031	625	395	727	1019	1335		1526	1575	450	146	1203	1203	799	1119	506	1115	1662	1019	1531	2731	730	1641	2545	861	688	2000	673	1960	2411	2799	521	1214	2933	970	958
1485	2995	963	1345	1622	1064	1381	1526		138	1134	1656	310	310	1680	1428	1417	414	2693	685	196	3090	822	1886	2883	665	1167	2359	2084	3051	3099	3034	1473	457	3168	551	1602
1446	2869	920	1306	1671	939	1255	1575	138		1094	1632	383	383	1625	1300	1466	454	2637	607	282	2963	871	1758	2756	714	1112	2232	2043	2931	2972	2907	1522	330	3041	600	1547
355	2054	175	215	907	569	886	450	1134	1094		539	906	906	703	747	686	818	1715	569	1234	2405	532	1269	2198	626	307	1675	954	2056	2360	2463	701	764	2597	679	748
455	1917	714	396	874	1020	1337	146	1656	1632	539		1332	1332	731	1121	653	1245	1548	1108	1660	2663	871	1643	2431	1002	690	1932	560	1846	2298	2731	668	1302	2865	1106	890
1262	2820	739	1123	1299	894	1211	1203	310	383	906	1332		430	1469	1258	1094	91	2481	367	313	2920	499	1716	2713	342	956	2189	1861	2839	2929	2864	1150	507	2998	228	1391
1076	2776	666	937	962	987	1303	891	753	801	720	1032	430		1424	1350	758	342	2436	428	757	3012	179	1808	2805	91	927	2282	1560	2725	3022	2957	814	747	3090	196	1368
355	1352	774	487	1609	880	793	799	1680	1625	703	731	1469	1424		463	1388	1408	1012	1124	1792	1934	1237	871	1727	1331	505	1204	466	1370	1657	2002	1403	1295	2136	1350	161
570	1567	704	724	1654	514	383	1119	1428	1300	747	1121	1258	1350	463		1433	1228	1440	928	1561	1662	1265	525	1455	1263	440	932	927	1630	1672	1719	1448	971	1853	1162	307
969	2538	863	830	232	1257	1573	506	1417	1466	686	653	1094	758	1388	1433		1006	2169	963	1422	3091	601	1955	2884	750	993	2360	1180	2467	2918	3149	82	1327	3283	860	1434
1175	2760	678	1035	1211	865	1181	1115	414	454	818	1245	91	342	1408	1228	1006		2420	306	419	2890	411	1686	2683	254	895	2160	1774	2779	2900	2835	1062	522	2968	140	1330
[illegible]	369	1786	1500	2390	1892	1805	1662	2693	2637	1715	1548	2481	2436	1012	1440	2169	2420		2136	2804	1335	2249	1308	883	2343	1517	651	987	358	750	1513	2184	2307	1655	2362	1173
920	2476	394	780	1167	564	881	1019	685	607	569	1108	367	428	1124	928	963	306	2136		690	2590	497	1386	2383	341	611	1859	1519	2494	2599	2534	1019	321	2668	240	1046
1590	3144	1062	1451	1627	1198	1515	1531	196	282	1234	1660	313	757	1792	1561	1422	419	2804	690		3223	827	2019	3016	670	1279	2493	2189	3162	3233	3168	1478	668	3301	556	1714
2237	971	2362	2382	3312	2063	1727	2731	3090	2963	2405	2663	2920	3012	1934	1662	3091	2890	1335	2590	3223		2923	1268	578	2925	2057	771	2322	1093	638	170	3106	2633	313	2824	1775
889	2588	564	749	805	956	1273	730	822	871	532	871	499	179	1237	1265	601	411	2249	497	827	2923		1777	2716	157	825	2193	1398	2563	2894	2926	656	820	3060	265	1266
1093	1309	1215	1247	2176	842	606	1641	1886	1758	1269	1643	1716	1808	871	525	1955	1686	1308	1386	2019	1268	1777		1151	1720	963	628	1335	1372	1368	1195	1970	1429	1328	1620	712
2030	519	2155	2175	3105	1970	1839	2545	2883	2756	2198	2431	2713	2805	1727	1455	2884	2683	883	2383	3016	578	2716	1151		2718	1850	524	1870	642	217	755	2899	2426	898	2617	1568
983	2682	572	843	954	899	1216	861	665	714	626	1002	342	91	1331	1263	750	254	2343	341	670	2925	157	1720	2718		834	2194	1530	2684	2934	2869	805	660	3003	108	1274
416	1856	264	294	1214	367	621	688	1167	1112	307	690	956	927	505	440	993	895	1517	611	1279	2057	825	963	1850	834		1326	968	1875	2066	2125	1008	782	2259	837	441
1507	691	1631	1652	2581	1446	1315	2000	2359	2232	1675	1932	2189	2282	1204	932	2360	2160	651	1859	2493	771	2193	628	524	2194	1326		1419	754	740	839	2375	1902	973	2094	1044
600	1356	1125	739	1401	1343	1257	673	2084	2043	954	560	1861	1560	466	927	1180	1774	987	1519	2189	2322	1398	1335	1870	1530	968	1419		1285	1737	2275	1195	1714	2410	1635	624
1703	124	2144	1841	2688	2145	2014	1960	3051	2931	2056	1846	2839	2725	1370	1630	2467	2779	358	2494	3162	1093	2563	1372	642	2684	1875	754	1285		508	1271	2481	2601	1414	2720	1531
2012	385	2372	2144	3140	2186	2055	2411	3099	2972	2360	2298	2929	3022	1657	1672	2918	2900	750	2599	3233	638	2894	1368	217	2934	2066	740	1737	508		816	2933	2643	958	2834	1784
2305	1148	2364	2440	3370	1991	1654	2799	3034	2907	2463	2731	2864	2957	2002	1719	3149	2835	1513	2534	3168	170	2926	1195	755	2869	2125	839	2275	1271	816		3164	2577	140	2769	1843
984	2553	878	845	274	1272	1588	521	1473	1522	701	668	1150	814	1403	1448	82	1062	2184	1019	1478	3106	656	1970	2899	805	1008	2375	1195	2481	2933	3164		1383	3297	916	1448
1115	2538	589	975	1532	607	924	1214	457	330	764	1302	507	747	1295	971	1327	522	2307	321	668	2633	820	1429	2426	660	782	1902	1714	2601	2643	2577	1383		2711	563	1217
2439	1291	2497	2574	3504	2124	1788	2933	3168	3041	2597	2865	2998	3090	2136	1853	3283	2968	1655	2668	3301	313	3060	1328	898	3003	2259	973	2410	1414	958	140	3297	2711		2902	1977
1036	2702	596	896	1065	799	1115	970	551	600	679	1106	228	196	1350	1162	860	140	2362	240	556	2824	265	1620	2617	108	837	2094	1635	2720	2834	2769	916	563	2902		1272
464	1513	705	597	1655	769	637	958	1602	1547	748	890	1391	1368	161	307	1434	1330	1173	1046	1714	1775	1266	712	1568	1274	441	1044	624	1531	1784	1843	1448	1217	1977	1272	

BORDER CROSSING

MEXICO

U.S. Citizens entering Mexico are required to present passports or proof of U.S. citizenship accompanied by photo identification. Visas are not requireed for stays of up to 180 days. Naturalized citizens should travel with their naturalizaton certificates, and alien permanent residents must present their Alien Registration Cards. Individuals under the age of 18 travelling alone, with one parent, or with other adults must carry notarized parental authorization or valid custodial documents.

In addition, all U.S. citizens visiting for up to 180 days must procure a tourist card, obtainable from Mexican consulates, tourism offices, and border crossing points, which must be surrendered upon departure. However, tourist cards are not needed for visits shorter than 72 hours to cities along the Mexico/U.S. border.

U.S. driver's licenses are valid in Mexico.

Visitors who wish to drive beyond the Baja California Peninsula or the Border Zone (extending approximately 25 km into Mexico) must obtain a temporary import permit for their vehicles. Permits may be obtained from a Mexican Customs Office at border crossings points as long as the original and two copies of the following documents bearing the driver's name are provided: passport/proof of U.S. citizenship, tourist card, vehicle registration, driver's license, and a major international credit card for use in paying the prevailing fee. Permits are valid for 180 days, and they must be surrendered upon final departure from Mexico.

All visitors driving in Mexico should be aware that U.S. auto insurance policies are not valid and that buying short-term tourist insurance is virtually mandatory. Many U.S. insurance companies sell Mexican auto insurance. American Automobile Association (for members only) and Sanborn's Mexico Insurance (800.638.9423) are popular companies with offices at most U.S. border crossings.

UNITED STATES (FROM MEXICO)

Everyone traveling by air, including U.S. citizens, is required to have a passport, U.S. Permanent Resident card, asylee or refugee document, Merchant Mariner's Document, or NEXUS Air card. Everyone, including U.S. citizens, traveling by land or sea, including ferries, may be required to have a passport or one of the other documents listed above. For additional information, contact http://www.travel.state.gov or http://www.dhs.gov before you travel.

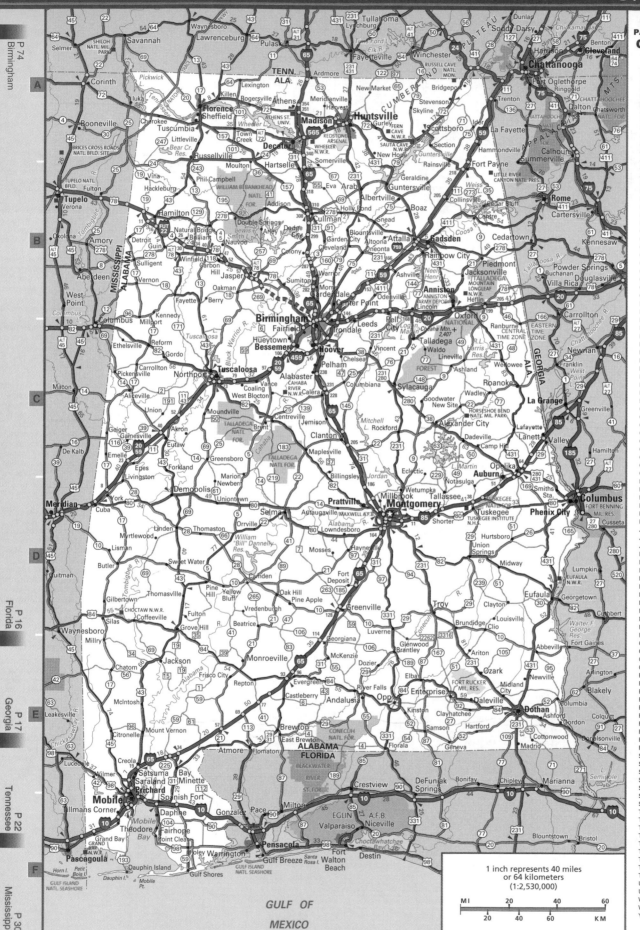

1 inch represents 40 miles
or 64 kilometers
(1:2,530,000)

© GeoNova Publishing, Inc.

GULF OF

MEXICO

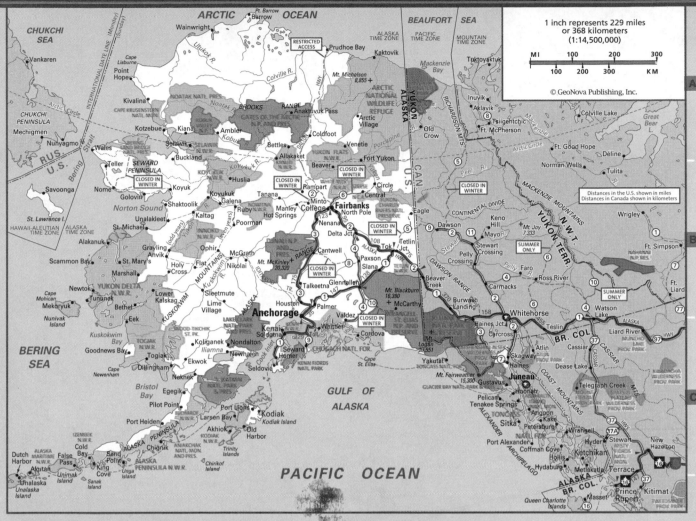

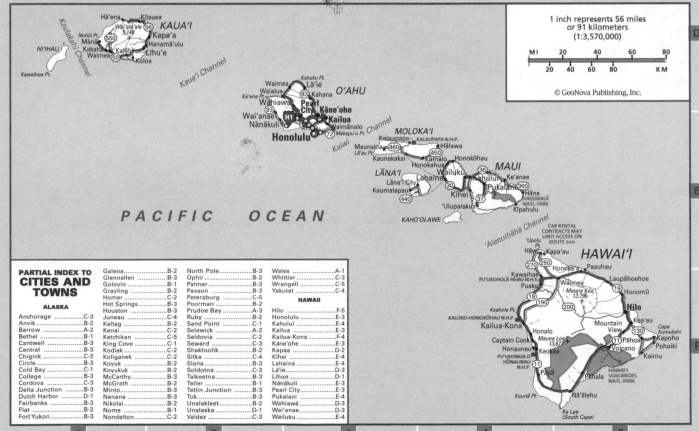

1 inch represents 229 miles or 368 kilometers (1:14,500,000)

1 inch represents 56 miles or 91 kilometers (1:3,570,000)

© GeoNova Publishing, Inc.

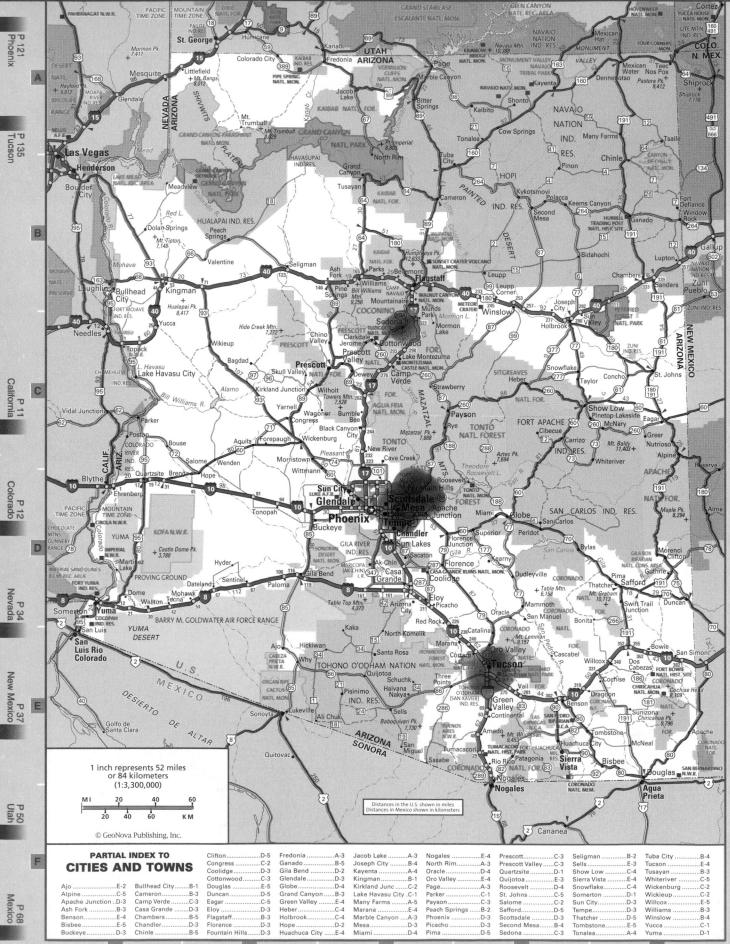

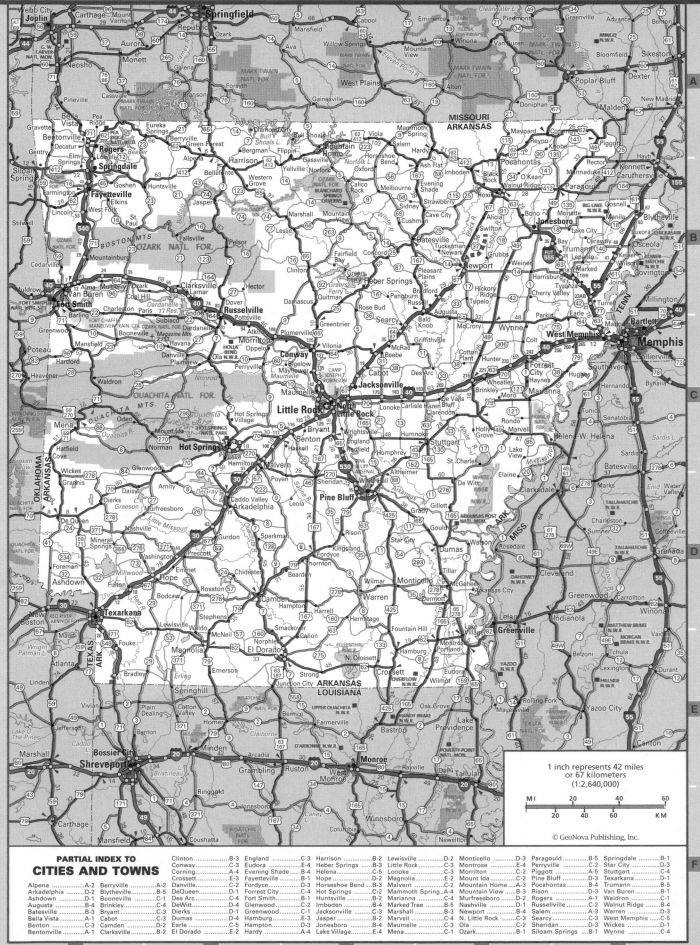

1 inch represents 42 miles
or 67 kilometers
(1:2,640,000)

© GeoNova Publishing, Inc.

PARTIAL INDEX TO CITIES AND TOWNS

P 22 Tennessee
P 25 Louisiana
P 30 Mississippi
P 31 Missouri
P 44 Oklahoma
P 48 Texas

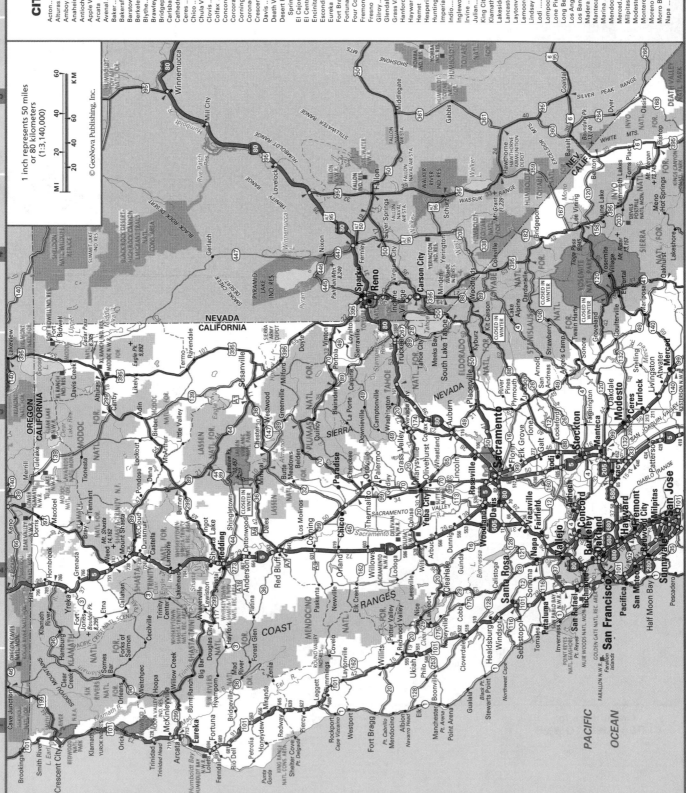

PARTIAL INDEX TO CITIES AND TOWNS

Acton	H-6	Needles	H-4
Alturas	A-3	Nevada City	C-3
Amboy	H-5	Newport Beach	J-4
Anaheim	J-4	Oakland	E-2
Antioch	E-2	Oceanside	K-4
Apple Valley	H-4	Ontario	J-4
Arcata	B-1	Orick	A-1
Avenal	G-2	Oxnard	J-5
Baker	G-5	Palm Springs	J-5
Bakersfield	G-3	Palmdale	H-4
Barstow	H-4	Paradise	C-3
Berkeley	E-2	Pasadena	J-4
Blythe	J-6	Petaluma	E-2
Brawley	K-5	Pismo Beach	H-2
Bridgeport	D-4	Pomona	J-4
Carlsbad	K-4	Porterville	G-3
Cathedral City	J-5	Poway	K-4
Ceres	E-3	Quincy	C-3
Chico	C-2	Ramona	K-4
Chula Vista	K-4	Redding	B-2
Clovis	F-2	Redlands	J-4
Colfax	C-3	Redwood City	E-2
Concord	E-2	Richmond	E-2
Corcoran	G-3	Ridgecrest	H-4
Corning	C-2	Riverside	J-4
Coronado	K-4	Roseville	C-3
Crescent City	A-1	Sacramento	D-2
Davis	D-2	Salinas	F-1
Death Valley	F-4	San Bernardino	J-4
Desert Hot Springs	J-5	San Clemente	J-4
El Cajon	K-4	San Diego	K-5
El Centro	K-4	San Fernando	H-4
Encinitas	K-4	San Francisco	E-2
Escondido	K-4	San Jose	E-2
Eureka	B-1	San Juan	K-4
Fort Bragg	D-1	San Luis Obispo	G-2
Fortuna	B-1	San Mateo	E-2
Four Corners	H-4	San Rafael	E-2
Fremont	E-2	San Simeon	G-1
Fresno	F-2	Santa Ana	J-4
Gilroy	F-1	Santa Barbara	H-2
Glendale	H-3	Santa Clarita	H-3
Grass Valley	C-3	Santa Cruz	F-1
Hanford	F-2	Santa Maria	H-2
Hayward	E-2	Santa Monica	J-3
Hemet	J-4	Santa Paula	H-3
Hesperia	H-4	Santa Rosa	G-5
Huntington Beach	J-3	Shoshone	H-3
Imperial Beach	K-4	Sierraville	H-3
Indio	J-5	Simi Valley	H-3
Inglewood	J-4	South Lake Tahoe	D-4
Irvine	J-4	Stockton	E-3
Julian	K-5	Sunnyvale	E-2
King City	G-2	Susanville	B-3
Klamath	A-1	Tehachapi	H-3
Lakeside	K-4	Temecula	J-4
Lancaster	H-4	Thousand Oaks	J-3
Laytonville	C-1	Torrance	J-3
Lemoore	F-2	Tracy	E-3
Lindsay	G-3	Tulare	G-3
Lodi	E-3	Turlock	F-4
Lompoc	H-2	Ukiah	D-1
Lone Pine	F-4	Vacaville	E-3
Long Beach	J-3	Vallejo	F-2
Los Angeles	J-3	Ventura	H-4
Madera	F-2	Victorville	H-4
Manteca	E-3	Visalia	F-3
Marina	F-1	Watsonville	F-1
Merced	F-2	Weed	A-2
Milpitas	E-3	Woodland	D-2
Modesto	E-3	Yosemite Village	E-4
Monterey	F-1	Yreka	A-2
Moreno Valley	J-4	Yuba City	D-2
Morro Bay	G-2	Yucaipa	J-4
Napa	E-2		

Scale:
1 inch represents 50 miles
or 80 kilometers
(1:3,140,000)

MI   0   20   40   60
KM   0   20   40   60

© GeoNova Publishing, Inc.

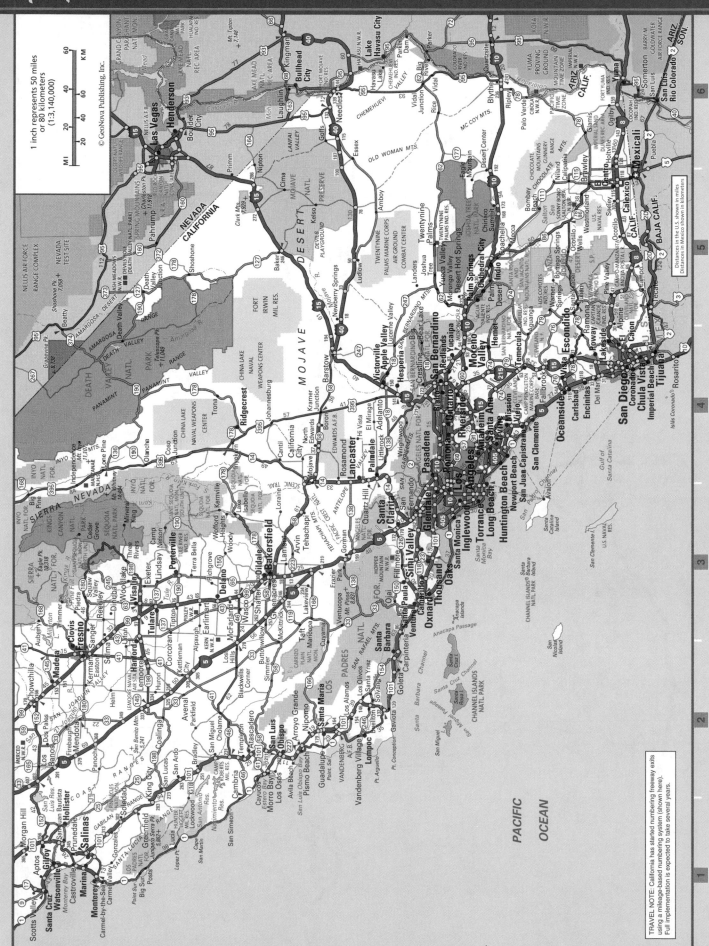

P 98
Los Angeles

P 130
San Diego

P 8
Arizona

P 10
California North

P 34
Nevada

P 68
Mexico

TRAVEL NOTE: California has started numbering freeway exits using a mileage-based numbering system (shown here). Full implementation is expected to take several years.

1 inch represents 50 miles or 80 kilometers (1:3,140,000)

© GeoNova Publishing, Inc.

PACIFIC OCEAN

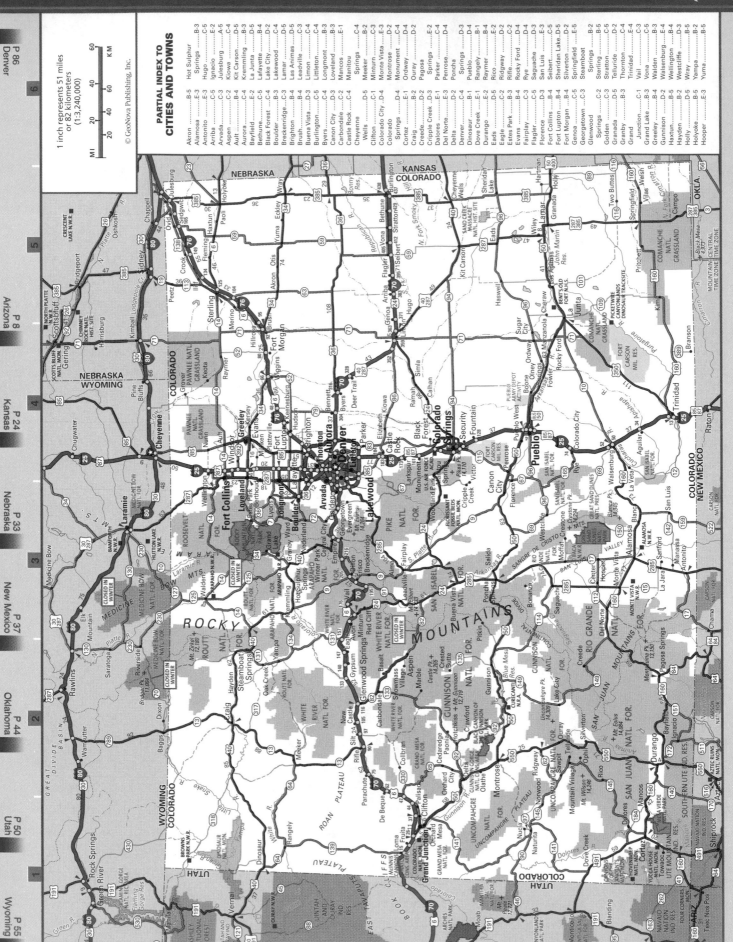

1 inch represents 51 miles
or 82 kilometers (1:3,240,000)

© GeoNova Publishing, Inc.

PARTIAL INDEX TO CITIES AND TOWNS

Akron	B-5	Hot Sulphur Springs	B-3	Meeker	B-2	Saguache	D-3
Alamosa	E-3	Hugo	C-4	Minturn	C-3	San Luis	E-3
Antonito	E-3	Ignacio	E-2	Monte Vista	D-2	Seibert	C-5
Arriba	C-5	Julesburg	A-5	Montrose	D-2	Sheridan Lake	D-5
Arvada	C-3	Kiowa	C-4	Monument	C-4	Silverton	E-2
Aspen	C-2	Kit Carson	C-4	Ordway	D-4	Springfield	E-5
Ault	B-4	Kremmling	B-3	Ouray	D-2	Steamboat Springs	B-2
Aurora	C-3	La Junta	D-5	Pagosa Springs	E-2	Sterling	B-5
Bayfield	E-2	Lafayette	B-4	Parker	C-4	Stratton	C-5
Bethune	B-4	Lake City	D-2	Penrose	D-4	Telluride	D-2
Black Forest	C-4	Lakewood	C-3	Poncha	D-3	Thornton	C-3
Boulder	B-3	Lamar	D-5	Pueblo	D-4	Trinidad	E-4
Breckenridge	C-3	Las Animas	D-5	Rangely	B-1	Vail	C-3
Brighton	B-4	Leadville	C-3	Raymer	B-4	Vona	C-5
Brush	B-4	Limon	C-4	Rico	E-2	Walden	B-3
Buena Vista	D-3	Littleton	C-4	Ridgway	D-2	Walsenburg	E-4
Burlington	C-4	Longmont	B-3	Rifle	C-2	Wellington	B-4
Byers	C-4	Loveland	B-3	Rocky Ford	D-4	Westcliffe	D-3
Canon City	D-3	Mancos	E-1	Rye	D-4	Wray	B-5
Carbondale	C-3	Manitou Springs	C-4			Yampa	B-3
Castle Rock	C-4					Yuma	B-5
Cheyenne Wells	D-5						
Clifton	C-1						
Colorado City	D-4						
Colorado Springs	C-4						
Cortez	E-1						
Craig	B-1						
Creede	D-2						
Cripple Creek	D-3						
Dolores	E-1						
Del Norte	E-3						
Delta	C-2						
Denver	C-4						
Dinosaur	B-1						
Dove Creek	E-1						
Durango	E-2						
Eads	D-5						
Eagle	C-2						
Estes Park	B-3						
Evans	B-4						
Fairplay	C-3						
Flagler	C-5						
Florence	D-3						
Fort Collins	B-4						
Fort Lupton	B-4						
Fort Morgan	B-4						
Genoa	C-5						
Georgetown	C-3						
Glenwood Springs	C-2						
Golden	C-3						
Granada	D-5						
Granby	B-3						
Grand Junction	C-1						
Grand Lake	B-3						
Greeley	B-4						
Gunnison	D-2						
Haxtun	B-5						
Hayden	B-2						
Holly	D-5						
Holyoke	B-5						
Hooper	E-3						

P 86 Denver
P 8 Arizona
P 24 Kansas
P 33 Nebraska
P 37 New Mexico
P 44 Oklahoma
P 50 Utah
P 55 Wyoming

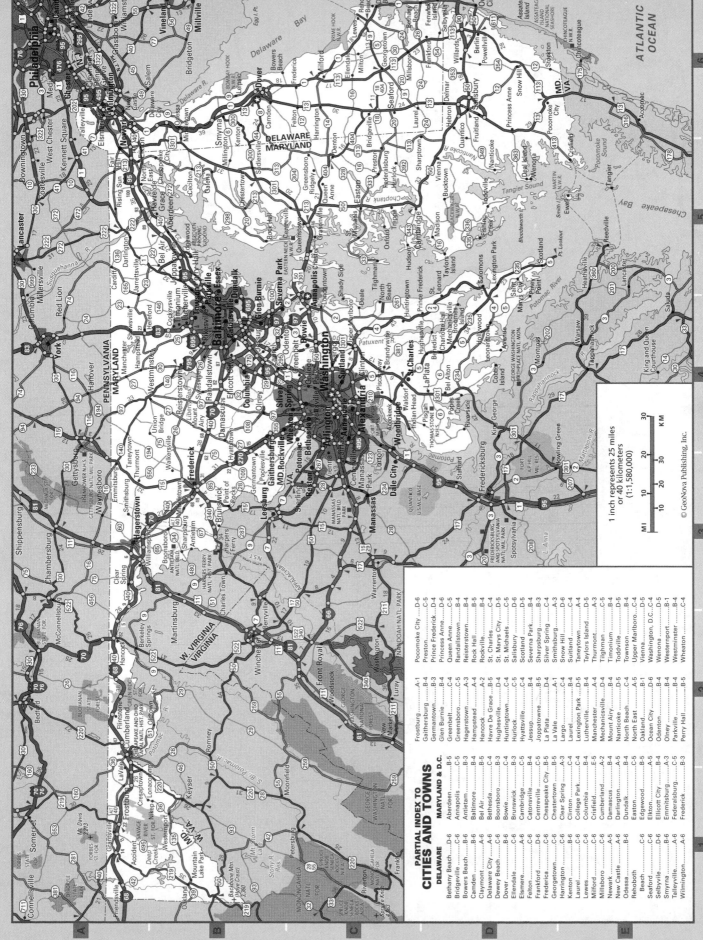

P 72
Baltimore

P 137
Washington, D.C.

P 36
New Jersey

P 46
Pennsylvania

P 52
Virginia

P 52
West Virginia

1 inch represents 25 miles
or 40 kilometers
(1:1,580,000)

© GeoNova Publishing, Inc.

ATLANTIC
OCEAN

DELAWARE
MARYLAND

PENNSYLVANIA
MARYLAND

W. VIRGINIA
VIRGINIA

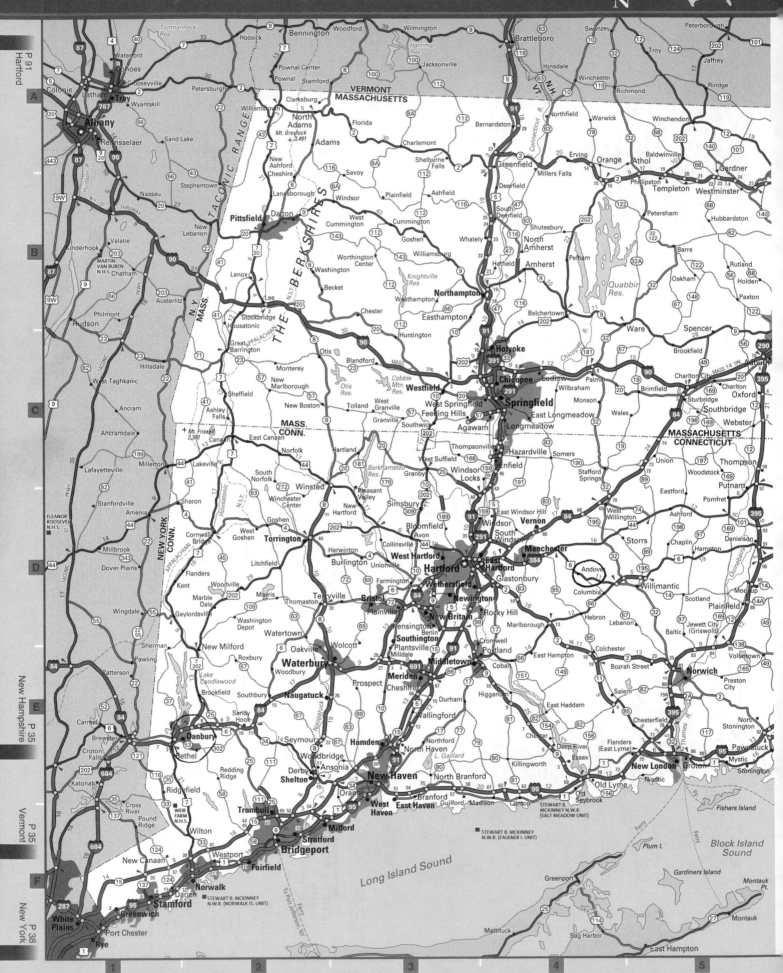

P 91 Hartford
P 35 New Hampshire
P 35 Vermont
P 38 New York

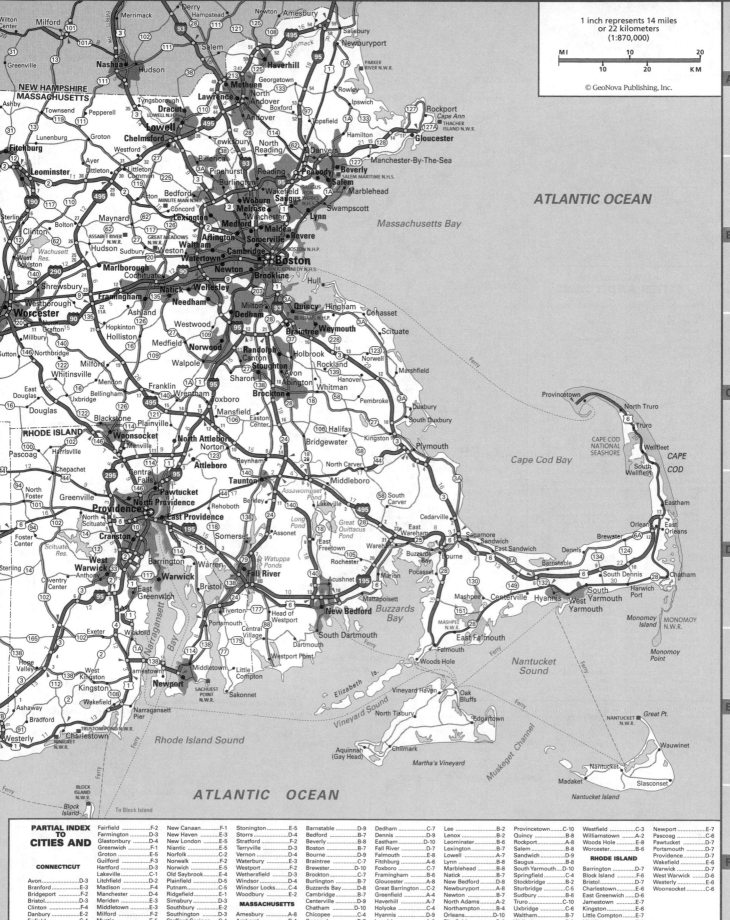

1 inch represents 14 miles
or 22 kilometers
(1:870,000)

N

1 inch represents 48 miles
or 77 kilometers
(1:3,020,000)

MI   20   40   60
20   40   60   KM

© GeoNova Publishing, Inc.

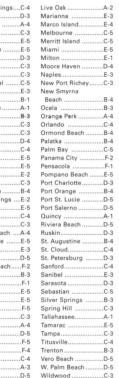

GULF
OF
MEXICO

ATLANTIC
OCEAN

GULF OF MEXICO

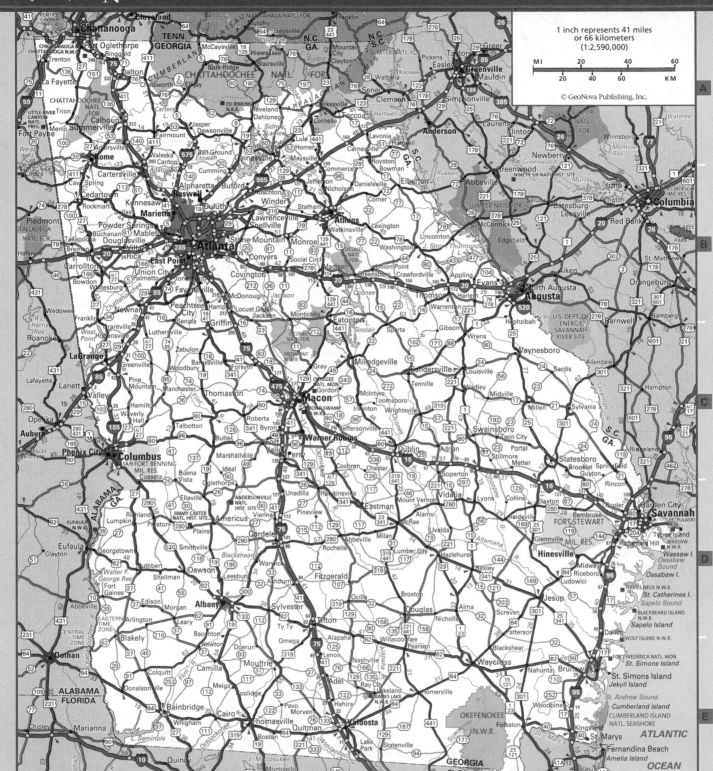

1 inch represents 41 miles
or 66 kilometers
(1:2,590,000)

© GeoNova Publishing, Inc.

P 71 Atlanta

P 6 Alabama

P 16 Florida

P 22 Tennessee

P 40 South Carolina

P 40 North Carolina

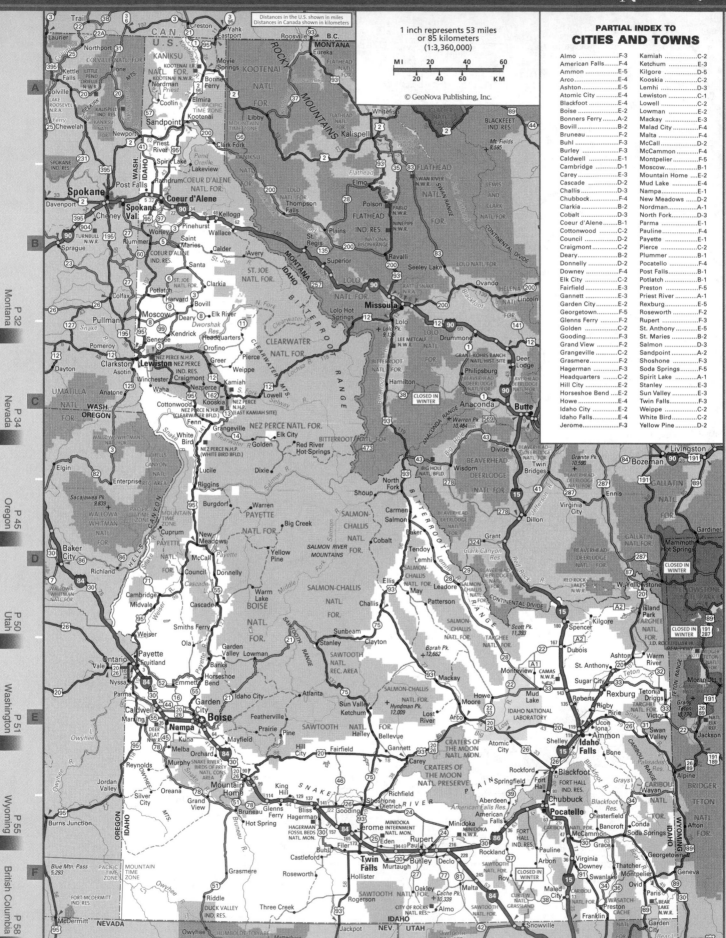

Distances in the U.S. shown in miles
Distances in Canada shown in kilometers

1 inch represents 53 miles
or 85 kilometers
(1:3,360,000)

MI   20   40   60

20   40   60   KM

© GeoNova Publishing, Inc.

PARTIAL INDEX TO CITIES AND TOWNS

P 32 Montana
P 34 Nevada
P 45 Oregon
P 50 Utah
P 51 Washington
P 55 Wyoming
P 58 British Columbia

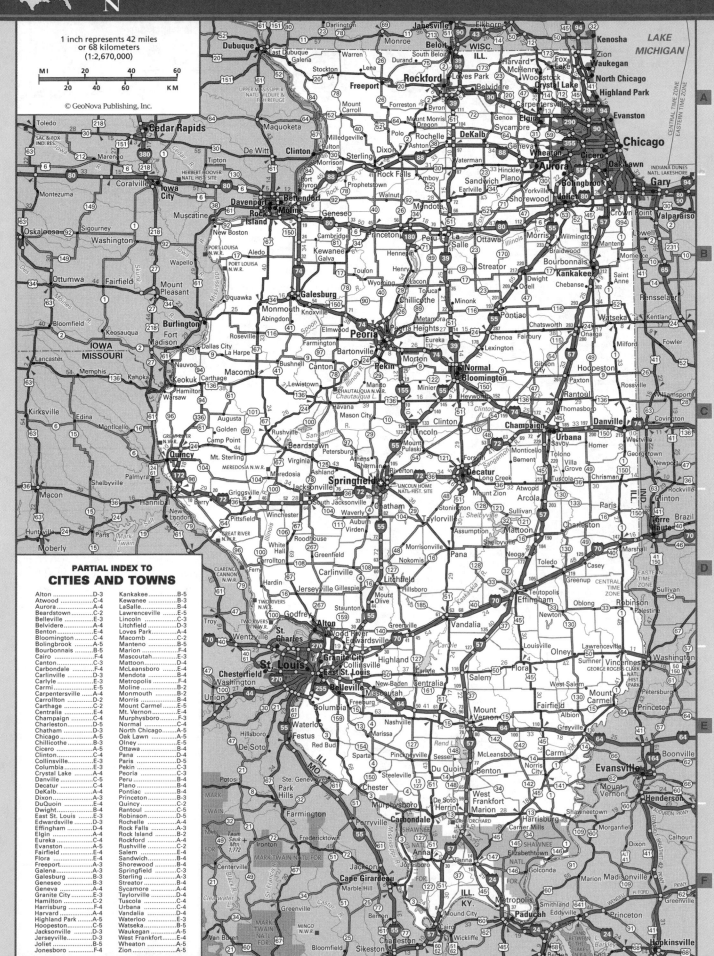

1 inch represents 42 miles
or 68 kilometers
(1:2,670,000)

MI   20   40   60
20   40   60
KM

© GeoNova Publishing, Inc.

LAKE MICHIGAN

IOWA
MISSOURI

PARTIAL INDEX TO
CITIES AND TOWNS

P 78 N. Chicago
P 80 S. Chicago
P 20 Indiana
P 21 Iowa
P 22 Kentucky
P 31 Missouri
P 54 Wisconsin

A B C D E F

1 2 3 4 5

Indiana

LAKE MICHIGAN

N

P 79 Gary
P 94 Indianapolis
P 19 Illinois
P 22 Kentucky
P 28 Michigan
P 43 Ohio

1 inch represents 35 miles
or 56 kilometers
(1:2,200,000)

MI   20   40
20   40 KM

© GeoNova Publishing, Inc.

PARTIAL INDEX TO CITIES AND TOWNS

Alexandria....C-4	Brazil....D-2	Crawfordsville....C-2
Anderson....C-4	Brookville....D-5	Crown Point....A-2
Angola....A-5	Brownsburg....C-3	Danville....C-3
Auburn....A-4	Brownstown....D-3	Decatur....B-5
Austin....D-4	Carmel....C-3	Delphi....B-3
Bedford....D-3	Charlestown....E-4	DeMotte....A-2
Bloomfield....D-2	Clinton....C-2	East Chicago....A-2
Bloomington....D-3	Columbus....D-4	Elkhart....A-4
Bluffton....B-4	Connersville....D-5	Elwood....C-4
Boonville....E-2	Covington....C-2	English....E-3

Evansville....E-2	Indianapolis....C-3	Lowell....A-2
Fort Wayne....B-4	Jasper....E-2	Madison....D-4
Fowler....B-2	Kendallville....A-4	Marion....B-4
Frankfort....C-3	Kentland....B-2	Martinsville....D-3
Franklin....D-3	Knox....A-3	Merrillville....A-2
French Lick....E-3	Kokomo....B-3	Michigan City....A-2
Garrett....A-4	La Porte....A-2	Mishawaka....A-3
Gary....A-2	Lafayette....B-2	Monticello....B-3
Gas City....B-4	Lawrence....C-3	Mt. Vernon....E-1
Goshen....A-4	Lawrenceburg....D-5	Muncie....C-4
Greencastle....C-3	Liberty....C-5	Nappanee....A-4
Greenfield....C-4	Linton....D-2	Nashville....D-3
Greensburg....D-4	Logansport....B-3	New Albany....E-4
Greentown....B-3	Logootee....E-2	New Castle....C-4
Greenwood....C-3		
Hammond....A-2		
Hartford City....B-4		
Huntington....B-4		

New Haven....B-4	Rensselaer....B-2	Sullivan....D-2
Newport....C-2	Richmond....C-5	Tell City....E-3
Noblesville....C-3	Rising Sun....D-5	Terre Haute....D-2
North	Rochester....B-3	Valparaiso....A-2
Manchester....B-4	Rockville....C-2	Versailles....D-4
North Vernon....D-4	Rushville....C-4	Vincennes....E-2
Palmyra....E-3	Salem....E-3	Wabash....B-4
Paoli....E-3	Santa Claus....E-2	Warsaw....A-4
Pendleton....C-4	Scottsburg....D-4	Washington....E-2
Peru....B-3	Seymour....D-4	Westville....A-3
Petersburg....E-2	Shelbyville....D-4	Williamsport....C-2
Portland....B-5	Shoals....E-3	Winchester....C-5
Princeton....E-2	South Bend....A-3	Zionsville....C-3
	Spencer....D-3	

N

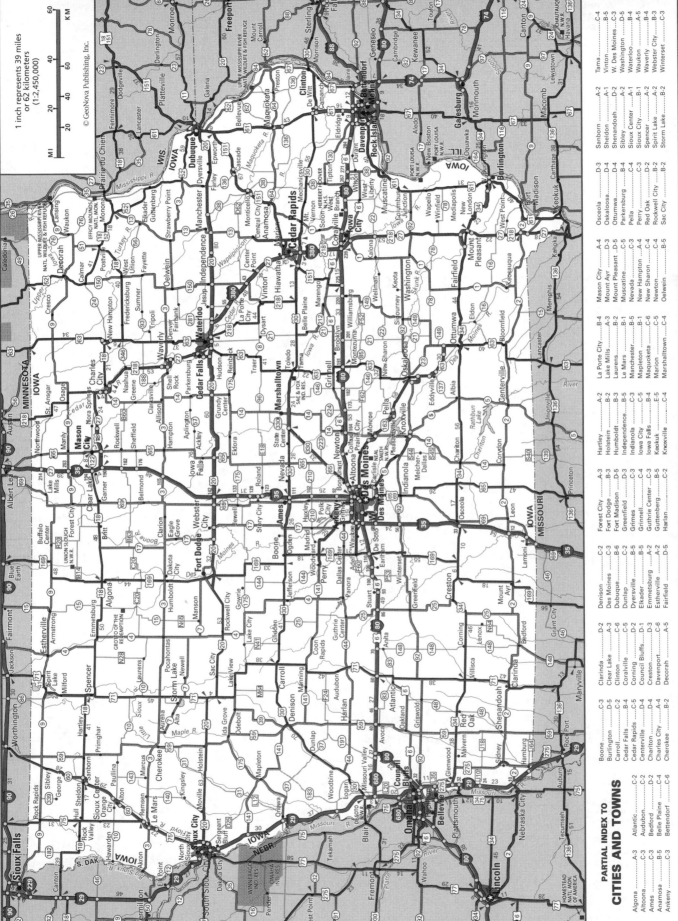

1 inch represents 39 miles
or 62 kilometers
(1:2,450,000)

© GeoNova Publishing, Inc.

P 87 Des Moines
P 19 Illinois
P 27 Minnesota
P 31 Missouri
P 33 Nebraska
P 47 South Dakota
P 54 Wisconsin

P 104 Memphis
P 110 Nashville
P 6 Alabama
P 9 Arkansas
P 19 Illinois
P 20 Indiana
P 30 Mississippi
P 31 Missouri

PARTIAL INDEX TO CITIES AND TOWNS

KENTUCKY

City	Grid	City	Grid	City	Grid
Albany	D-6	Glasgow	D-6	Mt. Sterling	B-8
Alexandria	A-7	Greenville	C-4	Mt. Vernon	C-7
Ashland	B-9	Hardin	D-3	Mt. Washington	B-6
Barbourville	D-8	Hardinsburg	C-5	Munfordville	C-6
Bardstown	C-6	Harlan	D-8	Murray	D-3
Beattyville	C-8	Harrodsburg	C-7	New Castle	B-6
Booneville	C-8	Hazard	C-8	Nicholasville	C-7
Bowling Green	D-5	Henderson	C-4	Owensboro	C-4
Brandenburg	B-5	Hickman	D-2	Owenton	B-7
Brooksville	B-8	Hindman	C-9	Paducah	D-3
Brownsville	C-5	Hopkinsville	D-4	Paintsville	C-9
Burkesville	D-6	Hyden	C-8	Paris	B-7
Cadiz	D-4	Independence	A-7	Pikeville	C-9
Calhoun	C-4	Inez	C-9	Pineville	D-8
Campbellsville	C-6	Jackson	C-8	Prestonburg	C-9
Carrollton	B-6	Jamestown	C-6	Providence	C-4
Catlettsburg	B-9	Lawrenceburg	B-7	Princeton	D-4
Cave City	D-6	Lebanon	C-6	Radcliff	C-6
Clinton	D-3	Leitchfield	C-5	Richmond	C-7
Columbia	D-6	Lexington	B-7	Russellville	D-5
Corbin	D-7	Liberty	C-7	Salyersville	C-8
Covington	A-7	London	C-7	Scottsville	D-5
Cynthiana	B-7	Louisa	B-9	Shelbyville	B-6
Danville	C-7	Louisville	B-6	Somerset	C-7
Dixon	C-4	Madisonville	C-4	Stanford	C-7
Eddyville	C-3	Marion	C-3	Taylorsville	B-6
Edmonton	D-6	Mayfield	D-3	Tompkinsville	D-6
Elizabethtown	C-6	Maysville	B-8	Vanceburg	B-8
Elkhorn City	C-9	McKee	C-8	Versailles	B-7
Falmouth	B-7	Middlesboro	D-8	Whitesburg	C-9
Flemingsburg	B-8	Monticello	D-7	Whitley City	D-7
Frankfort	B-7	Morehead	B-8	Wickliffe	D-2
Franklin	D-5	Morganfield	C-4	Williamsburg	D-7
Fulton	D-3	Morgantown	C-5	Williamstown	B-7
Georgetown	B-7	Mt. Olivet	B-7	Winchester	B-7

TENNESSEE

City	Grid	City	Grid	City	Grid
Adamsville	F-3	Franklin	E-5	New Johnsonville	E-4
Allardt	D-7	Gatlinburg	E-8	New Market	E-8
Ashland City	D-4	Germantown	F-2	Newport	E-8
Athens	F-7	Greeneville	E-9	Oak Ridge	E-7
Baileyton	D-9	Harriman	E-7	Parsons	E-3
Bartlett	F-2	Harrogate	D-8	Pigeon Forge	E-8
Benton	F-7	Henderson	E-3	Pikeville	E-6
Big Sandy	E-3	Hendersonville	E-5	Portland	D-5
Blaine	E-8	Hohenwald	E-4	Pulaski	F-4
Brentwood	E-5	Hornsby	F-3	Ripley	E-2
Bristol	D-9	Huntingdon	E-3	Rockwood	E-7
Brownsville	E-2	Jackson	E-3	Rogersville	D-9
Bulls Gap	D-8	Jamestown	D-7	Rutledge	D-8
Calhoun	F-7	Jefferson City	D-8	Savannah	F-3
Camden	E-3	Johnson City	D-9	Selmer	F-3
Centerville	E-4	Jonesborough	D-9	Sevierville	E-8
Chattanooga	F-6	Kingsport	D-9	Shelbyville	F-5
Clarksville	D-4	Knoxville	E-8	Signal Mountain	F-6
Cleveland	F-7	La Follette	D-7	Smyrna	E-5
Collegedale	F-7	Lake City	E-7	Soddy-Daisy	F-6
Collinwood	F-4	Lawrenceburg	F-4	Somerville	F-2
Columbia	E-4	Lebanon	E-5	Sparta	E-6
Cookeville	E-6	Lenoir City	E-7	Spencer	E-6
Covington	E-2	Lexington	E-3	Springfield	D-5
Crab Orchard	E-7	Linden	E-4	Sweetwater	E-7
Crossville	E-7	Livingston	D-6	Tazewell	D-8
Dandridge	E-8	Madisonville	E-7	Trenton	E-3
Dayton	E-7	Manchester	F-5	Tullahoma	F-5
Dickson	E-4	Maryville	E-8	Union City	D-2
Dover	D-4	McKenzie	E-3	Wartburg	E-7
Dresden	D-3	McMinnville	E-6	Waverly	E-4
Ducktown	F-7	Memphis	F-1	Waynesboro	F-4
Dunlap	F-6	Milan	E-3	Westmoreland	D-5
Dyersburg	E-2	Milledgeville	F-3	Whiteville	F-2
Elizabethton	D-9	Millington	F-2	Whitewell	F-6
Elkton	F-5	Monteagle	F-6	Winchester	F-5
Erin	D-4	Monterey	E-6	Winfield	D-7
Fayetteville	F-5	Morristown	E-8	
		Murfreesboro	E-5	
		Nashville	E-5	

1 2 3 4 5

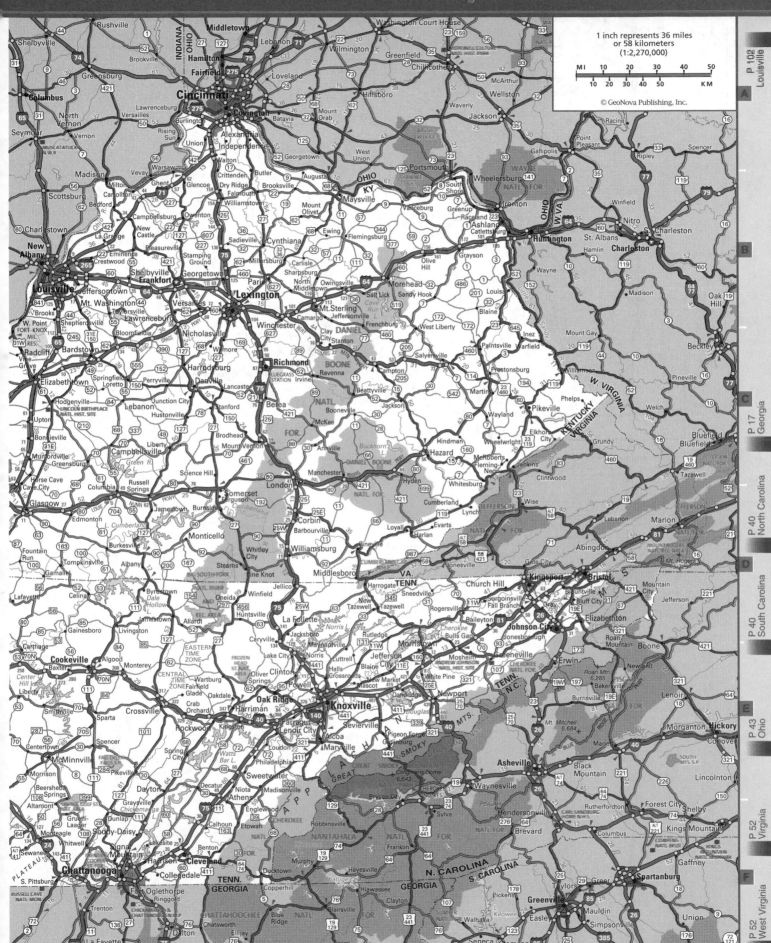

© GeoNova Publishing, Inc.

1 inch represents 36 miles
or 58 kilometers
(1:2,270,000)

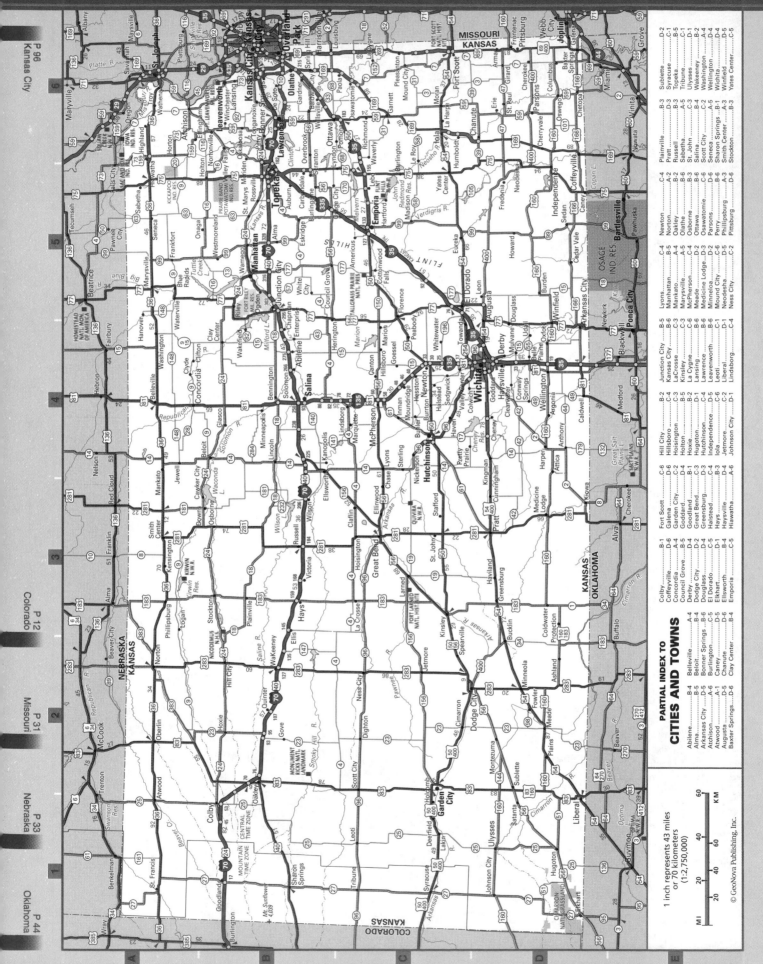

PARTIAL INDEX TO
CITIES AND TOWNS

Abilene	B-4
Alma	C-5
Arkansas City	D-5
Atchison	A-6
Atwood	A-1
Augusta	D-5
Baxter Springs	D-6

Belleville	A-4
Beloit	B-4
Bonner Springs	C-5
Burlington	C-5
Caney	D-6
Chanute	D-5
Clay Center	B-4

Colby	B-1
Coffeyville	D-6
Concordia	A-4
Council Grove	C-4
Derby	D-5
Dodge City	D-2
Douglass	D-5
El Dorado	D-5
Elkhart	D-1
Ellsworth	B-4
Emporia	C-5

Fort Scott	C-6
Galena	D-6
Garden City	C-2
Goddard	D-4
Great Bend	C-3
Greensburg	D-3
Halstead	C-4
Hays	B-3
Haysville	D-4
Hiawatha	A-6

Hill City	B-2
Hillsboro	C-4
Hoisington	C-3
Holton	B-5
Hoxie	B-2
Hugoton	D-1
Hutchinson	C-4
Iola	C-5
Independence	D-6
Jetmore	C-2
Johnson City	D-1

Junction City	B-4
Kansas City	C-6
Kinsley	C-3
La Cygne	C-6
Lansing	C-6
Lawrence	C-5
Leavenworth	C-6
Leoti	C-1
Liberal	D-1
Lindsborg	C-4

Lyons	C-3
Mankato	A-4
Marion	C-4
McPherson	C-4
Meade	D-2
Medicine Lodge	D-3
Minneola	D-2
Mound City	C-6
Ness City	C-2

Newton	C-4
Norton	A-2
Oakley	B-1
Olathe	C-5
Osborne	B-3
Ottawa	C-5
Osawatomie	C-6
Parsons	D-5
Perry	C-5
Phillipsburg	A-3
Pittsburg	D-6

Plainville	B-3
Pratt	D-3
Russell	B-3
Sabetha	A-5
St. John	C-3
Salina	B-4
Scott City	C-2
Seneca	A-5
Sharon Springs	B-1
Smith Center	A-3
Stockton	B-3

Sublette	D-2
Syracuse	C-1
Topeka	B-5
Tribune	C-1
Ulysses	D-1
Wakeeney	B-2
Washington	A-4
Wellington	D-4
Wichita	D-4
Winfield	D-5
Yates Center	C-5

1 inch represents 43 miles
or 70 kilometers
(1:2,750,000)

© GeoNova Publishing, Inc.

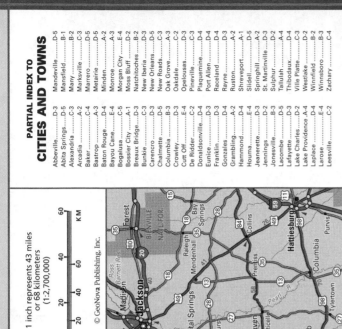

PARTIAL INDEX TO CITIES AND TOWNS

Abbeville	D-3	Jeanerette	D-4	Pineville	C-3
Abita Springs	B-1	Jennings	D-3	Plaquemine	C-4
Alexandria	C-3	Jonesville	B-3	Port Allen	D-4
Arcadia	A-2	Lacombe	C-5	Raceland	D-4
Baker	C-4	Lafayette	D-3	Rayne	D-3
Bastrop	A-3	Lake Charles	D-2	Ruston	A-2
Baton Rouge	C-4	Lake Providence	A-4	St. Martinville	D-5
Bayou Cane	D-5	Larose	E-4	Slidell	C-5
Bogalusa	B-2	Leesville	C-2	Springhill	A-1
Bossier City	B-2	Mandeville	D-3	Sulphur	D-2
Breaux Bridge	D-3	Mansfield	B-1	Tallulah	A-4
Bunkie	C-3	Many	C-3	Thibodaux	D-4
Carencro	D-3	Marksville	C-3	Ville Platte	C-3
Chalmette	C-5	Marrero	C-4	Westlake	D-2
Columbia	B-3	Metairie	D-5	Winnfield	B-2
Crowley	D-3	Minden	A-2	Winnsboro	B-3
Cut Off	D-5	Monroe	A-3	Zachary	C-4
De Ridder	C-2	Morgan City	E-4		
Donaldsonville	C-4	Moss Bluff	D-2		
Eunice	D-3	Natchitoches	B-2		
Franklin	D-4	New Iberia	D-5		
Gonzales	C-4	New Roads	C-3		
Grambling	A-2	Oak Grove	A-3		
Hammond	C-4	Oakdale	C-2		
Houma	E-4	Opelousas	D-3		

1 inch represents 43 miles
or 68 kilometers
(1:2,700,000)

© GeoNova Publishing, Inc.

P 73 Baton Rouge

P 111 New Orleans

P 9 Arkansas

P 30 Mississippi

P 48 Texas

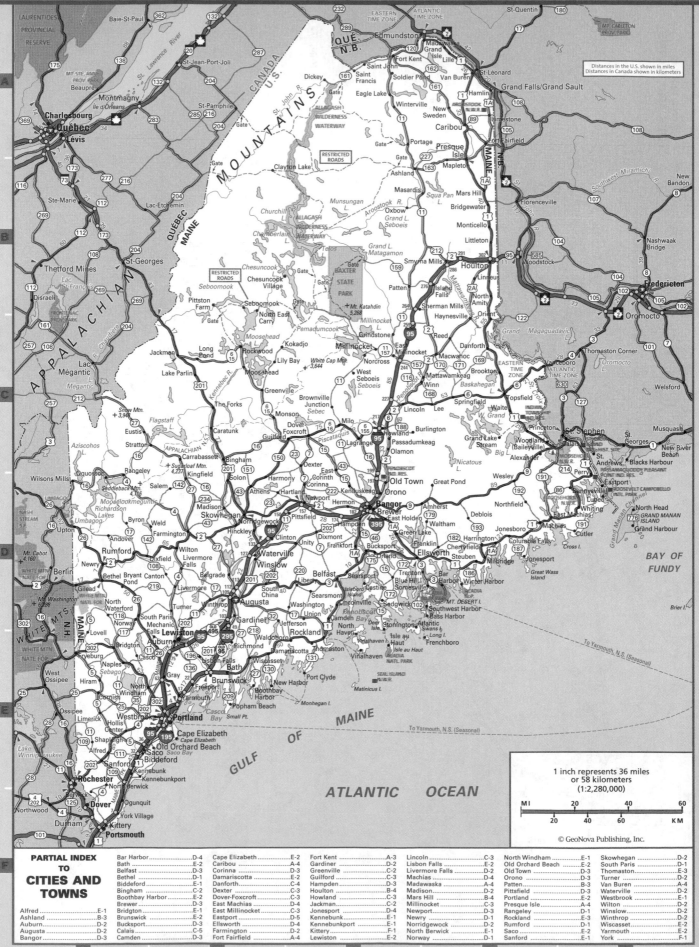

1 inch represents 36 miles
or 58 kilometers
(1:2,280,000)

MI   20   40   60

20   40   60   KM

© GeoNova Publishing, Inc.

BAY OF FUNDY

ATLANTIC OCEAN

GULF OF MAINE

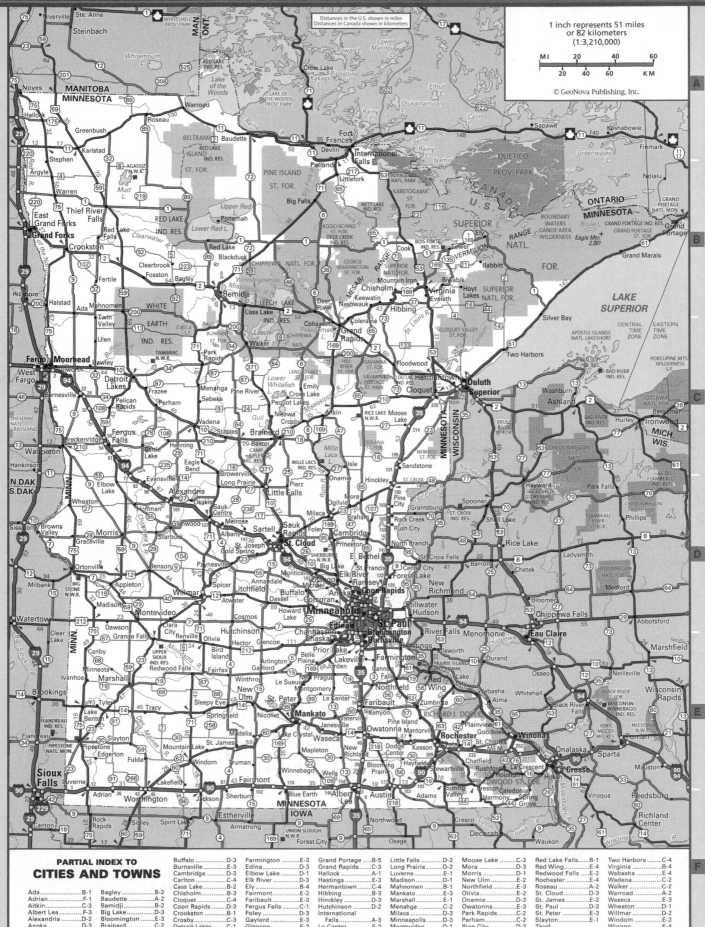

P 106 Minneapolis

P 21 Iowa

P 42 North Dakota

P 47 South Dakota

P 54 Wisconsin

P 61 Manitoba

P 62 Ontario

1 inch represents 51 miles
or 82 kilometers
(1:3,210,000)

MI 20 40 60

20 40 60 KM

© GeoNova Publishing, Inc.

Distances in the U.S. shown in miles
Distances in Canada shown in kilometers

PARTIAL INDEX TO
CITIES AND TOWNS

Ada B-1	Buffalo D-3	Farmington E-3	Grand Portage B-5	Little Falls D-2	Moose Lake C-3	Red Lake Falls .. B-1	Two Harbors C-4
Adrian F-1	Burnsville E-3	Edina D-3	Grand Rapids C-3	Long Prairie D-2	Mora D-3	Red Wing E-4	Virginia B-4
Aitkin C-3	Cambridge D-3	Elbow Lake D-1	Hallock A-1	Luverne E-1	Morris D-1	Redwood Falls E-2	Wabasha E-4
Albert Lea F-3	Carlton C-4	Elk River D-3	Hastings E-3	Madison D-1	New Ulm E-2	Rochester E-4	Wadena C-2
Alexandria D-2	Cass Lake B-2	Ely B-4	Hermantown C-4	Mahnomen B-1	Northfield E-3	Roseau A-2	Walker C-2
Anoka D-3	Chisholm B-3	Fairmont F-2	Hibbing B-3	Mankato E-3	Olivia E-2	St. Cloud D-3	Warroad A-2
Austin F-3	Cloquet C-4	Faribault E-3	Hinckley D-3	Marshall E-1	Onamia D-3	St. James E-2	Waseca E-3
	Coon Rapids D-3	Fergus Falls C-1	Hutchinson D-2	Menahga C-2	Owatonna E-3	St. Paul D-3	Wheaton D-1
Bagley B-2	Crookston B-1	Foley D-3	International	Milaca D-3	Park Rapids C-2	St. Peter E-2	Willmar D-2
Baudette A-2	Crosby C-3	Gaylord E-2	Falls A-3	Minneapolis D-3	Perham C-2	Slayton E-1	Windom E-2
Bemidji B-2	Detroit Lakes C-1	Glencoe E-3	Le Center E-3	Montevideo D-1	Pine City D-3	Thief	Winona E-4
Big Lake D-3	Duluth C-4	Grand Marais B-5	Litchfield D-2	Moorhead C-1	Pipestone E-1	River Falls B-1	Worthington F-2
Bloomington ... E-3							
Brainerd D-3							
Breckenridge .. C-1							

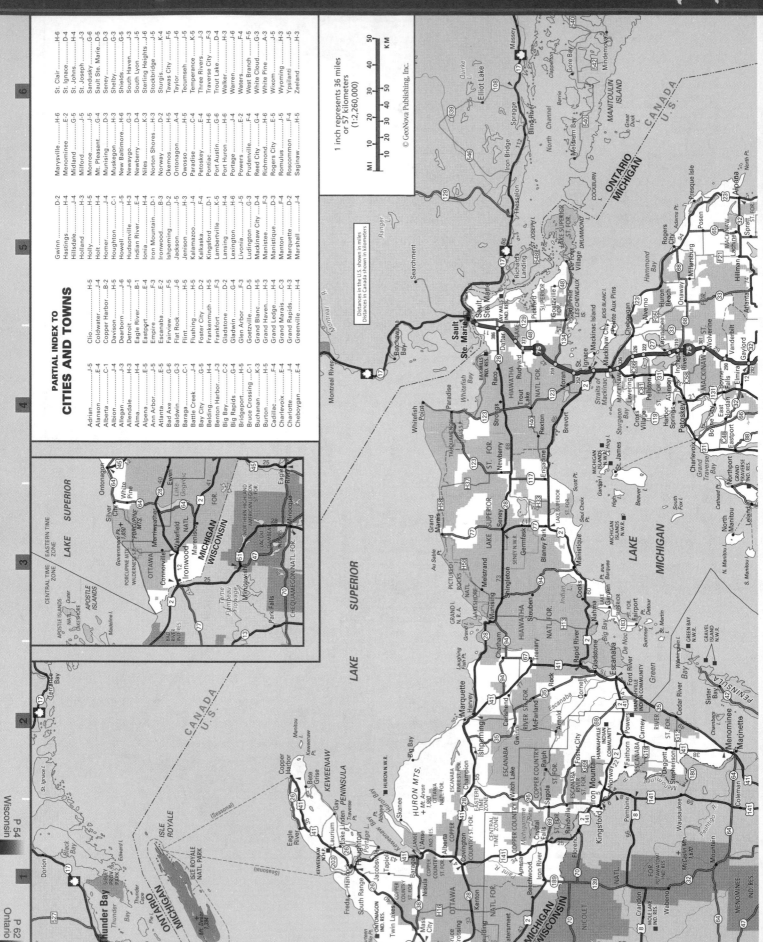

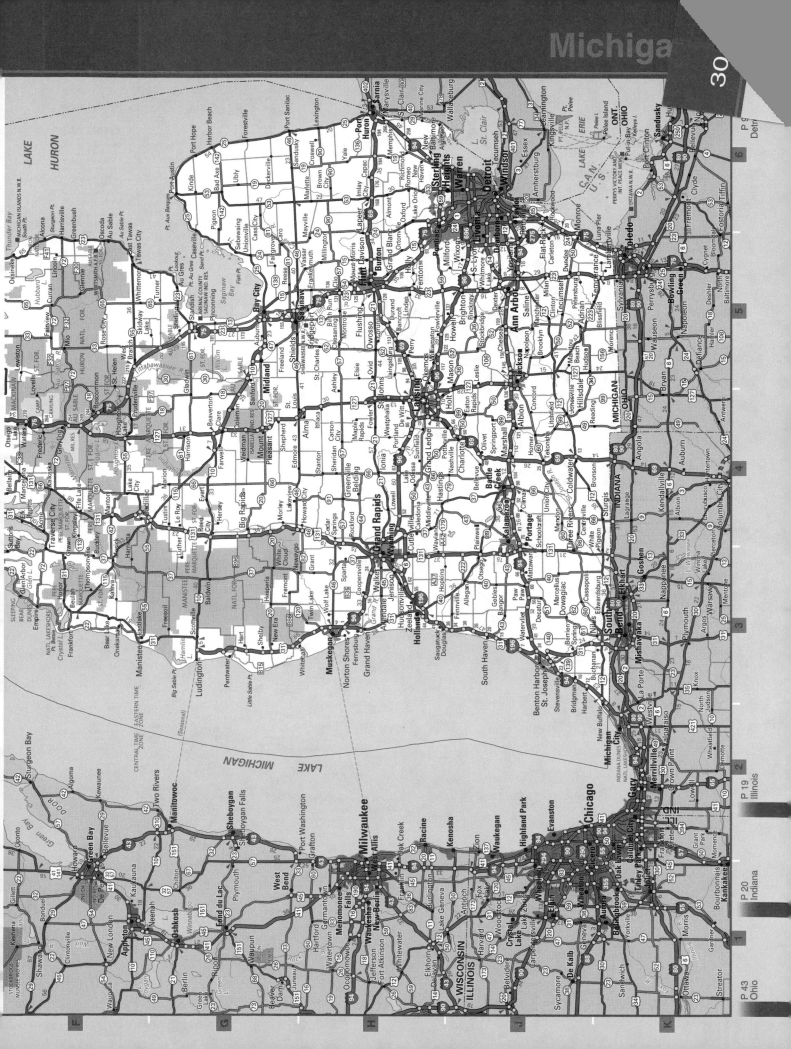

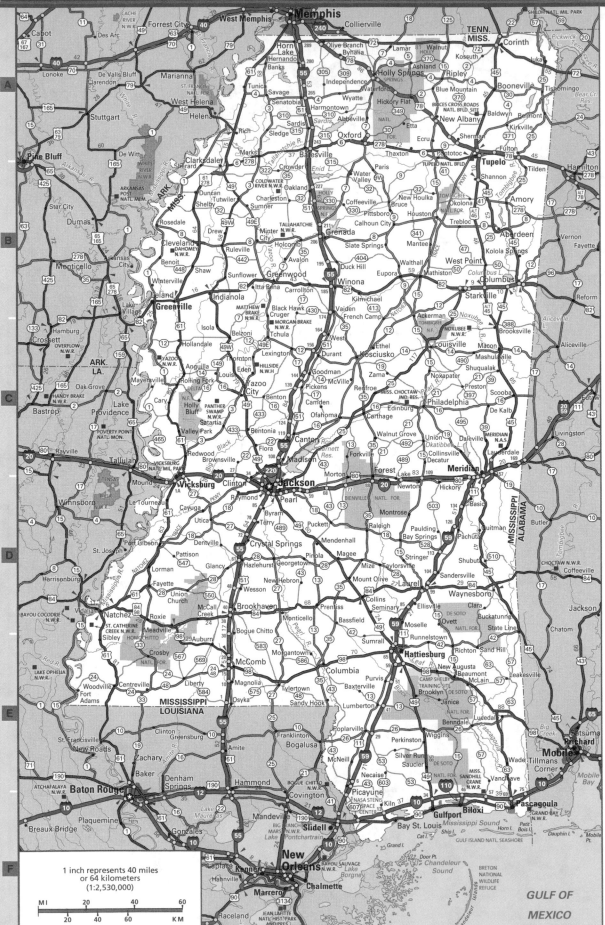

1 inch represents 40 miles
or 64 kilometers
(1:2,530,000)

© GeoNova Publishing, Inc.

GULF OF MEXICO

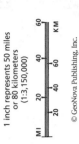

1 inch represents 50 miles
or 80 kilometers
(1:3,150,000)

© GeoNova Publishing, Inc.

MI
KM

0 20 40 60
0 20 40 60 80

PARTIAL INDEX TO
CITIES AND TOWNS

Alton	A-3	Lancaster	E-4	
Anderson	E-2	LaPlata	A-3	
Appleton City	C-2	Lebanon	D-3	
Ash Grove	D-2	Liberty	B-2	
Aurora	D-2	Licking	D-3	
Bethany	A-2	Louisiana	C-1	
Belton	B-3	Macon	B-3	
Bethany	A-2	Madison	E-5	
Bolivar	D-2	Malden	D-2	
Bonne Terre	C-4	Marshall	B-2	
Boonville	B-3	Marshfield	D-3	
Bowling Green	B-4	Maryville	A-1	
Branson	E-2	Memphis	B-3	
Brunswick	B-2	Mexico	B-3	
Cabool	D-3	Moberly	B-3	
Camdenton	C-3	Monett	A-4	
Canton	A-4	Monett	D-5	
Cape Girardeau	B-3	Montgomery City	B-4	
Carrollton	B-2	Mountain Grove	D-3	
Carthage	D-2	Neosho	E-5	
Caruthersville	D-5	Nevada	D-2	
Cassville	E-2	O'Fallon	B-4	
Charleston	D-5	Owensville	C-4	
Chesterfield	B-4	Ozark	D-2	
Chillicothe	B-2	Paris	B-3	
Clinton	C-2	Perryville	C-4	
Columbia	B-3	Piedmont	D-4	
Cuba	C-4	Poplar Bluff	E-4	
DeSoto	C-4	Potosi	C-4	
Dexter	D-4	Princeton	A-2	
Doniphan	E-4	Republic	A-3	
Edina	A-3	Richland	C-3	
Eldorado Springs	C-2	Richmond	B-2	
Ellington	D-4	Rock Port	A-1	
Elsberry	B-4	Rolla	C-3	
Eminence	D-4	Salem	C-3	
Excelsior Springs	B-2	St. Charles	B-4	
Farmington	C-4	St. James	C-3	
Festus	C-4	St. Joseph	B-1	
Flat River	C-4	St. Louis	B-4	
Forsyth	E-2	Salem	C-4	
Fredericktown	D-4	Savannah	A-1	
Fulton	B-3	Sedalia	C-2	
Gainesville	E-3	Shelbina	A-2	
Gallatin	A-2	Sikeston	D-5	
Greenfield	D-2	Stanberry	A-2	
Greenville	D-4	Sullivan	C-4	
Hamilton	B-2	Summersville	D-4	
Hannibal	B-4	Trenton	A-2	
Harrisonville	B-2	Union	C-4	
Hermitage	D-2	Unionville	A-3	
Houston	D-3	Vandalia	B-4	
Independence	B-2	Versailles	C-3	
Ironton	D-4	Vienna	C-4	
Jackson	C-5	Vienna	C-4	
Jefferson City	B-3	Warrenton	B-4	
Joplin	D-1	Warsaw	C-2	
Kansas City	B-1	Washington	B-4	
Kennett	E-5	Waynesville	C-3	
Keytesville	B-3	Webb City	D-2	
King City	A-2	West Plains	E-3	
Kirksville	A-3	Wentzville	B-4	
LaBelle	A-4	Willow Springs	D-3	
LaGrange	A-4	Winona	C-3	
Lake Ozark	C-3			

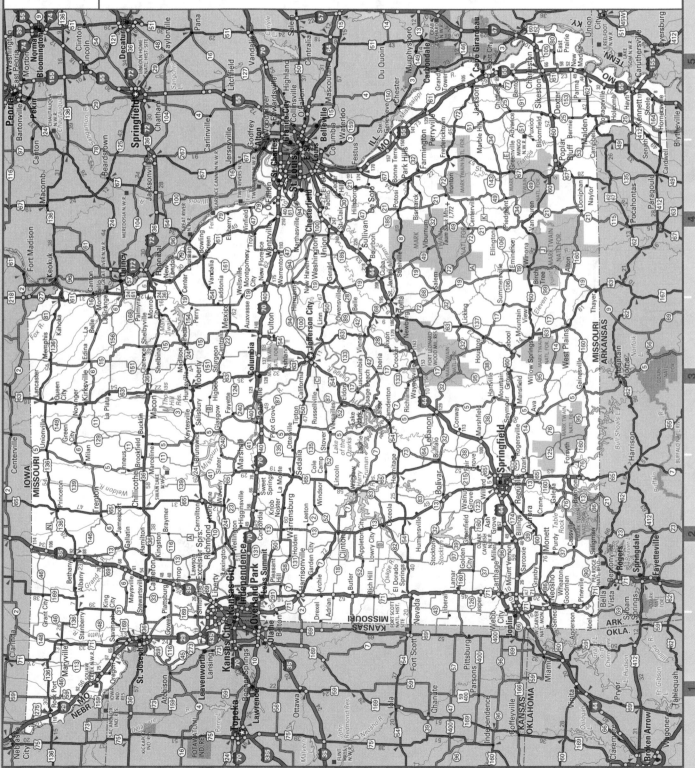

P 96   Kansas City

P 128   St. Louis

P 9   Arkansas

P 19   Illinois

P 21   Iowa

P 22   Tennessee

P 24   Kansas

P 33   Nebraska

P 44   Oklahoma

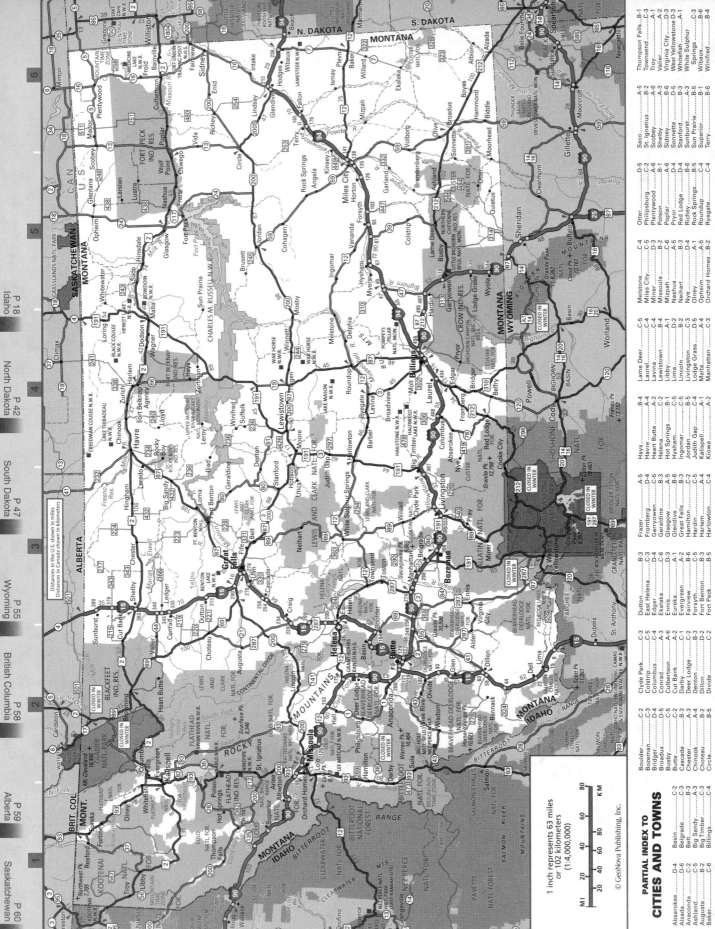

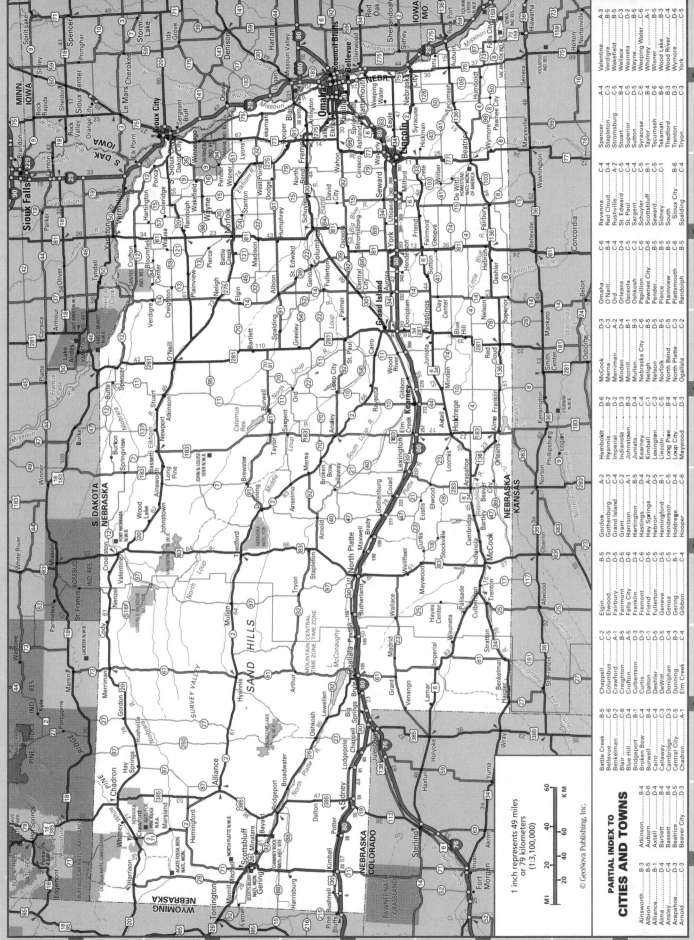

1 inch represents 49 miles
or 79 kilometers
(1:3,100,000)

© GeoNova Publishing, Inc.

PARTIAL INDEX TO
CITIES AND TOWNS

Ainsworth	B-3		Battle Creek	B-5
Albion	B-5		Bellevue	C-6
Alliance	A-1		Blair	D-2
Alma	C-4		Blue Hill	C-4
Ansley	C-4		Bridgeport	B-1
Arapahoe	D-3		Broken Bow	C-4
Arnold	C-3		Burwell	B-4
Atkinson	B-4		Cairo	C-4
Auburn	D-6		Callaway	C-3
Axtell	D-4		Cambridge	C-3
Bartlett	B-4		Central City	C-5
Bassett	B-4		Chadron	D-3
Beatrice	D-5		Chappell	B-2
Beaver City	D-3			

Chappell	B-2		Elgin	C-2
Columbus	C-5		Elwood	C-3
Crawford	A-1		Fairbury	D-5
Creighton	B-5		Fairfield	C-2
Crofton	A-5		Falls City	C-6
Culbertson	C-3		Franklin	C-4
Curtis	C-4		Fremont	C-6
Dalton	B-1		Friend	D-5
Deshler	D-5		Fullerton	C-5
DeWitt	D-5		Genoa	C-5
Doniphan	C-4		Geneva	D-5
Dunning	B-3		Gibbon	C-4
Elm Creek	C-4			

Gordon	B-5		Humboldt	A-2
Gothenburg	D-3		Hyannis	C-3
Grand Island	C-4		Imperial	C-2
Grant	C-2		Innavale	A-5
Harrison	A-1		Johnstown	A-1
Hartington	B-5		Juniata	B-5
Hastings	C-4		Kearney	C-4
Hay Springs	A-2		Kimball	C-1
Hebron	D-5		Lexington	C-3
Hemingford	C-5		Lincoln	B-1
Henderson	C-5		Long Pine	B-4
Holdrege	B-1		Loup City	C-5
Hooper	C-6		Maywood	D-3

McCook	D-6		Omaha	D-3
Merna	B-2		O'Neill	B-2
Minden	D-4		Ord	C-2
Morrill	B-3		Orleans	D-4
Mullen	B-3		Osceola	C-5
Nebraska City	C-1		Oshkosh	B-3
Neligh	B-5		Papillion	B-4
Nelson	C-3		Pawnee City	C-6
Norfolk	B-5		Pender	D-5
North Bend	C-3		Pierce	C-5
North Platte	C-5		Plainview	B-4
Ogallala	C-2		Plattsmouth	C-3
			Randolph	B-5

Ravenna	C-6		Spencer	A-3
Red Cloud	D-4		Stapleton	B-5
Stuart	D-4		Stromsburg	C-3
St. Edward	A-2		Stuart	C-4
St. Paul	C-4		Superior	C-4
Sargent	C-5		Sutton	C-5
Schuyler	D-6		Syracuse	C-5
Scottsbluff	B-1		Taylor	B-4
Seward	C-5		Tecumseh	D-6
Sidney	C-1		Tekamah	B-3
South			Thedford	B-3
Sioux City	B-6		Trenton	D-6
Spalding	B-5		Tryon	C-3

Valentine	A-3			
Verdigre	B-5			
Wakefield	C-3			
Wallace	D-2			
Wauneta	C-2			
Wayne	B-5			
Weeping Water	C-6			
Whitney	A-1			
Wisner	B-5			
Wood Lake	B-3			
Wood River	C-4			
Wymore	D-6			
York	C-5			

P 117 Omaha
P 12 Colorado
P 21 Iowa
P 24 Kansas
P 31 Missouri
P 47 South Dakota
P 55 Wyoming

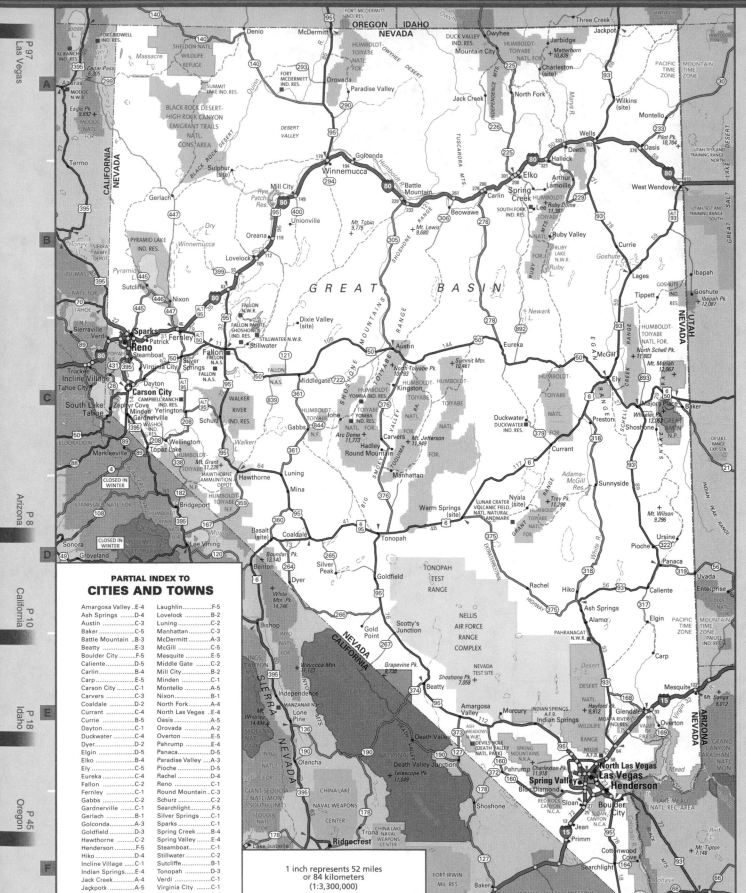

PARTIAL INDEX TO
CITIES AND TOWNS

1 inch represents 52 miles
or 84 kilometers
(1:3,300,000)

MI   20   40   60
20   40   60
KM

© GeoNova Publishing, Inc.

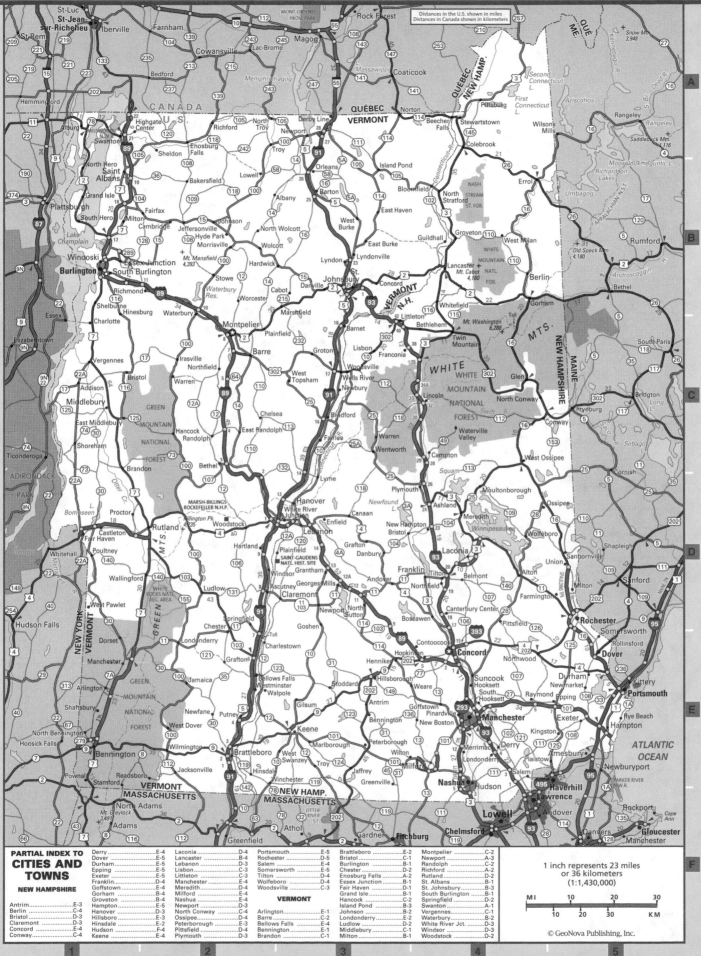

Distances in the U.S. shown in miles
Distances in Canada shown in kilometers

QUÉBEC
NEW HAMP.
VERMONT
N.H.
NEW HAMPSHIRE
MAINE
MASSACHUSETTS
NEW YORK
ATLANTIC OCEAN
CANADA
U.S.
QUÉBEC

PARTIAL INDEX TO CITIES AND TOWNS

NEW HAMPSHIRE

Antrim	E-3
Berlin	C-4
Bristol	D-3
Claremont	D-2
Concord	E-4
Conway	C-4
Derry	E-4
Dover	E-5
Durham	E-5
Epping	E-5
Exeter	E-5
Franklin	D-4
Goffstown	E-4
Gorham	B-4
Groveton	B-4
Hampton	E-5
Hanover	D-3
Hillsboro	E-3
Hinsdale	E-2
Hudson	F-4
Keene	E-4
Laconia	D-4
Lancaster	B-4
Lebanon	D-3
Littleton	C-3
Manchester	E-4
Meredith	D-4
Milford	E-4
Nashua	E-4
Newport	D-3
North Conway	C-4
Ossipee	D-4
Peterborough	E-3
Pittsfield	E-4
Plymouth	D-3
Portsmouth	E-5
Rochester	D-5
Salem	E-4
Somersworth	D-4
Tilton	D-4
Wolfeboro	D-4
Woodsville	C-3

VERMONT

Arlington	E-1
Barre	C-2
Bellows Falls	D-2
Bennington	E-1
Brandon	C-1
Brattleboro	E-2
Bristol	C-1
Burlington	B-1
Chester	D-2
Enosburg Falls	A-2
Essex Junction	B-1
Fair Haven	D-1
Grand Isle	B-1
Hancock	C-2
Island Pond	B-3
Johnson	B-2
Londonderry	E-2
Ludlow	D-2
Middlebury	C-1
Milton	B-1
Montpelier	C-2
Newport	A-3
Randolph	C-2
Richford	A-2
Rutland	D-2
St. Albans	B-1
St. Johnsbury	B-3
South Burlington	B-1
Springfield	D-2
Swanton	A-1
Vergennes	C-1
Waterbury	B-2
White River Jct.	D-3
Windsor	D-3
Woodstock	D-2

1 inch represents 23 miles or 36 kilometers
(1:1,430,000)

MI   10   20   30
10   20   30   KM

© GeoNova Publishing, Inc.

P 14 Massachusetts
P 26 Maine
P 38 New York
P 64 Québec

N

PARTIAL INDEX TO CITIES AND TOWNS

1 inch represents 18 miles
or 29 kilometers
(1:1,160,000)

MI   10   20

10   20   KM

© GeoNova Publishing, Inc.

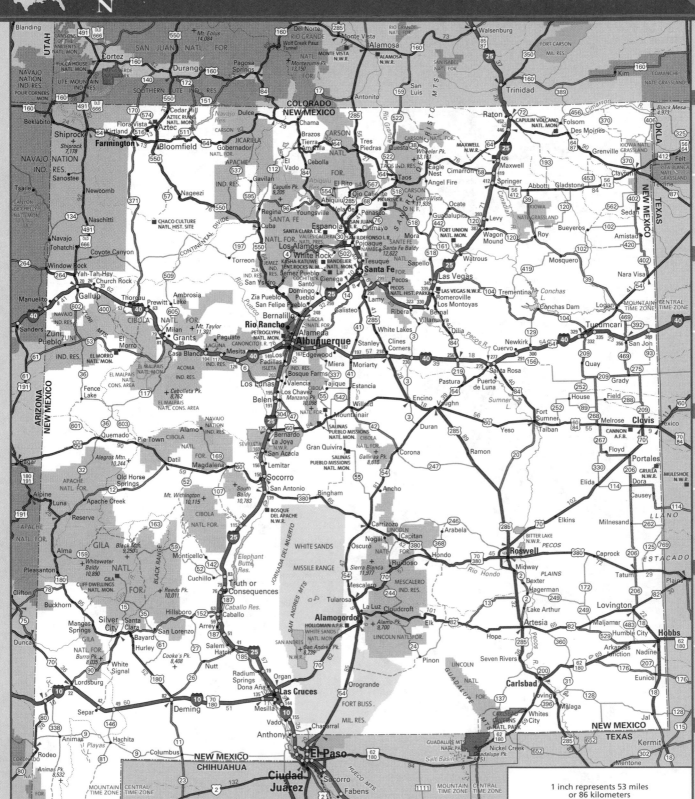

Map Legend and Scale

1 inch represents 53 miles
or 86 kilometers
(1:3,380,000)

MI 20 40 60

20 40 60 KM

© GeoNova Publishing, Inc.

Distances in the U.S. shown in miles
Distances in Mexico shown in kilometers

P 76 Buffalo
P 112 New York City
P 125 Rochester
P 36 New Jersey
P 46 Pennsylvania
P 62 Ontario

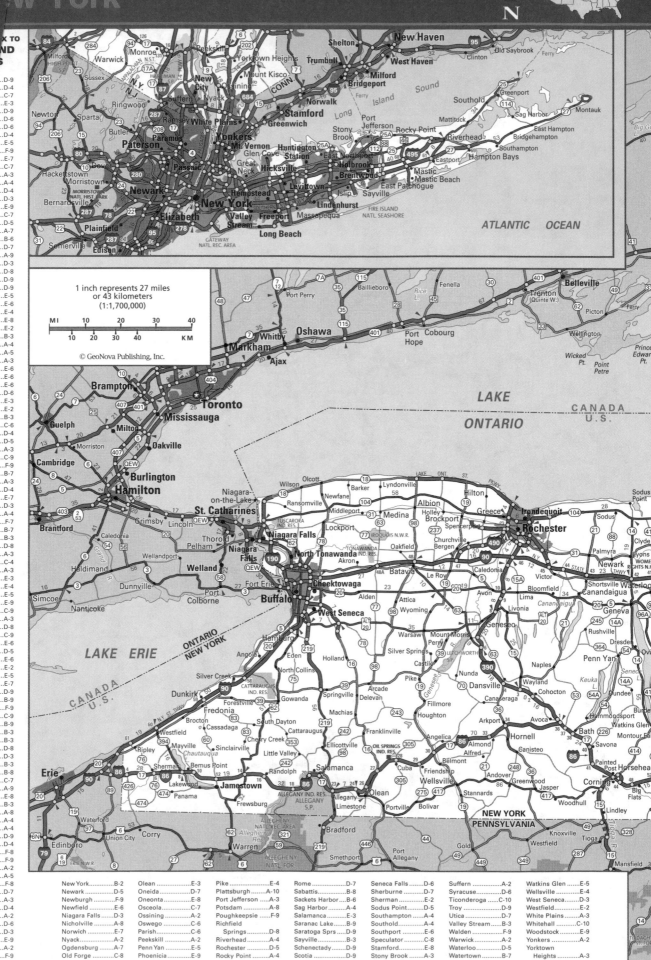

1 inch represents 27 miles
or 43 kilometers
(1:1,700,000)

© GeoNova Publishing, Inc.

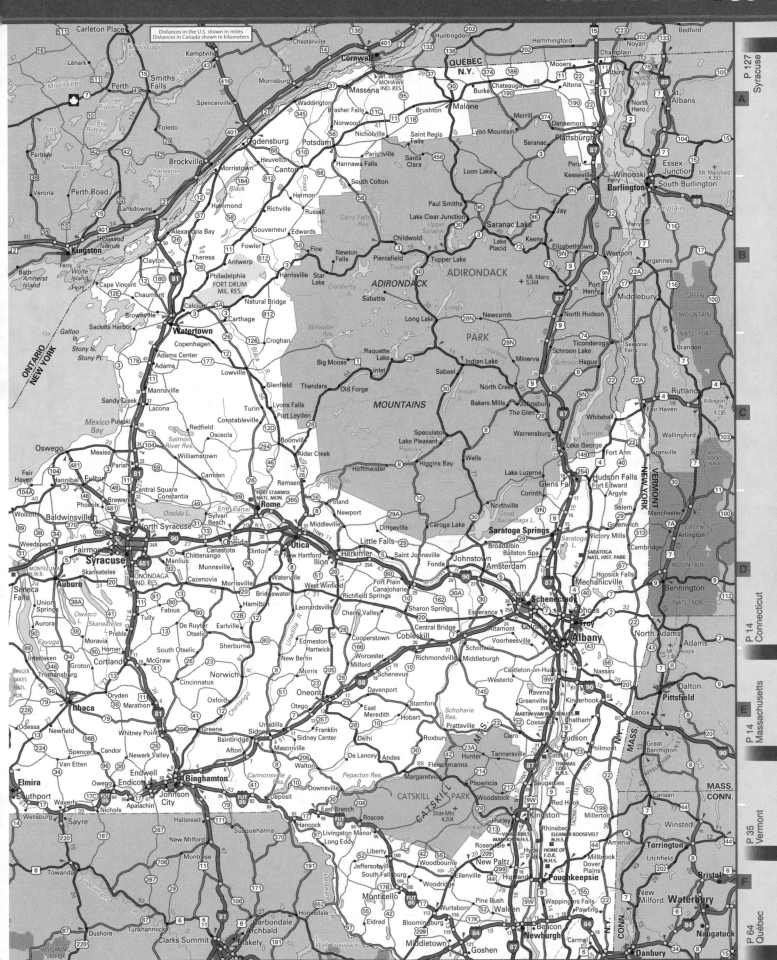

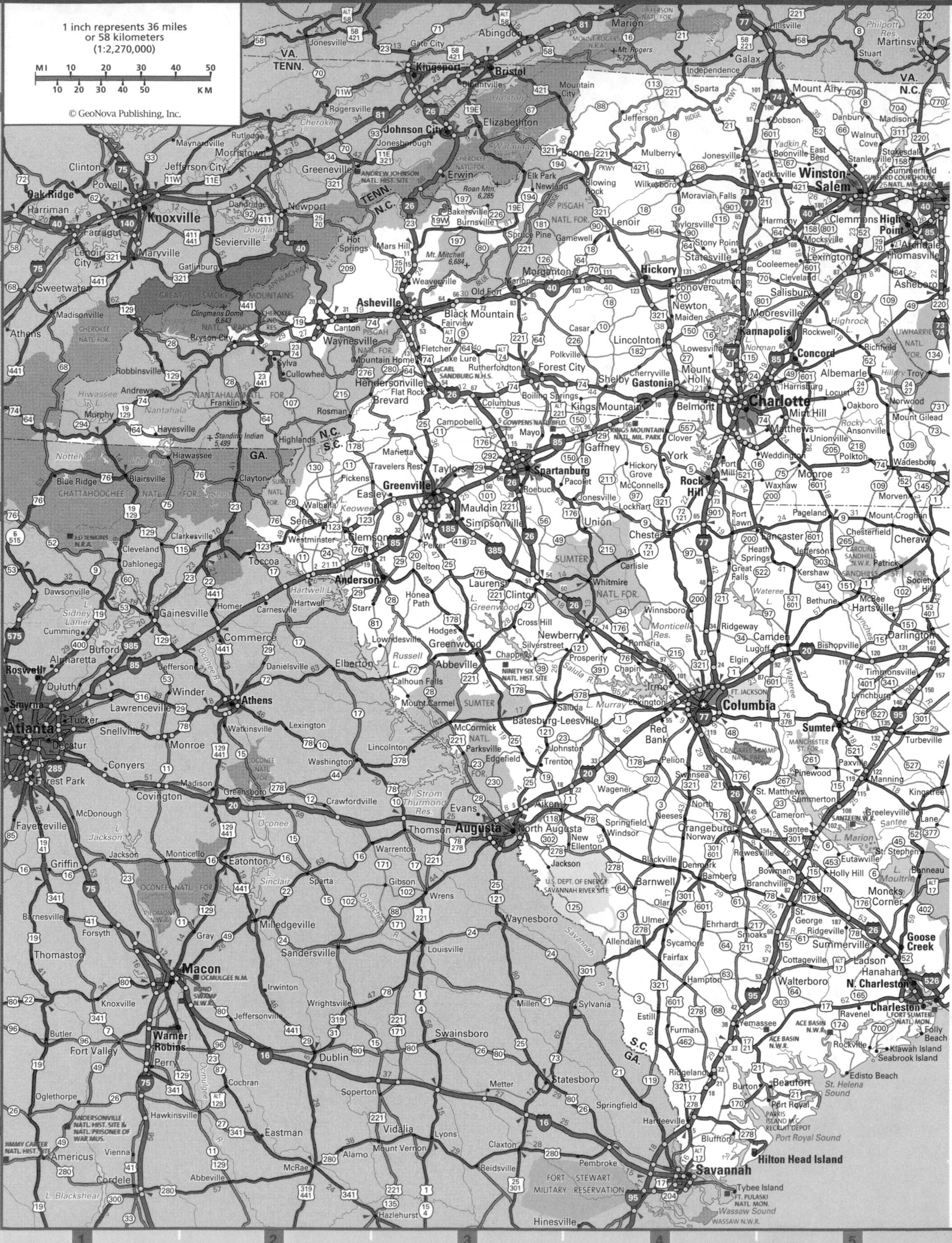

N

1 inch represents 36 miles
or 58 kilometers
(1:2,270,000)

MI 10 20 30 40 50
10 20 30 40 50 KM

© GeoNova Publishing, Inc.

P 73 Charleston
P 77 Charlotte
P 138 Winston-Salem
P 17 Georgia
P 22 Tennessee
P 52 Virginia

VA.
TENN.
TENN.
N.C.
N.C.
S.C.
S.C.
GA.
GA.
VA.
N.C.

Kingsport
Bristol
Johnson City
Knoxville
Oak Ridge
Harriman
Maryville
Sweetwater
Asheville
Black Mountain
Hickory
Winston-Salem
High Point
Clemmons
Mooresville
Kannapolis
Concord
Charlotte
Gastonia
Rock Hill
Spartanburg
Greenville
Anderson
Columbia
Sumter
Augusta
North Augusta
Aiken
Orangeburg
Summerville
Goose Creek
Hanahan
N. Charleston
Charleston
Savannah
Hilton Head Island
Macon
Warner Robins
Atlanta
Athens
Gainesville
Roswell
Smyrna
Decatur

1 2 3 4 5
A B C D E F

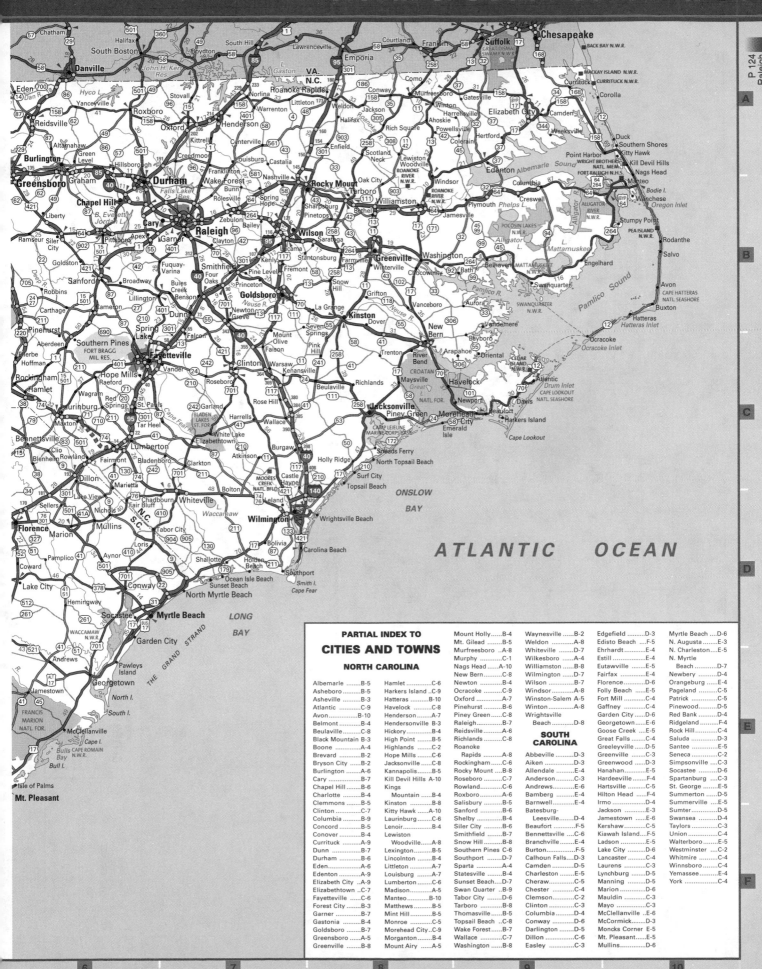

P 124
Raleigh

ATLANTIC OCEAN

ONSLOW BAY

LONG BAY

THE GRAND STRAND

PARTIAL INDEX TO
CITIES AND TOWNS

NORTH CAROLINA

Albemarle B-5	Hamlet C-6	Mount Holly......B-4	Waynesville B-2
Asheboro B-5	Harkers Island ..C-9	Mt. Gilead B-5	Weldon A-8
Asheville B-3	Hatteras B-10	Murfreesboro ..A-8	Whiteville D-7
Atlantic C-9	Havelock C-8	Murphy C-1	Wilkesboro A-4
Avon B-10	Henderson A-7	Nags Head A-10	Williamston B-8
Belmont B-4	Hendersonville B-3	New Bern C-8	Wilmington D-7
Beulaville C-8	Hickory B-4	Newton B-4	Wilson B-7
Black Mountain B-3	High Point B-5	Ocracoke C-9	Windsor A-8
Boone A-4	Highlands C-2	Oxford A-7	Winston-Salem A-5
Brevard B-2	Hope Mills C-6	Pinehurst B-6	Winton A-8
Bryson City B-2	Jacksonville C-8	Piney Green C-8	Wrightsville
Burlington A-6	Kannapolis.......B-5	Raleigh B-7	Beach D-8
Cary B-7	Kill Devil Hills A-10	Reidsville A-6	
Chapel Hill B-6	Kings	Richlands C-8	### SOUTH
Charlotte B-4	Mountain B-4	Roanoke	### CAROLINA
Clemmons B-5	Kinston B-8	Rapids A-8	
Clinton C-7	Kitty Hawk A-10	Rockingham C-6	Abbeville D-3
Columbia B-9	Laurinburg C-6	Rocky Mount ...B-8	Aiken D-3
Concord B-5	Lenoir B-4	Roseboro C-7	Allendale E-4
Conover B-4	Lewiston	Rowland C-6	Anderson C-3
Currituck A-9	Woodville ...A-8	Roxboro A-6	Andrews E-6
Dunn B-7	Lexington B-5	Salisbury B-5	Bamberg E-4
Durham B-6	Lincolnton B-4	Sanford B-6	Barnwell E-4
Eden A-6	Littleton A-7	Shelby B-4	Batesburg-
Edenton A-9	Louisburg A-7	Siler City B-6	Leesville D-4
Elizabeth City ..A-9	Lumberton C-6	Smithfield B-7	Beaufort F-5
Elizabethtown ..C-7	Madison A-5	Snow Hill B-8	Bennettsville C-6
Fayetteville C-6	Manteo B-10	Southern Pines C-6	Branchville E-4
Forest City B-3	Matthews B-5	Southport D-7	Burton F-5
Garner B-7	Mint Hill B-5	Sparta A-4	Calhoun Falls ...D-3
Gastonia B-4	Monroe C-5	Statesville B-4	Camden D-5
Goldsboro B-7	Morehead City...C-9	Tabor City D-7	Charleston E-5
Greensboro A-5	Morganton B-4	Tarboro B-8	Cheraw C-5
Greenville B-8	Mount Airy A-5	Thomasville B-5	Chester C-4
		Topsail Beach ..C-8	Clemson C-2
		Wake Forest B-7	Clinton C-3
		Wallace C-7	Columbia D-4
		Washington B-8	Conway D-6
			Darlington D-5
			Dillon C-6
			Easley C-3

Edgefield D-3	Myrtle Beach D-6
Edisto Beach F-5	N. Augusta E-3
Ehrhardt E-4	N. Charleston E-5
Estill E-4	N. Myrtle
Eutawville E-5	Beach D-7
Fairfax E-4	Newbery D-4
Florence D-6	Orangeburg E-4
Folly Beach E-5	Pageland C-5
Fort Mill C-4	Patrick C-5
Gaffney C-4	Pinewood D-5
Garden City D-6	Red Bank D-4
Georgetown E-6	Ridgeland F-4
Goose Creek E-5	Rock Hill C-4
Great Falls C-4	Saluda D-3
Greeleyville D-5	Santee E-5
Greenville C-3	Seneca C-2
Greenwood D-3	Simpsonville C-3
Hanahan E-5	Socastee D-6
Hardeeville F-4	Spartanburg C-3
Hartsville D-5	St. George E-4
Hilton Head F-4	Summerton D-5
Irmo D-4	Summerville E-5
Jackson E-3	Sumter D-5
Jamestown D-4	Swansea D-4
Kershaw C-5	Taylors C-3
Kiawah Island ..F-5	Union C-4
Ladson E-5	Walterboro E-5
Lake City D-6	Westminster C-2
Lancaster C-4	Whitmire C-3
Laurens C-3	Winnsboro C-4
Lynchburg D-5	Yemassee E-4
Manning D-5	York C-4
Marion D-6	
Mauldin C-3	
Mayo C-3	
McClellanville ..E-6	
McCormick D-3	
Moncks Corner E-5	
Mt. Pleasant E-5	
Mullins D-6	

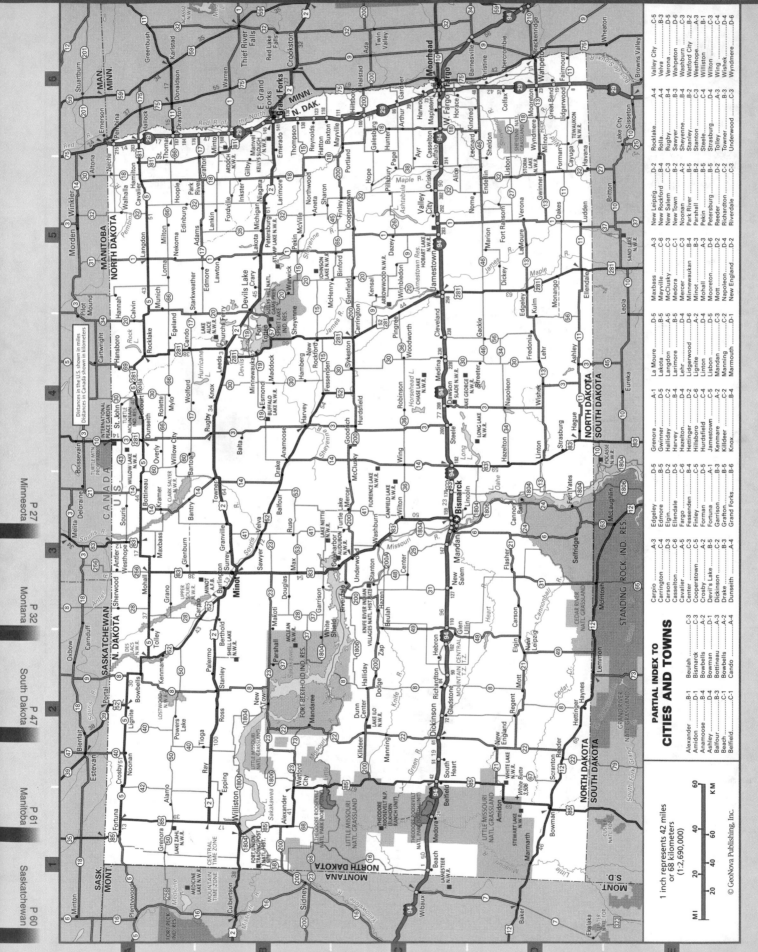

Distances in the U.S. shown in miles
Distances in Canada shown in kilometers

1 inch represents 42 miles
or 68 kilometers
(1:2,690,000)

© GeoNova Publishing, Inc.

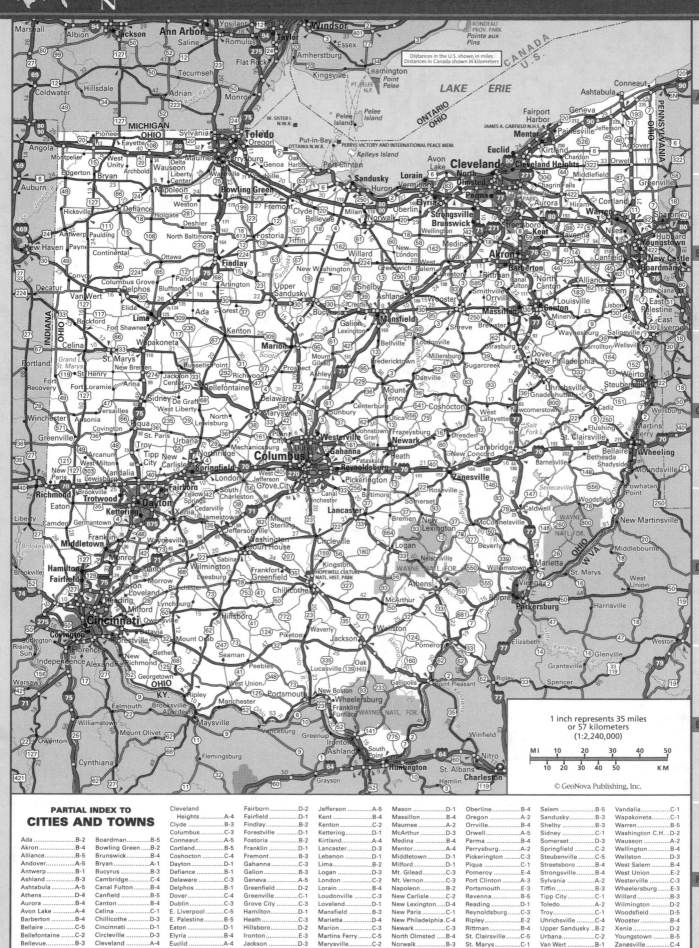

1 inch represents 35 miles
or 57 kilometers
(1:2,240,000)

MI 10   20   30   40   50
KM 10 20 30 40 50

© GeoNova Publishing, Inc.

PARTIAL INDEX TO CITIES AND TOWNS

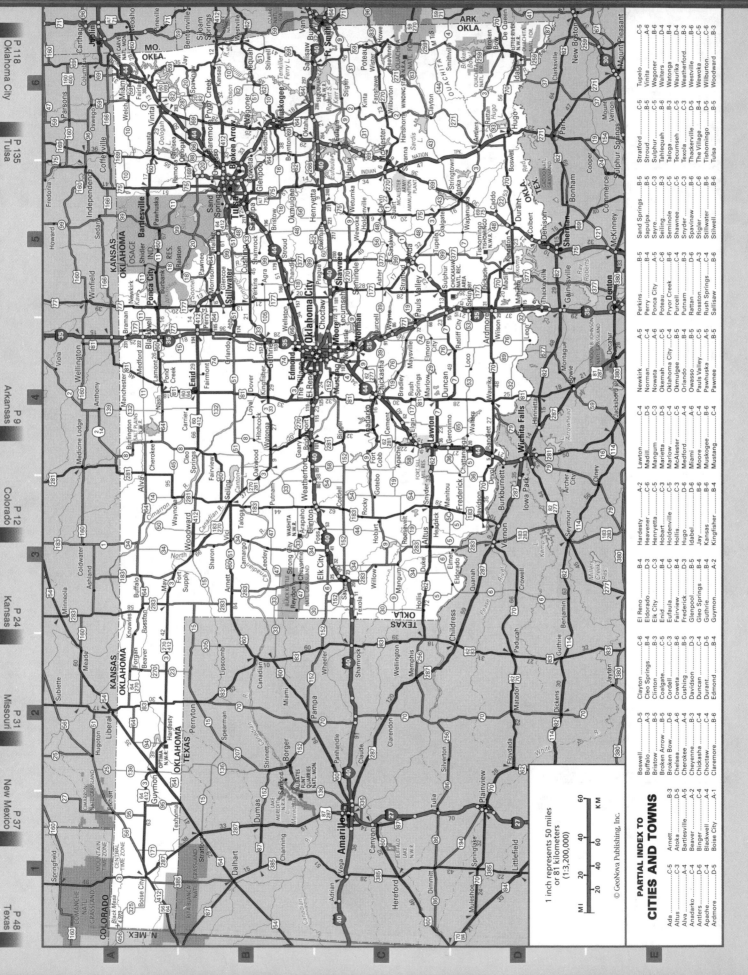

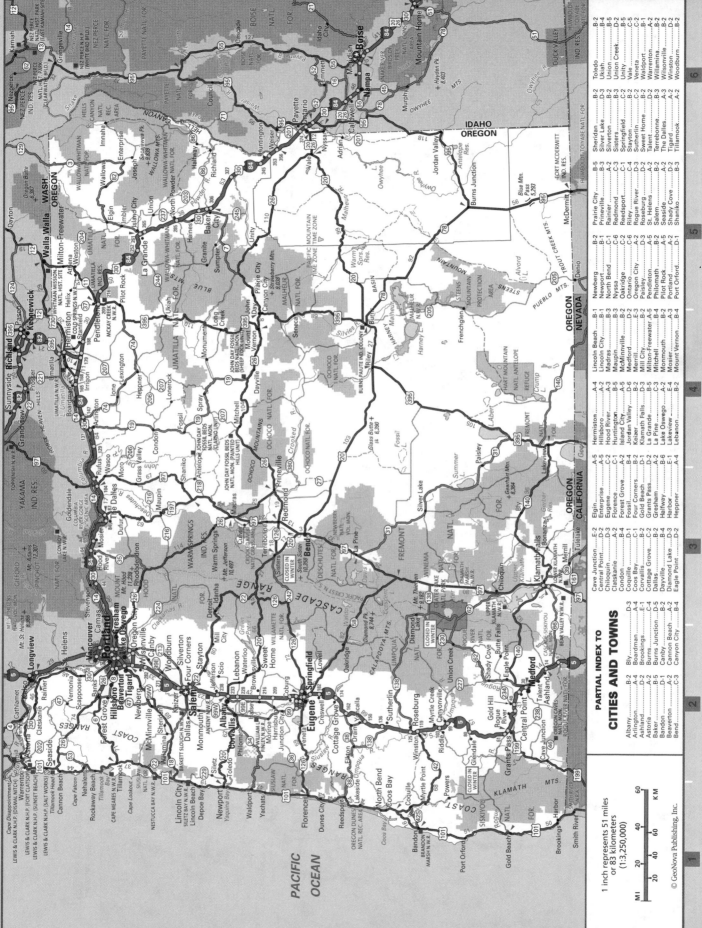

N

P 120 Philadelphia
P 122 Pittsburgh
P 13 Delaware
P 13 Maryland
P 36 New Jersey
P 38 New York
P 43 Ohio
P 52 West Virginia

1 inch represents 33 miles
or 53 kilometers
(1:2,100,000)

© GeoNova Publishing, Inc.

CATSKILL PARK

LAKE ERIE

CANADA
U.S.

NEW YORK

PENNSYLVANIA

OHIO

PA.
W. VA.

N.J.
PA.

PA.
MD.

DEL.

APPALACHIAN MTS.

PARTIAL INDEX TO CITIES AND TOWNS

Allentown	C-6	Breezewood	D-3	Corry	D-3
Altoona	D-3	Brookville	C-2	Danville	C-4
Ambridge	C-1	Butler	C-1	Downingtown	D-6
Bangor	C-6	Carbondale	B-6	Doylestown	C-6
Beaver	C-1	Carlisle	D-4	Du Bois	C-2
Bedford	D-3	Chambersburg	D-3	Easton	C-6
Bellefonte	C-3	Chester	D-6	Edinboro	A-1
Berwick	C-5	Clarion	C-2	Ellwood City	C-1
Bethel Park	D-1	Clearfield	C-2	Emmaus	C-6
Bethlehem	C-6	Connellsville	D-2	Emporium	B-3
Bloomsburg	C-5				
Bradford	A-3				

Ephrata	D-5	Hollidaysburg	D-3	Lebanon	D-5
Erie	A-1	Huntingdon	D-3	Levittown	D-6
Franklin	B-1	Indiana	C-2	Lewisburg	C-4
Gettysburg	D-4	Jim Thorpe	C-5	Lewistown	C-4
Greensburg	D-2	Johnstown	D-2	Linglestown	D-4
Greenville	B-1	King of Prussia	D-6	Lock Haven	C-4
Hanover	E-4	Kittanning	C-2	McCandless	C-1
Harrisburg	D-4	Lansdale	C-6	McConnellsburg	D-3
Hazleton	C-5	Latrobe	D-2	McKeesport	D-1
Hershey	D-4			Meadville	B-1

Mechanicsburg	D-4	New Castle	C-1	Shenandoah	C-5
Media	D-6	New Kensington	D-1	Shippensburg	D-4
Mercer	B-1	Norristown	D-6	Somerset	D-2
Mifflintown	C-4	Oil City	B-2	Souderton	C-6
Milford	B-6	Philadelphia	D-6	State College	C-3
Milton	C-4	Phoenixville	D-6	Sugarcreek	B-1
Monessen	D-1	Pine Grove	C-5	Sunbury	C-4
Monroeville	D-1	Pittston	B-5	Scotrun	A-6
Nanticoke	B-5	Pottstown	D-5	Scranton	B-5
Nazareth	C-6	Pottsville	C-5	Selinsgrove	C-4
Punxsutawney	C-1			Shamokin	C-5
Quakertown	D-6				
Reading	D-5				
Ridgway	B-2			Uniontown	D-1
St. Marys	B-3			Vandergrift	A-2
Sayre	A-5			Warren	A-2
				Washington	D-1
				Waynesboro	E-4
				West Chester	D-5
				Westmont	D-2
				Williamsport	C-5
				Wilkes-Barre	B-5
				York	D-4

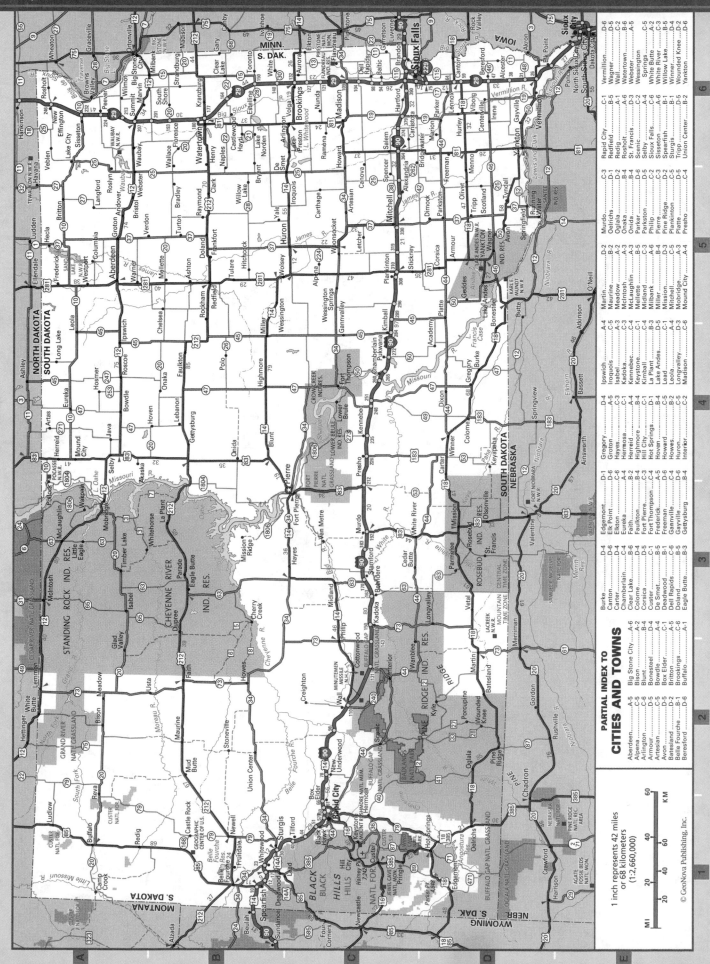

PARTIAL INDEX TO

CITIES AND TOWNS

Aberdeen	A-6	
Alpena	C-5	
Arlington	D-6	
Armour	D-5	
Artesian	D-5	
Avon	D-5	
Batesland	D-2	
Belle Fourche	B-1	
Beresford	D-6	

Big Stone City	A-6	
Bison	A-2	
Blunt	B-4	
Bonesteel	D-4	
Bowdle	A-4	
Box Elder	C-1	
Britton	A-5	
Brookings	D-6	
Buffalo	A-1	

Burke	D-4	
Canton	D-6	
Carter	D-4	
Chamberlain	C-4	
Clear Lake	A-6	
Colome	C-4	
Corsica	D-5	
Custer	C-1	
Deadwood	B-1	
Dell Rapids	D-6	
Doland	C-5	
Eagle Butte	B-3	

Edgemont	D-6	
Elk Point	D-6	
Elkton	D-6	
Eureka	A-4	
Faith	B-2	
Faulkton	B-4	
Fort Pierre	C-3	
Fort Thompson	C-4	
Frederick	A-5	
Freeman	D-6	
Gann Valley	C-4	
Gayville	D-5	
Gettysburg	B-4	

Gregory	D-4	
Groton	A-5	
Hayes	C-3	
Hermosa	C-1	
Herreid	A-4	
Highmore	B-4	
Hill City	C-1	
Hot Springs	C-1	
Howard	D-5	
Howes	B-2	
Huron	C-5	
Interior	C-3	

Ipswich	B-4	
Iroquois	C-5	
Isabel	A-3	
Kadoka	C-3	
Kennebec	C-4	
Keystone	C-1	
Kimball	C-4	
La Plant	B-3	
Lake Andes	D-5	
Lead	B-1	
Leola	A-4	
Longvalley	C-3	
Madison	C-6	

Martin	D-2	
Maurine	B-2	
Meadow	A-2	
McIntosh	A-3	
McLaughlin	A-3	
Mellette	B-5	
Midland	C-3	
Milbank	A-6	
Miller	B-4	
Mission	D-3	
Mitchell	C-5	
Mobridge	A-3	
Mound City	A-4	

Murdo	C-3	
Oelrichs	D-1	
Ogala	A-2	
Onida	B-4	
Parker	D-5	
Parkston	C-3	
Philip	C-3	
Pierre	B-4	
Pine Ridge	D-2	
Plankinton	C-5	
Platte	D-4	
Presho	C-4	

Rapid City	C-1	
Redfield	B-5	
Redig	A-2	
Rosholt	A-6	
Scenic	C-2	
Selby	A-4	
Sioux Falls	C-6	
Spearfish	B-1	
Sisseton	A-6	
Sturgis	B-1	
Tripp	D-5	
Union Center	B-2	

Vermillion	D-6	
Wagner	D-5	
Wall	C-2	
Watertown	B-6	
Webster	A-5	
Wessington	C-5	
White Butte	A-2	
White River	C-3	
Winner	C-4	
Wounded Knee	D-2	
Yankton	D-6	

1 inch represents 42 miles
or 68 kilometers
(1:2,660,000)

MI 0 20 40 60
KM 0 20 40 60

© GeoNova Publishing, Inc.

P 21 Iowa
P 27 Minnesota
P 32 Montana
P 33 Nebraska
P 42 North Dakota
P 55 Wyoming

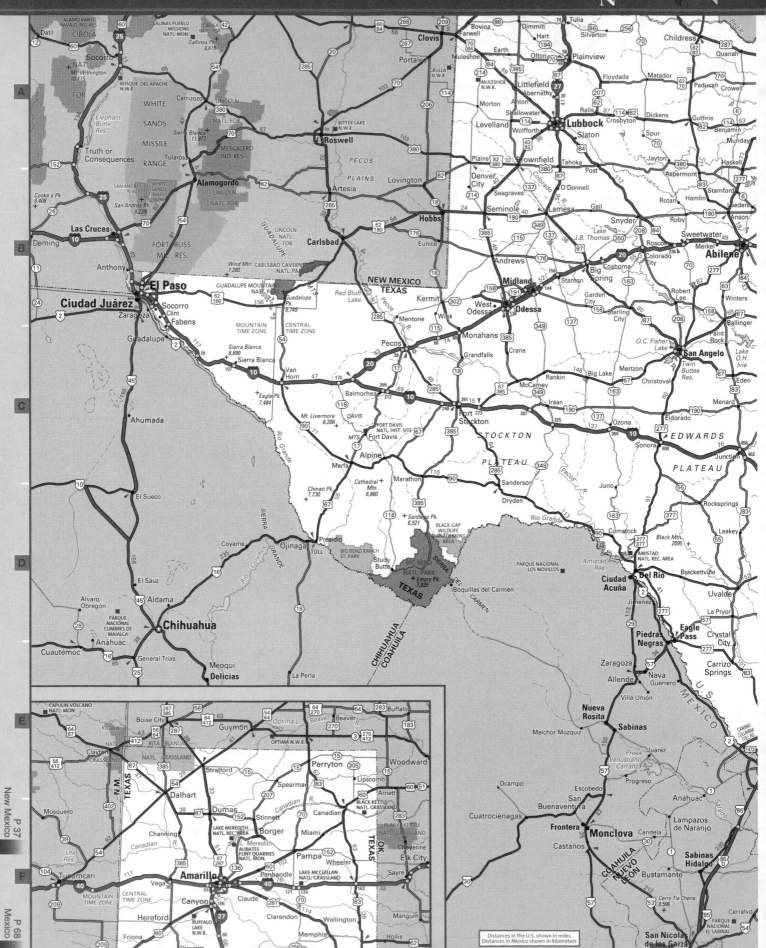

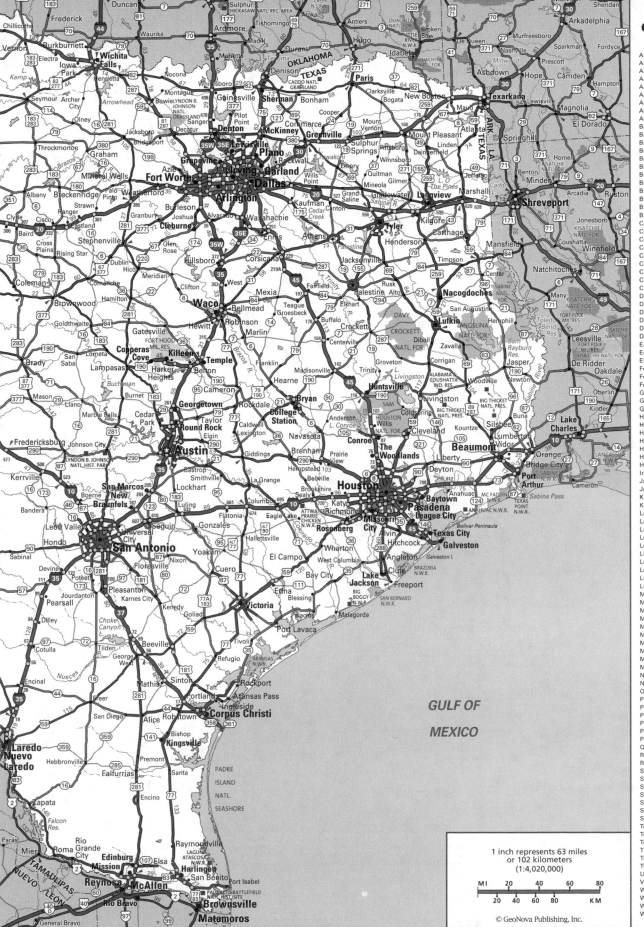

© GeoNova Publishing, Inc.

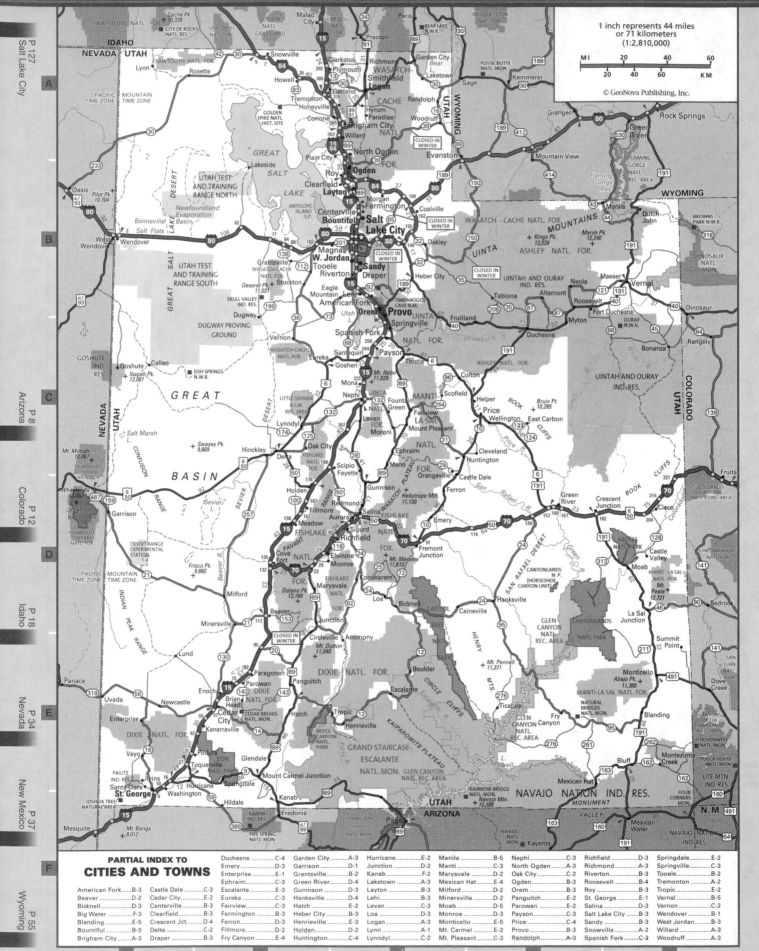

P 127 Salt Lake City

P 8 Arizona

P 12 Colorado

P 18 Idaho

P 34 Nevada

P 37 New Mexico

P 55 Wyoming

1 inch represents 44 miles
or 71 kilometers
(1:2,810,000)

© GeoNova Publishing, Inc.

PARTIAL INDEX TO
CITIES AND TOWNS

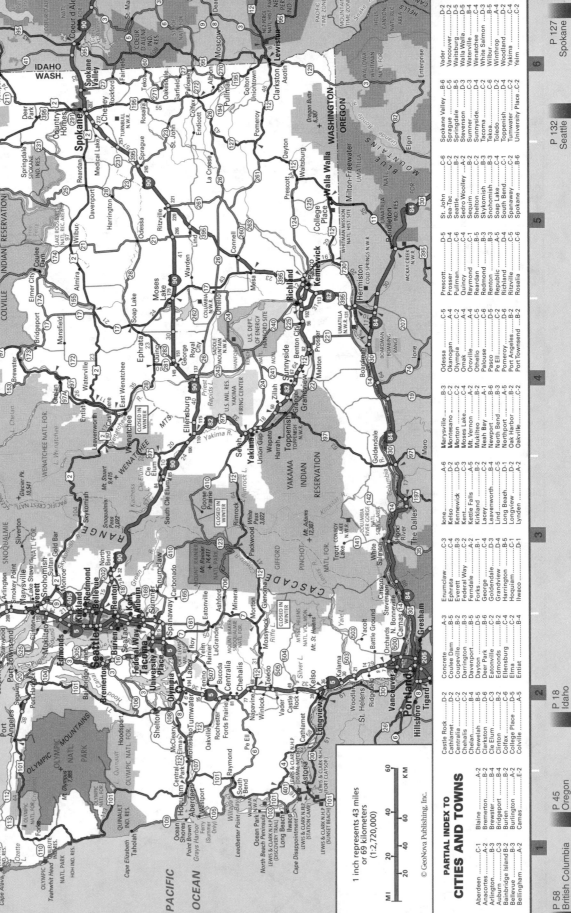

1 inch represents 43 miles
or 69 kilometers
(1:2,720,000)

© GeoNova Publishing, Inc.

PARTIAL INDEX TO
CITIES AND TOWNS

P 127 Spokane

P 132 Seattle

P 18 Idaho

P 45 Oregon

P 58 British Columbia

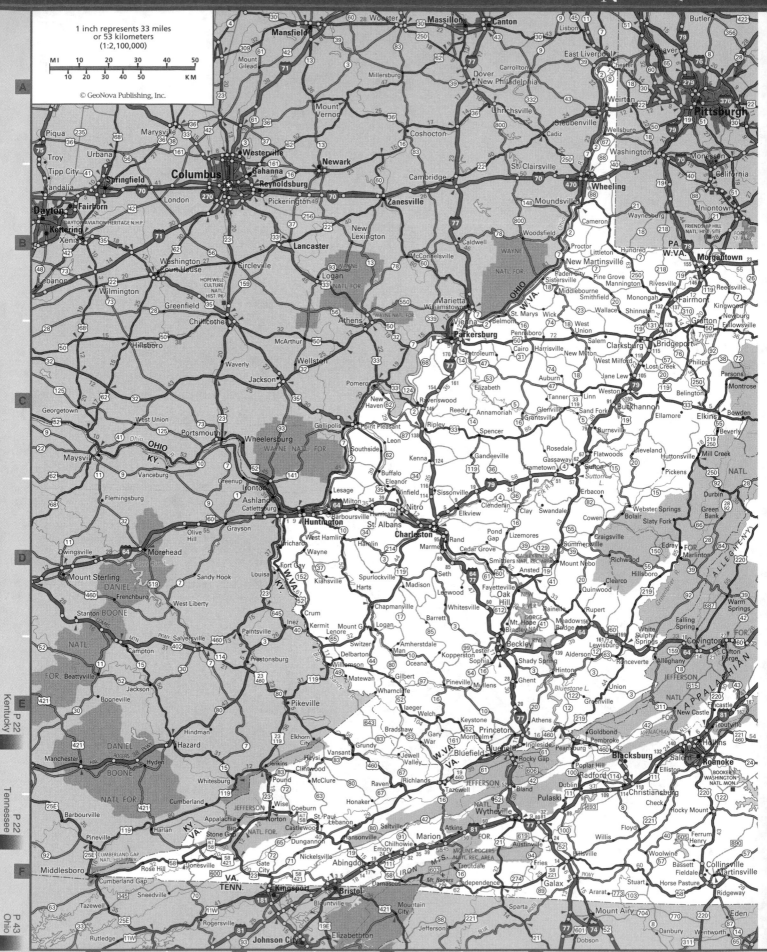

PARTIAL INDEX TO CITIES AND TOWNS

VIRGINIA

WEST VIRGINIA

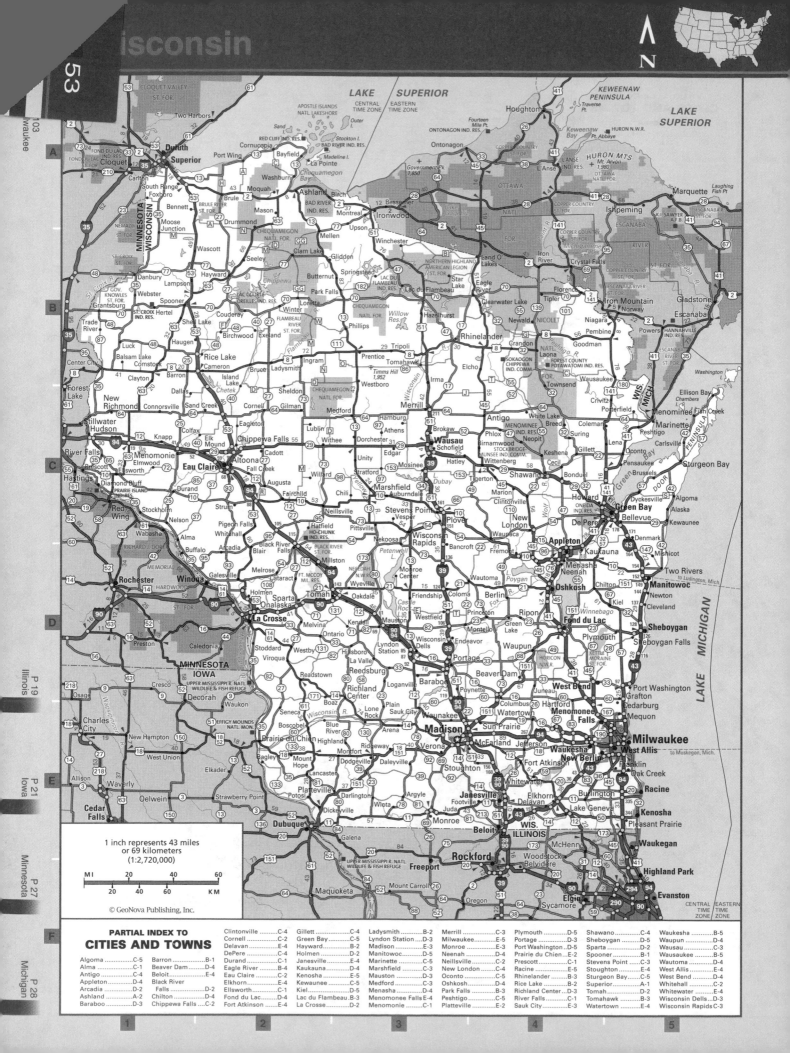

LAKE SUPERIOR

CENTRAL TIME ZONE EASTERN TIME ZONE

KEWEENAW PENINSULA

LAKE SUPERIOR

1 inch represents 43 miles
or 69 kilometers
(1:2,720,000)

MI 20 40 60

20 40 60 KM

© GeoNova Publishing, Inc.

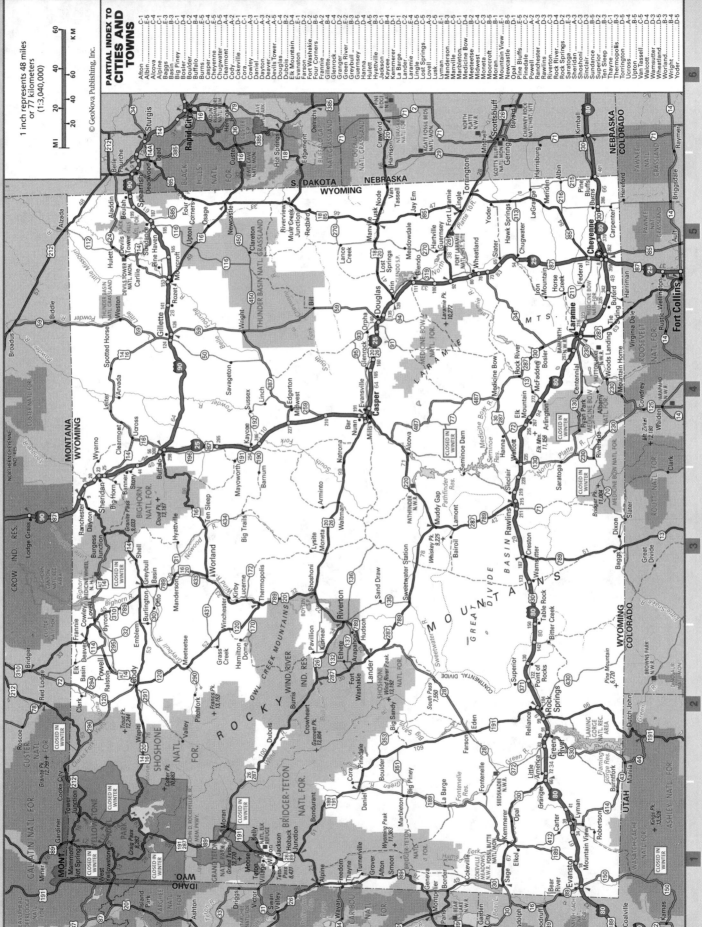

N

1 inch represents 48 miles
or 77 kilometers
(1:3,040,000)

© GeoNova Publishing, Inc.

1 inch represents 259 miles
or 417.5 kilometers
(1:16,457,143)

MI   400
      200   400
200   400   KM

© GeoNova Publishing, Inc.

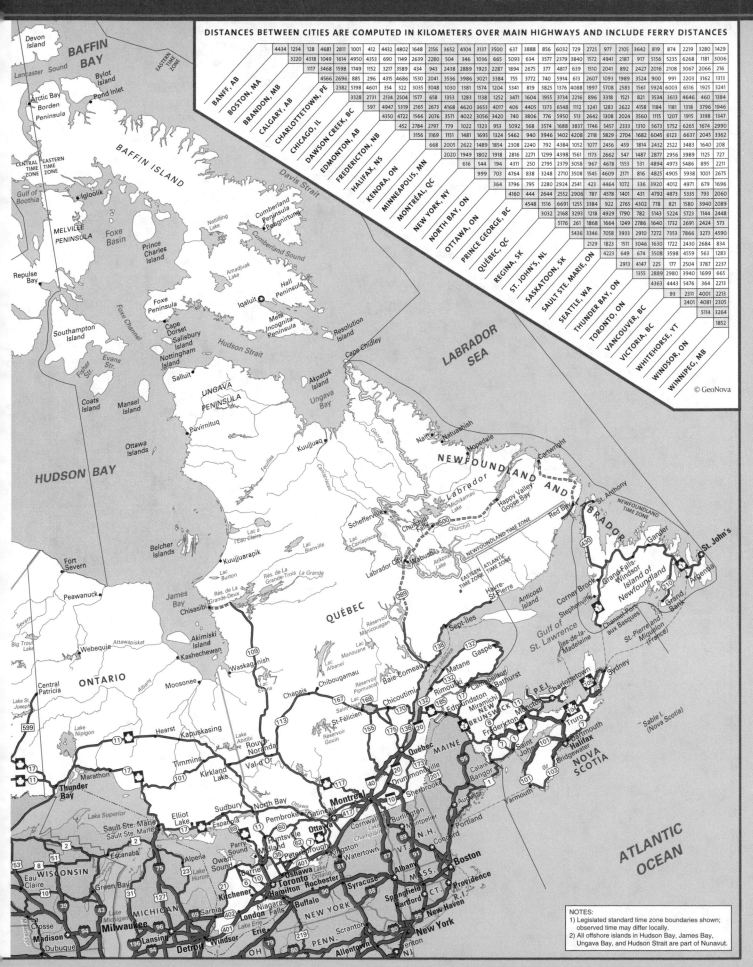

DISTANCES BETWEEN CITIES ARE COMPUTED IN KILOMETERS OVER MAIN HIGHWAYS AND INCLUDE FERRY DISTANCES

Distance chart (triangular matrix). Distances listed for each origin city to the following cities in the chart:

From	Distances (to the cities listed below it in the chart)
BANFF, AB	4434 1234 128 4681 2811 1001 412 4432 4802 1648 2156 3652 4104 3137 3500 637 3888 856 6032 729 2725 977 2105 3642 819 874 2219 3280 1429
BOSTON, MA	3220 4318 1049 1614 4950 4353 690 1149 2639 2280 504 346 1036 665 5093 634 3577 2379 3840 1572 4941 2187 917 5156 5235 6268 1181 3006
BRANDON, MB	1117 3468 1598 1749 1152 3217 3589 434 943 2438 2889 1923 2287 1894 2675 377 3772 740 5914 613 2607 1093 1989 3524 900 991 2203 3162 216
CALGARY, AB	4566 2696 885 296 4315 4686 1530 2041 3536 3986 3021 3384 755 5914 613 2607 1093 1989 3524 900 991 2203 3162 1313
CHARLOTTETOWN, PE	2382 5198 4601 354 322 3035 3048 1030 1381 1574 1204 5341 819 3825 1376 4088 1997 5708 2583 1561 5924 6003 6516 1925 3241
CHICAGO, IL	3328 2731 2134 2504 1577 658 1353 1138 1252 3471 1604 1955 3734 2216 896 3318 1521 821 3534 3613 4646 460 1384
DAWSON CREEK, BC	597 4947 5319 2165 2673 4168 4620 3653 4017 406 4405 1373 6548 1112 3241 1283 2622 4158 1184 1181 1318 3796 1946
EDMONTON, AB	4350 4722 1566 2076 3571 4022 3056 3420 740 3806 776 5950 513 2642 1308 2024 3560 1115 1207 1915 3198 1347
FREDERICTON, NB	452 2784 2797 1751 1022 1323 953 5092 568 3574 1688 3837 1746 5457 2333 1310 5673 5752 6265 1674 2990
HALIFAX, NS	3156 3169 1151 1481 1695 1324 5829 940 3946 1402 4208 2118 5829 2704 1682 6045 6123 6637 2045 3362
KENORA, ON	668 2005 2622 1489 1854 2308 2240 792 4384 1052 1077 2456 459 1814 2432 2522 3483 1640 208
MINNEAPOLIS, MN	2020 1949 1802 1918 2816 2271 1299 4398 1561 1173 2662 547 1487 2877 2956 3989 1125 727
MONTRÉAL, QC	616 544 194 4311 250 2795 3058 967 4678 1553 531 4894 4973 5673 895 2211
NEW YORK, NY	999 703 4764 838 3248 2710 3508 1545 4609 2171 618 4825 4905 5938 1001 2675
NORTH BAY, ON	364 3796 795 2280 2924 2541 423 4464 1072 336 3920 4012 4971 679 1696
OTTAWA, ON	4160 444 2644 2552 2906 787 4578 1401 431 4792 4873 5335 793 2060
PRINCE GEORGE, BC	4548 1516 6691 1255 3384 922 2765 4302 778 821 1580 3940 2089
QUÉBEC, QC	3032 2168 3293 1218 4929 1790 782 5143 5224 5723 1144 2448
REGINA, SK	5176 261 1868 1249 2786 1640 1732 2691 2424 573
ST. JOHN'S, NL	5436 3346 7058 3933 2910 7272 7353 7866 3273 4590
SASKATOON, SK	2129 1823 1511 3046 1630 1722 2430 2684 834
SAULT STE. MARIE, ON	4223 649 674 3508 3598 4559 563 1283
SEATTLE, WA	2913 4347 225 177 2504 3787 2237
THUNDER BAY, ON	1355 2889 2980 3940 1699 665
TORONTO, ON	4363 4443 5476 364 2213
VANCOUVER, BC	93 2311 4001 2213
VICTORIA, BC	2401 4081 2305
WHITEHORSE, YT	5114 3264
WINDSOR, ON	1852
WINNIPEG, MB	

© GeoNova

NOTES:
1) Legislated standard time zone boundaries shown; observed time may differ locally.
2) All offshore islands in Hudson Bay, James Bay, Ungava Bay, and Hudson Strait are part of Nunavut.

N

PARTIAL INDEX TO CITIES AND TOWNS

Abbotsford D-4	Merritt D-4	Radium
Ainsworth	Nanaimo D-3	Hot Springs D-6
Hot Springs E-4	Needles D-5	Revelstoke D-5
Burnaby E-3	Nelson E-5	Richmond E-4
Burns Lake B-3	New Hazelton A-2	Rossland E-5
Cache Creek D-4	Oliver E-5	Salmon Arm D-5
Campbell River D-3	Parksville D-3	Sicamous D-5
Castlegar E-5	Peachland E-5	Sorrento D-5
Chase D-4	Penticton E-5	Squamish E-4
Chetwynd B-4	Port Alberni D-3	Summerland E-5
Chilliwack D-4	Port Coquitlam E-4	Terrace A-2
Christina Lake E-5	Port Hardy D-2	Tofino E-2
Comox D-3	Port McNeill D-3	Trail E-5
Courtenay D-3	Port Moody E-4	Vancouver E-3
Cranbrook E-5	Powell River D-3	Vanderhoof B-3
Creston E-5	Prince George B-4	Vernon D-5
Dawson Creek B-4	Prince Rupert A-1	Victoria E-3
Duncan D-3	Princeton E-4	Whistler E-3
Elkford D-5	Queen Charlotte B-1	White Rock E-3
Elko E-5	Quesnel C-3	Williams Lake C-4
Enderby D-5		
Fernie E-5		
Fort St. John B-4		
Golden D-5		
Grand Forks E-5		
Greenwood E-5		
Hope D-4		
Houston B-2		
Hudson's Hope A-4		
Hundred Mile		
House C-4		
Invermere D-6		
Kamloops D-4		
Kelowna D-5		
Kimberley E-5		
Kitimat A-2		
Lac La Hache C-4		
Langley E-4		
Lytton D-4		
Mackenzie A-3		

1 inch represents 83 miles
or 134 kilometers
(1:5,300,000)

Distances in the U.S. shown in miles
Distances in Canada shown in kilometers

MI 0 50 100
KM 0 50 100

© GeoNova Publishing, Inc.

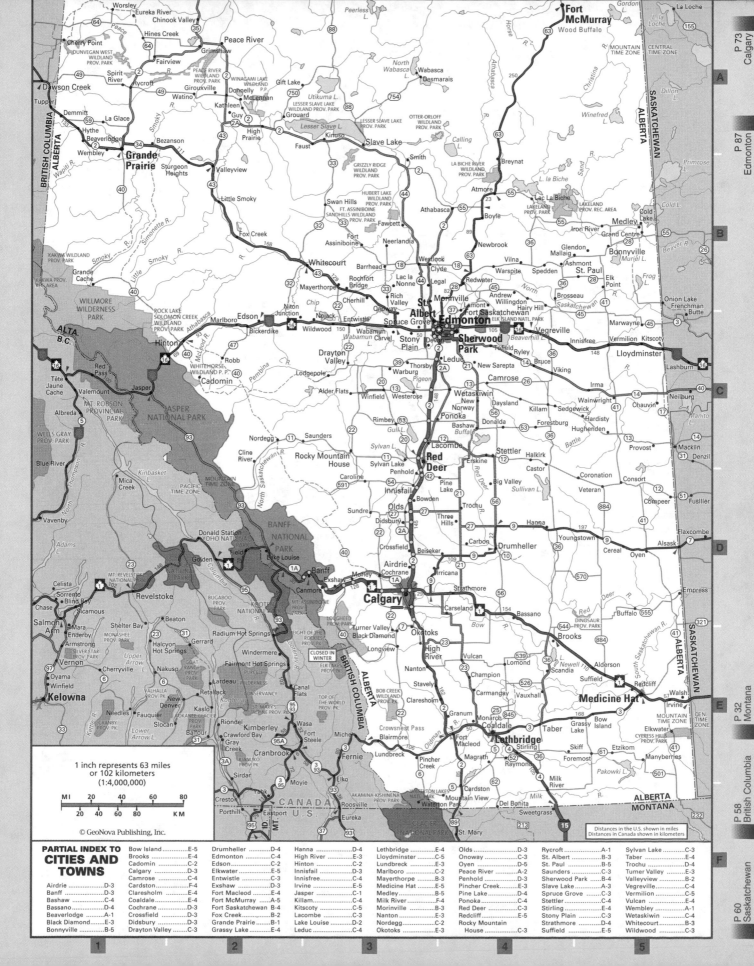

1 inch represents 63 miles
or 102 kilometers
(1:4,000,000)

MI 20   40   60   80

20 40 60 80 KM

© GeoNova Publishing, Inc.

Distances in the U.S. shown in miles
Distances in Canada shown in kilometers

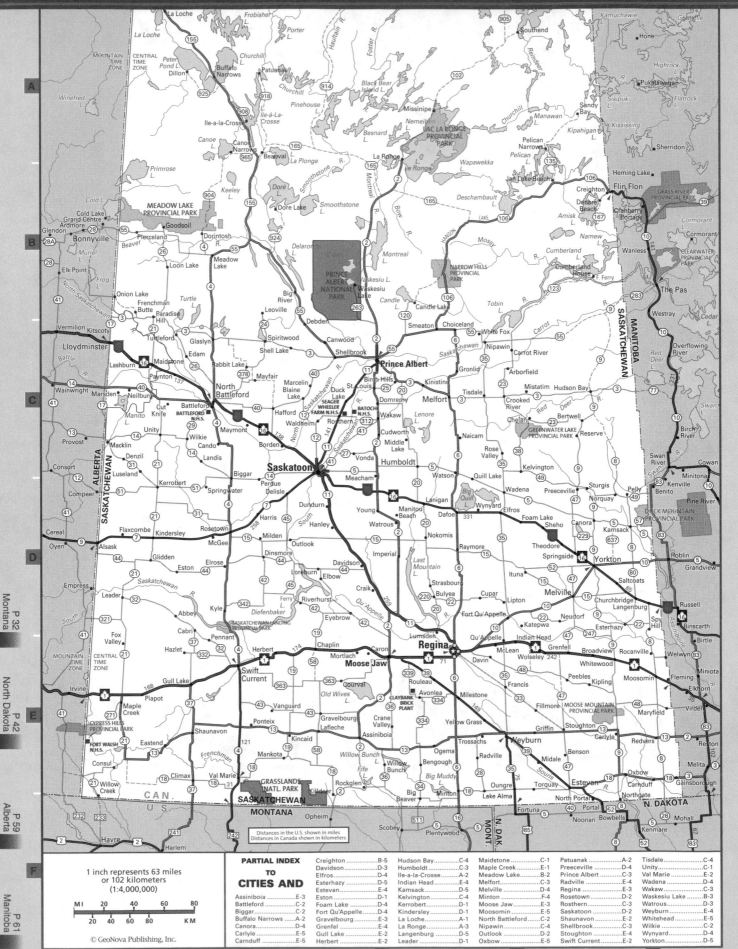

1 inch represents 63 miles
or 102 kilometers
(1:4,000,000)

MI 20   40   60   80
KM 20 40 60 80

Distances in the U.S. shown in miles
Distances in Canada shown in kilometers

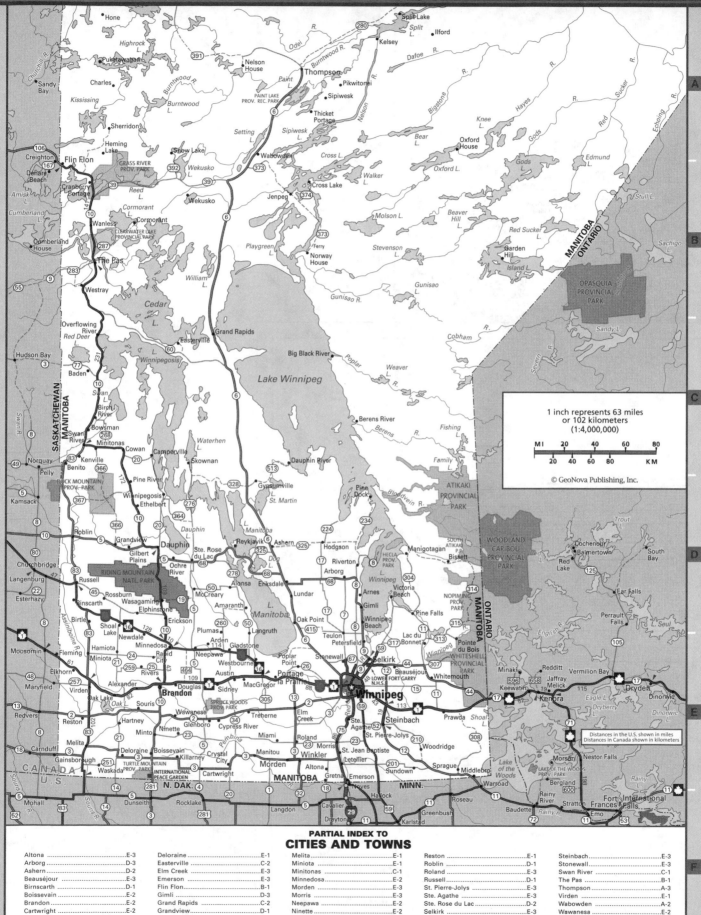

1 inch represents 63 miles
or 102 kilometers
(1:4,000,000)

MI   20   40   60   80
20   40   60   80   KM

© GeoNova Publishing, Inc.

Distances in the U.S. shown in miles
Distances in Canada shown in kilometers

PARTIAL INDEX TO
CITIES AND TOWNS

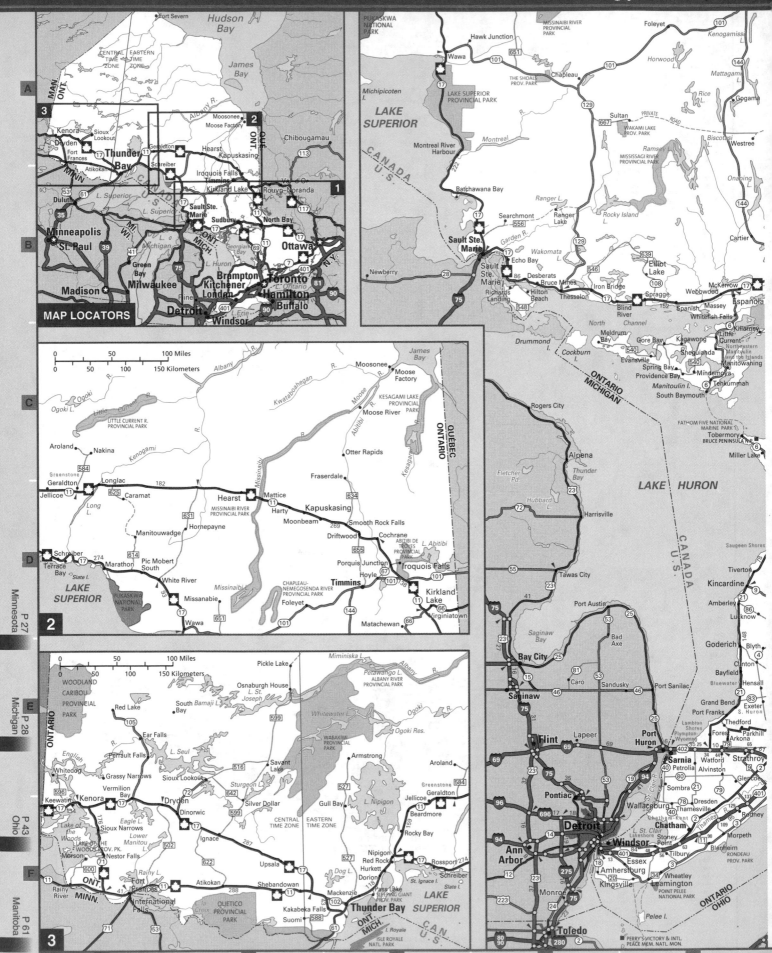

N

MAP LOCATORS

Map 1 (Top Right)

Hudson Bay

James Bay

PUKASKWA NATIONAL PARK

Foleyet · 101

Kenogamissi L.

Hawk Junction · 101

Wawa · 651

Chapleau · 101 · 144

Horwood · L.

Mattagami · L.

THE SHOALS PROV. PARK

Michipicoten I.

LAKE SUPERIOR

LAKE SUPERIOR PROVINCIAL PARK

Montreal · R.

129

Sultan · PRIVATE ROAD

WAKAMI LAKE PROV. PARK

667

Rice L.

Gogama

Montreal River Harbour

222

Batchawana Bay

Searchmont · 556

Ranger L.

Ranger Lake

Rocky Island L.

RAMSEY L.

MISSISSAGI RIVER PROVINCIAL PARK

Biscotasi L.

Westree

Onaping

144

CANADA / U.S.

Newberry

Echo Bay

28

Sault Ste. Marie

17

Garden R.

Wakomata L.

Bruce Mines · 638

Elliot Lake

McKerrow · 17

Cartier

Sault Ste. Marie · 75 · 86

Richards Landing

Hilton Beach · 548

Desbarats

Iron Bridge · 546

Thessalon · 108

Blind River

Spragge · 152 · Spanish

Webbwood

Massey

Espanola

North Channel

Meldrum Bay

Gore Bay · 540

Evansville

Spring Bay · 540

Providence Bay

Kagawong

Sheguiandah

Mindemoya

Manitoulin I.

Killarney · 6

Little Current

Northeastern Manitoulin and the Islands

Manitowaning

Tehkummah · 6

South Baymouth

ONTARIO / MICHIGAN

Drummond I.

Cockburn I.

Rogers City

Alpena

FATHOM FIVE NATIONAL MARINE PARK

Tobermory · BRUCE PENINSULA N.P. · 6

Miller Lake

LAKE HURON

Thunder Bay

Fletcher Pd.

Hubbard L.

Harrisville

Saugeen Shores

CANADA / U.S.

Tiverton

Kincardine · 21 · 9

Amberley · 86

Lucknow

72

23

Tawas City

Port Austin

41

Goderich · 148

Blyth · 4

Clinton

Bayfield

Hensall · 83

55

Bay City · 25

Port Sanilac

46

Saginaw · 75 · 15

Caro · 81

Bad Axe · 53

Sandusky

Port Sanilac · 46

Grand Bend

Port Franks

Exeter · S. Huron

Thedford

Parkhill · 81 · 79 · 65 · 83

Arkona

Lambton Shores

Plympton-Wyoming

Forest

16

27

Flint · 69

Lapeer

Port Huron · 25

Watford

Petrolia

Alvinston

Strathroy

Pontiac · 69 · 75 · 96 · 23 · 35

Sarnia · 402 · 40 · 80

Sombra · 79

Glencoe

Dresden · 21

Detroit · 696 · 18 · 14 · 94

Wallaceburg

Thamesville

Chatham · 40

Ridgetown · 401 · 125

Ann Arbor · 275 · 23

Windsor · 401

Stoney Point

Tilbury

Blenheim · 11 · 3

Morpeth

Essex · 18 · 13

RONDEAU PROV. PARK

Amherstburg · 20 · 34

Kingsville

Wheatley

Leamington

POINT PELEE NATIONAL PARK

Monroe · 24 · 75 · 56

12

Toledo · 80 · 90 · 2 · 280

Pelee I.

ONTARIO / OHIO

PERRY'S VICTORY & INTL. PEACE MEM. NATL. MON.

223

Map 2 (Middle Left)

0 — 50 — 100 Miles

0 — 50 — 100 — 150 Kilometers

Ogoki L.

Albany R.

James Bay

Moosonee

Moose Factory

KESAGAMI LAKE PROVINCIAL PARK

Little Current R.

LITTLE CURRENT R. PROVINCIAL PARK

Ogoki R.

Kwataboahegan R.

Moose River

Moose R.

Abitibi R.

QUÉBEC / ONTARIO

Aroland

Nakina

Kenogami R.

Otter Rapids

Greenstone · 584

Geraldton

Longlac · 182

Fraserdale

Missinaibi R.

Jellicoe · 11

625 · Caramat

Hearst · 634

Mattice

631

Kapuskasing

L. Abitibi

Long L.

MISSINAIBI RIVER PROVINCIAL PARK

Harty

ABITIBI DE TROYES PROV. PARK

Manitouwadge

Hornepayne

Moonbeam · 269

Smooth Rock Falls

Driftwood

Cochrane · 655

Schreiber · 274

614

Pic Mobert South

Porquis Junction

Hoyle · 67

Iroquois Falls

Terrace Bay

Marathon

White River

Slate I.

101 · 38

LAKE SUPERIOR

Slate I.

CHAPLEAU-NEMEGOSENDA RIVER PROVINCIAL PARK

Timmins · 101

Kirkland Lake · 11 · 66

PUKASKWA NATIONAL PARK

93

Missanabie

Missinaibi R.

Foleyet

144 · Virginiatown

Wawa · 651

101

Matachewan · 66

Map 3 (Bottom Left)

0 — 50 — 100 Miles

0 — 50 — 100 — 150 Kilometers

ONTARIO

Miminiska L.

Albany R.

Pickle Lake

Osnaburgh House

L. St. Joseph

Petawanga L.

ALBANY RIVER PROVINCIAL PARK

WOODLAND CARIBOU PROVINCIAL PARK

South Bay

Bamaji L.

Whitewater L.

Ogoki R.

Ogoki Res.

Red Lake · 105

Armstrong

WABAKIMI PROVINCIAL PARK

Aroland

Ear Falls

Perrault Falls

L. Seul

599

Savant Lake

527

Greenstone · 584

English R.

Whitedog

Grassy Narrows

516

Sioux Lookout · 642

Silver Dollar

Jellicoe · 11 · 159

Geraldton

596

Keewatin · Kenora · 17 · 176

Vermilion Bay

Dryden · 72

599

Sturgeon L.

Gull Bay

Beardmore

Rocky Bay

Eagle L.

Sioux Narrows

Dinorwic

L. Nipigon

Lower Manitou

Ignace · 287

CENTRAL TIME ZONE

EASTERN TIME ZONE

527

Nipigon · 17 · 274

Red Rock

Rossport

LAKE OF THE WOODS PROV. PK.

Lake of the Woods

502

Morson · 71

Nestor Falls · 600

622

Upsala

Hurkett

Dorion

St. Ignace I.

Schreiber

Rainy R.

International Falls

Fort Frances · 41

MINN.

288

Atikokan

Shebandowan

Mackenzie · 102

Dog L.

118

SLEEPING GIANT PROV. PARK

Kakabeka Falls · 588

Suomi

Thunder Bay

LAKE SUPERIOR

QUETICO PROVINCIAL PARK

71 · 53

61

ONT. / MICH.

CAN. / U.S.

ISLE ROYALE NATL. PARK

I. Royale

Map Locators (Inset Top Left)

Fort Severn

Hudson Bay

James Bay

CENTRAL TIME ZONE / EASTERN TIME ZONE

MAN. / ONT.

Moosonee · 2

Moose Factory

Chibougamau

Albany R.

Kenora

Sioux Lookout

Dryden

Geraldton · 11

Hearst

Kapuskasing

113

QUE. / ONT.

Fort Frances

Thunder Bay · 11

Atikokan

Schreiber

Iroquois Falls

Timmins

Kirkland Lake

Rouyn-Noranda · 1

53 · 61

L. Superior

Duluth

L. Superior

Sault Ste. Marie

Sudbury · 11

North Bay · 117

35 · 41

Minneapolis

St. Paul · 39

Green Bay

Mackinac · 69

Georgian Bay

L. Huron

7

Ottawa · 17

N.Y.

75

Madison

Milwaukee

Kitchener

Brampton

Toronto · 401

Hamilton

81

London

Flint

Detroit · 401

L. Erie

Buffalo · 90

Windsor

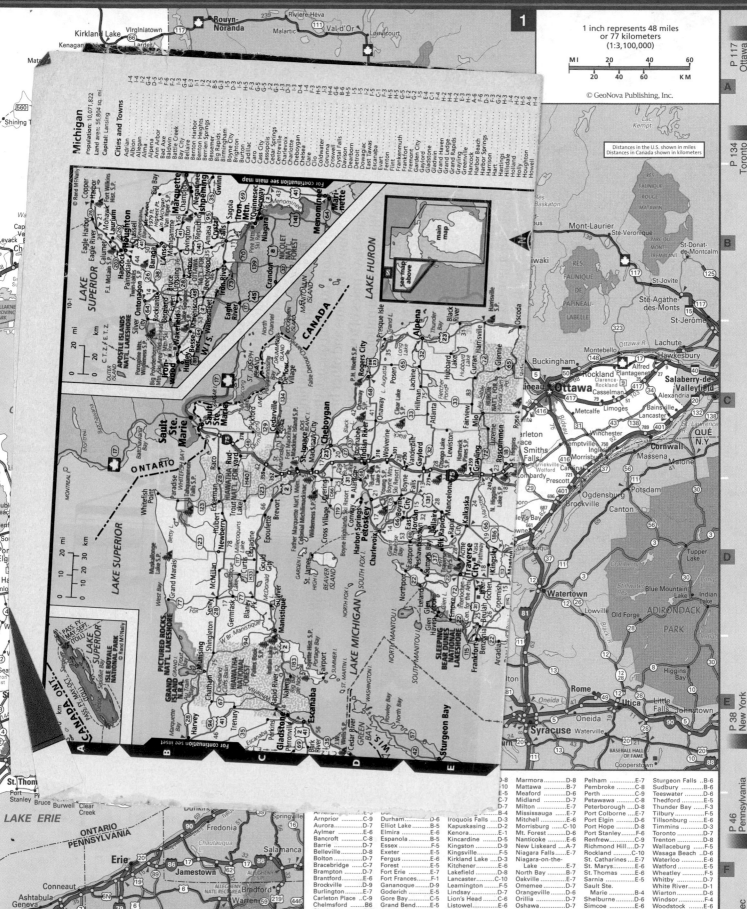

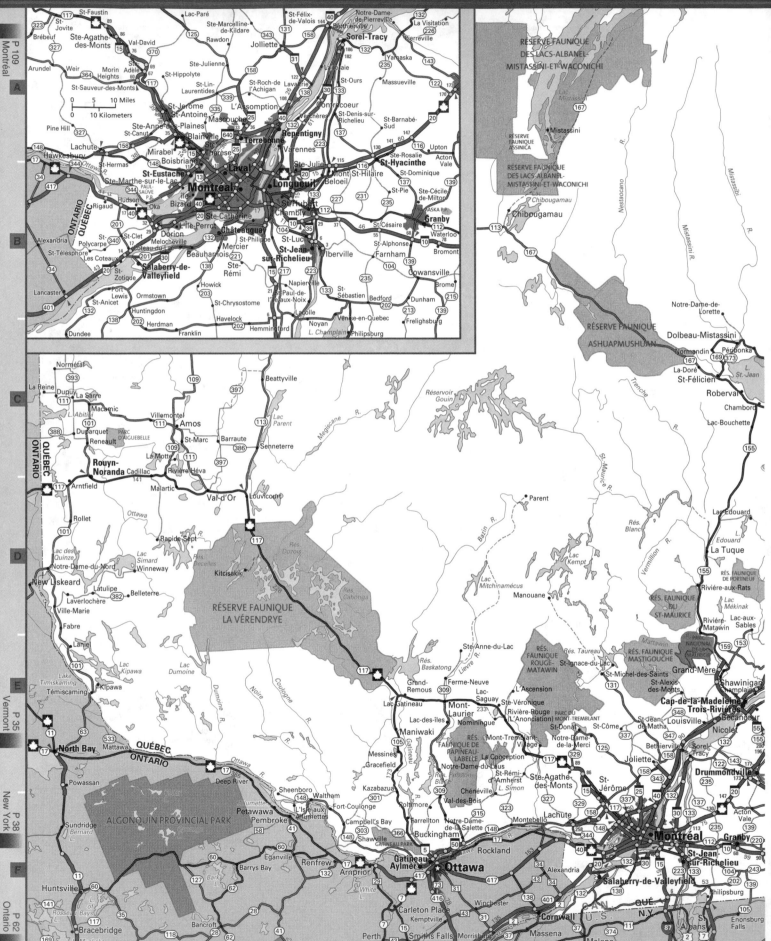

P 109 Montreal

P 35 Vermont

P 38 New York

P 62 Ontario

ONTARIO
QUÉBEC

QUÉBEC
ONTARIO

RÉSERVE FAUNIQUE DES LACS-ALBANEL-MISTASSINI-ET-WACONICHI

RÉSERVE FAUNIQUE ASSINICA

RÉSERVE FAUNIQUE DES LACS-ALBANEL-MISTASSINI-ET-WACONICHI

RÉSERVE FAUNIQUE ASHUAPMUSHUAN

RÉSERVE FAUNIQUE LA VÉRENDRYE

ALGONQUIN PROVINCIAL PARK

PARC D'AIGUEBELLE

RÉS. FAUNIQUE ROUGE-MATAWIN

RÉS. FAUNIQUE MASTIGOUCHE

RÉS. FAUNIQUE DU ST-MAURICE

RÉS. FAUNIQUE DE PORTNEUF

PARC DU MONT-TREMBLANT

RÉS. FAUNIQUE DE PAPINEAU-LABELLE

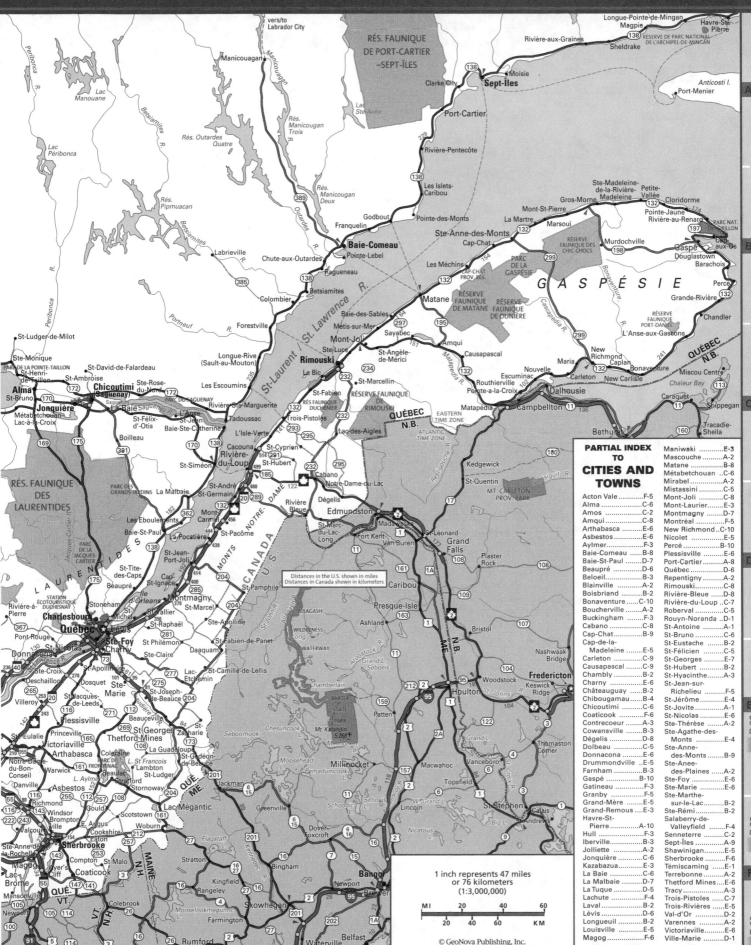

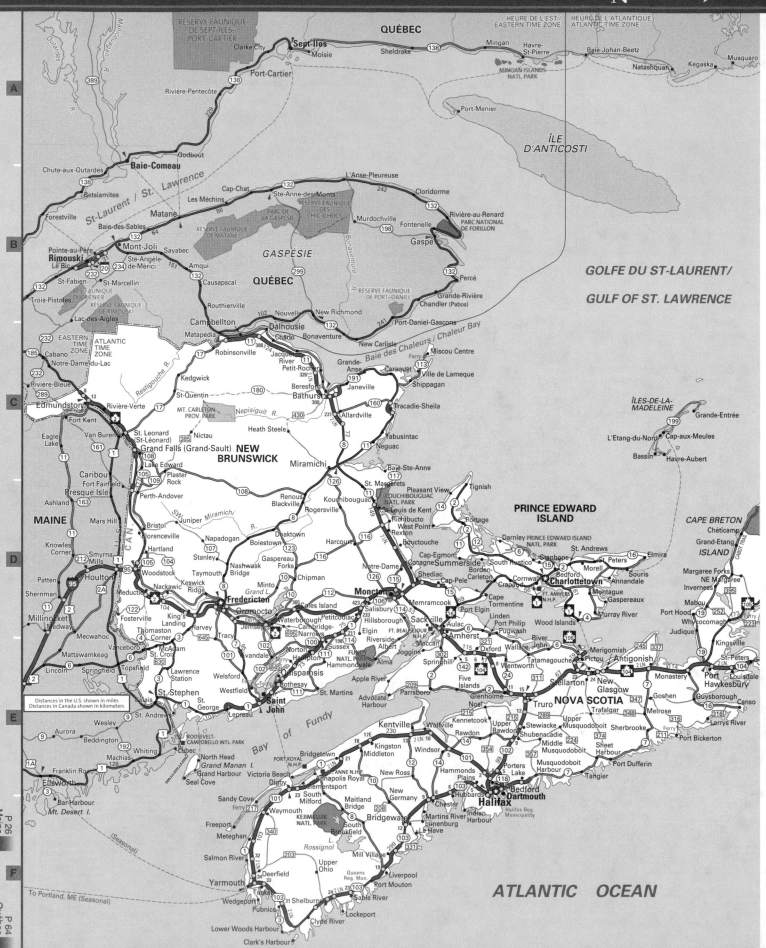

QUÉBEC

RÉSERVE FAUNIQUE
DE SEPT-ÎLES—
PORT-CARTIER

HEURE DE L'EST /
EASTERN TIME ZONE

HEURE DE L'ATLANTIQUE
ATLANTIC TIME ZONE

Sept-Îles
Clarke City
Moisie
Sheldrake
138
Mingan
Havre-
St-Pierre
Baie-Johan-Beetz
Natashquan
Kegaska
Musquaro

Port-Cartier
MINGAN ISLANDS
NATL. PARK

Rivière-Pentecôte

ÎLE
D'ANTICOSTI

Port-Menier

Godbout

Baie-Comeau

Chute-aux-Outardes

L'Anse-Pleureuse
Cloridorme

138
Betsiamites
Cap-Chat
132
Ste-Anne-des-Monts
242
132
Rivière-au-Renard
PARC NATIONAL
DE FORILLON

Les Méchins
96
PARC DE
LA GASPÉSIE
Murdochville
198
Fontenelle

Forestville
Matane
RÉSERVE FAUNIQUE
DES
CHIC-CHOCS

Baie-des-Sables
132
64
RÉSERVE FAUNIQUE
DE MATANE
Gaspé

Pointe-au-Père
Mont-Joli
Sayabec
GASPÉSIE

Rimouski
20
234
Ste-Angèle-
de-Mérici
151
Amqui
132
Bonaventure
299
QUÉBEC
Percé
GOLFE DU ST-LAURENT/
GULF OF ST. LAWRENCE

Le Bic
232
St-Fabien
St-Marcellin
Causapscal
132
Grande-Rivière
Chandler (Pabos)

132
Trois-Pistoles
RÉSERVE FAUNIQUE
DUCHÉNIER
Routhierville
RÉSERVE FAUNIQUE
DE PORT-DANIEL
Port-Daniel-Gascons
241

232
Lac-des-Aigles
RÉSERVE FAUNIQUE
DE RIMOUSKI
Campbellton
102
Nouvelle
New Richmond
Baie des Chaleurs / Chaleur Bay

185
Cabano
Notre-Dame-
du-Lac
EASTERN
TIME ZONE
ATLANTIC
TIME ZONE
Matapédia
Dalhousie
Charlo
Bonaventure
New Carlisle

232
Rivière-Bleue
11
388
24
Jacquet
River
Miscou Centre

289
17
Robinsonville
326
Petit-Rocher
11
Grande-
Anse
191
Caraquet
113
Ferry
Ville de Lameque

Rivière-Verte
Kedgwick
Beresford
Janeville
Shippagan

Edmundston
St-Quentin
180
MT. CARLETON
PROV. PARK
300
Bathurst
160
Tracadie-Sheila
ÎLES-DE-LA-
MADELEINE

Fort Kent
430
231
Allardville
199
Grande-Entrée

Eagle
Lake
Van Buren
161
St. Leonard
(St-Léonard)
Nictau
385
Nepisiguit R.
72
L'Étang-du-Nord
Cap-aux-Meules

11
Grand Falls (Grand-Sault)
108
NEW
BRUNSWICK
Heath Steele
8
11
Tabusintac
Bassin
Havre-Aubert

Caribou
Fort Fairfield
Presque Isle
105
Lake Edward
109
Plaster
Rock
Miramichi
126
Neguac
Baie-Ste-Anne
117

Ashland
163
Perth-Andover
108
Renous
Blackville
Rogersville
KOUCHIBOUGUAC
NATL. PARK
St. Margarets
Pleasant View
Tignish
CAPE BRETON

MAINE
Mars Hill
Bristol
SW. Juniper Miramichi R.
149
St-Louis de Kent
2
14
Chéticamp
Grand-Etang
ISLAND

Knowles
Corner
11
Florenceville
Hartland
Napadogan
Boiestown
123
Harcourt
116
Richibucto
West Point
Rexton
Portage
Darnley
PRINCE EDWARD ISLAND
NATL. PARK
St. Andrews
16
Elmira
Margaree Forks
NE Margaree
Inverness
395
105

Patten
Smyrna
Mills
212
Woodstock
105
104
Stanley
Taymouth
Nashwaak
Bridge
10
Gaspereau
Forks
116
Bouctouche
Cap-Egmont
Cornwall
Summerside
South Rustico
15
Stanhope
Bedford
St. Peters
Morell
Mabou
Port Hood
19
252
13

Houlton
95
2A
Meductic
2
Nackawic
Keswick
Ridge
8
Minto
Grand L.
Chipman
112
126
Notre-Dame
115
Shediac
Cap-Pele
Borden-
Carleton
Crapaud
Charlottetown
Montague
Gaspereaux
Murray River
4
Whycocomagh
Judique

Shernman
122
Fosterville
104
Fredericton
Oromocto
365
Coles Island
Salisbury
423
106
Moncton
114
Memramcook
15
69
Cape
Tormentine
Wood Islands
106
Merigomish
245
337
Kingsville
St-Péters
104

Mecwahoc
Thomaston
Corner
645
Harvey
Tracy
Jemseg
Waterborough
Petitcodiac
233
173
Hillsborough
Elgin
FT. BEAUSÉJOUR
N.H.P.
Aulac
Port Elgin
Linden
Oxford
321
Wallace
Pugwash
River
John
106
Pictou
New
Glasgow
114
Antigonish
19
Port
Hawkesbury

Vanceboro
St. Croix
630
McAdam
101
Evandale
Cambridge-
Narrows
695
100
198
114
Sussex
111
Riverside-
Albert
FUNDY
NATL. PARK
Maccan
302
Springhill
115
142
104
Wentworth
24
Stellarton
Monastery
Canso
Guysborough

Lincoln
6
Springfield
Topsfield
Hampton
845
Ferry
Alma
Joggins
9
Five Islands
311
Glenholme
New
Glasgow
7
Goshen
16
316

2
Lawrence
Station
Welsford
Rothesay
Quispamsis
111
Apple River
209
Parrsboro
215
Truro
289
NOVA SCOTIA
347
Melrose
Larrys River

St. Stephen
St.
George
Westfield
St. Martins
Advocate
Harbour
Kentville
17E
Walville
Kennetcook
Rawdon
14
Upper
Rawdon
Upper
Stewiacke
Musquodoboit
Trafalgar
348
374
Sherbrooke
211
Port Bickerton

Calais
Distances in the U.S. shown in miles
Distances in Canada shown in kilometers
Saint
John
Lepreau
Bay of Fundy
18
Bridgetown
21
Kingston
Middleton
Windsor
101
14
Hammonds
Plains
354
102
Middle
Musquodoboit
Sheet
Harbour
7
Port Dufferin

St. Andrew
9
Wesley
Aurora
9
Beddington
192
Whiting
ROOSEVELT-
CAMPOBELLO INTL. PARK
PORT ROYAL
N.H.P.
ANNE N.H.P.
New Ross
New
Germany
8
103
Chester
Shubenacadie
224
Porters
Lake
Musquodoboit
Harbour
Tangier

1A
Franklin Road
129
Lubec
North Head
Grand Manan I.
Grand Harbour
Seal Cove
Victoria Beach
Digby
Clementsport
Annapolis Royal
10
208
Hubbards
103
Indian
Harbour
Halifax Reg.
Municipality

Machias
Ellsworth
3
Bar Harbour
Mt. Desert I.
Sandy Cove
Ferry
217
South
Milford
23
Weymouth
Maitland
Bridge
KEJIMKUJIK
NATL. PARK
8
Martins River
Lunenburg
La Have
Bridgewater
103
Bedford
Dartmouth
Halifax
118

(Seasonal)
Freeport
Meteghan
340
Upper Ohio
Rossignol
L.
South
Brookfield
Mill Village
209
331

Salmon River
32
203
19
Liverpool

Yarmouth
34
33
Deerfield
Queens
Reg. Mun.
Port Mouton

To Portland, ME (Seasonal)
Tusket
103
Wedgeport
Pubnico
Shelburne
Sable River
103
ATLANTIC   OCEAN

Lower Woods Harbour
Clyde River
Lockeport

Clark's Harbour

1   2   3   4   5

ATLANTIC OCEAN

NEWFOUNDLAND AND LABRADOR

NEWFOUNDLAND ISLAND

GROS MORNE NATL PARK

TERRA NOVA NATL. PARK

BARACHOIS PROV. PARK

JIPUJIJKUEI KUESPEM PROV. PARK

PORT AU PORT PEN.

HEURE DE L'ATLANTIQUE / ATLANTIC TIME ZONE

NEWFOUNDLAND TIME ZONE

CANADA FRANCE

ST-PIERRE AND MIQUELON

CAPE BRETON HIGHLANDS NATL PARK

ALEXANDER GRAHAM BELL N.H.P.

FORTRESS OF LOUISBOURG N.H.P.

ATLANTIC OCEAN

1 inch represents 51 miles
or 83 kilometers
(1:3,250,000)

MI   20   40   60
      20   40   60   KM

© GeoNova Publishing, Inc.

N

OCÉANO PACÍFICO / PACIFIC OCEAN

Golfo de California

PACIFIC OCEAN

PARTIAL INDEX TO CITIES AND TOWNS

P 8 Arizona
P 11 California
P 37 New Mexico

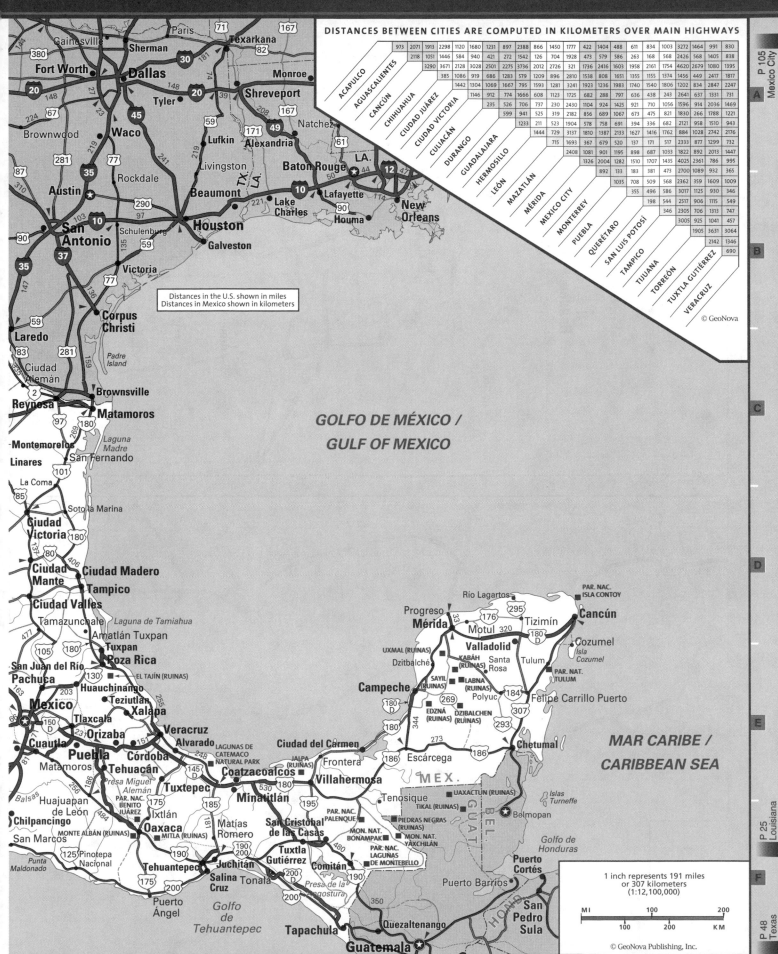

Albuquerque & Austin

P 37
New Mexico

1 inch represents 3.9 miles
or 6.3 kilometers (1:246,297)
© GeoNova Publishing, Inc.

CIBOLA NATIONAL FOREST

Albuquerque

KIRTLAND AIR FORCE BASE

Rio Rancho

Paradise Hills

Bernalillo

Corrales

Alameda

Los Ranchos de Albuquerque

Armijo

Five Points

SANDIA PUEBLO

ISLETA PUEBLO

ISLETA PUEBLO

MESA DEL SOL

1 inch represents 2.3 miles
or 3.7 kilometers (1:145,488)
© GeoNova Publishing, Inc.

Austin

Austin-Bergstrom International Airport (AUS)

West Lake Hills

McKinney Falls State Park

P 48
Texas

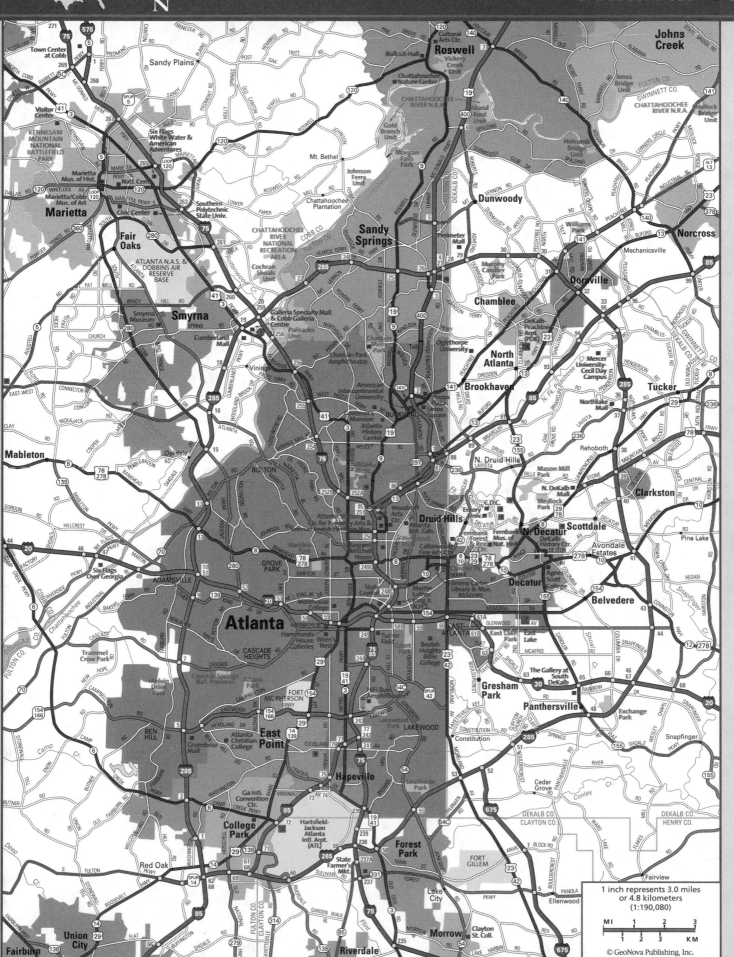

N

Johns Creek

Roswell

Town Center at Cobb

Sandy Plains

Marietta

Fair Oaks

Smyrna

Dunwoody

Norcross

Sandy Springs

Chamblee

Doraville

North Atlanta

Tucker

Brookhaven

Mableton

Clarkston

N. Druid Hills

Scottdale

Druid Hills

N. Decatur

Avondale Estates

Decatur

Belvedere

Atlanta

Pine Lake

CASCADE HEIGHTS

East Atlanta

East Lake

The Gallery at South DeKalb

Gresham Park

Panthersville

FORT MC PHERSON

Exchange Park

East Point

LAKEWOOD

Hapeville

Snapfinger

Cedar Grove

College Park

Forest Park

Fort Gillem

Red Ok

Lake City

Union City

Morrow

Fairburn

Riverdale

Ellenwood

1 inch represents 3.0 miles
or 4.8 kilometers
(1:190,080)

MI
0   1   2   3
0 1 2 3 4 5
KM

© GeoNova Publishing, Inc.

N

Worthington
Owings Mills
Owings Mills Town Center
Soldiers Delight Natural Environment Area
Delight
Garrison
Chattolanee
Randallstown
Rockdale
Kings Park
Milford
Hebbville
Lochearn
Woodmoor
Western Area Park
Patapsco Valley State Park
Mt. Hebron
Woodlawn
Security Square Mall
Westview
Ellicott City
Court House
Catonsville
Banneker Historical Park & Mus.
McAlpine
B&O Railroad Station Museum
Ilchester
Worthington
Cider Mill Farm
Rockburn
Patapsco Valley State Park
Rockburn Branch Park
Long Reach
Pfeiffer Corners
Arbutus
Univ. of Md., Baltimore County
Halethorpe
Elkridge
Harwood Park
Hanover
Historical Electronics Museum
Linthicum
Lansdowne
Baltimore Highlands
Brooklyn Park
Pumphrey
Arundel Village
Dorsey
Waterloo
Montevideo
Ferndale
Jessup
Savage
Savage Mill
Maryland City
Annapolis Junction
Natl. Cryptologic Museum
FORT GEORGE G. MEADE MIL. RES.
National Security Agency
Odenton
Patuxent Wildlife Research Center
Gambrills
Arundel Mills
Joe Cannon Stadium
Harmans
Baltimore-Washington International Thurgood Marshall Airport (BWI)
Glen Burnie
Severn
Harundale
Marley Station Mall
South Gate
Marley
Ridgeway Run
Benfield
Severn Run Natural Environment Area
Kinder Park
Elvaton
Pasadena
Mays Chapel
Timonium
Maryland State Fairgrounds
TIMONIUM
Lutherville
Fire Museum
Hampton Natl. Hist. Site
Hampton
Providence
Germantown
Loch Raven Reservoir
Loch Raven Res.
Gunpowder Falls S.P.
Texas
Villa Julie College
Brooklandville
Stevenson
Irvine Natural Science Center
Cloisters Children's Museum
Riderwood
Ruxton
Robert E. Lee Park
Lake Roland
Towson Town Ctr.
Goucher College
Towson
Towson Univ.
Rodgers Forge
Putty Hill
Pikesville
Perry Hall
Carney
Parkville
Overlea
White Marsh Mall
White Marsh
Fullerton
Rossville
Nottingham
Pimlico Race Course
Cylburn Arboretum
Evergreen House
College of Notre Dame of Md.
Loyola College in Maryland
Morgan St. Univ.
Kenwood
Rosedale
Middle River
Maryland Zoo in Baltimore
Johns Hopkins University
Baltimore Mus. of Art
Druid Hill
Clifton Park
Herring Run Park
Coppin State Coll.
Gwynns Falls Park
The Heritage Museum
Middleborough
Chesaco Park
Essex
Univ. of Baltimore
Johns Hopkins Hosp.
Eastpoint Mall
Gwynns Falls
North Ave.
City Hall
Loudon Park Natl. Cem.
Baltimore Natl. Cem.
Franklin St.
Fayette
Camden Yards
B&O Mus.
Mt. Clare Mansion
M&T Bank Stadium
Oriole Park
Mus. of Industry
Boston
Eastern
O'Donnell St.
Ft. McHenry Natl. Mon. & Hist. Shrine
North Point Village
Dundalk
Edgemere
Evergreen Park
PATAPSCO
NECK
RIVER
Old Road Bay
North Point State Park
Fort Howard Park
Fort Howard
North Point
Sparrows Point
Middle Br.
Baltimore
Curtis Bay
Fort Carroll
Francis Scott Key Bridge
Sparrows Point
Patapsco
HOG NECK
Orchard Beach
Riviera Beach
Fort Smallwood Park
Rock Pt.
Rock Cr.
Venice on the Bay
Paradise Beach
Boyd Pond
Bayside Beach
Bellhaven Beach
Main Cr.
Bodkin Cr.
Bayside Beach
Chesapeake Bay
Green Haven
Lipins Corner
Margate
Solley
Jacobsville
Lake Shore
Chelsea Beach
Pinehurst
Ventnor
Mount Carmel
Downs Mem. Park
North Shore
Gibson Island
Gibson Island
Mago Vista Beach
Severna Park
Round Bay
Twin Harbors
Mountain Pt.
Sunshine Beach Rd.
Arden-on-the-Severn
Dorrs Corner

1 inch represents 3.0 miles or 4.8 kilometers (1:190,080)

MI   1   2   3
KM   1   2   3

© GeoNova Publishing, Inc.

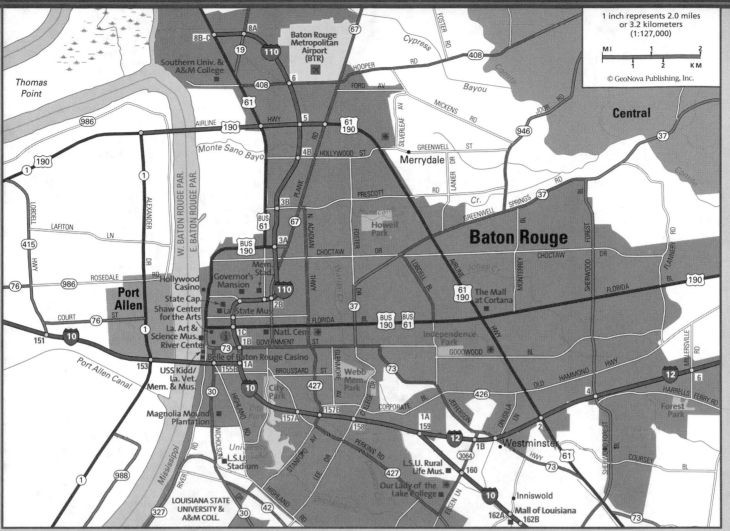

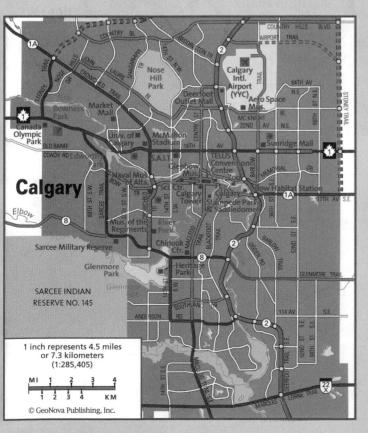

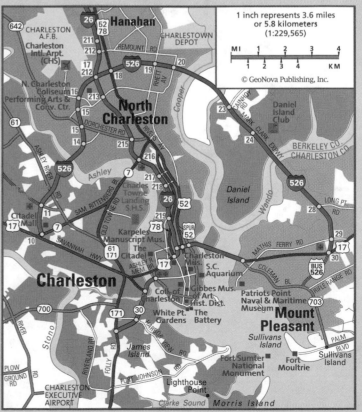

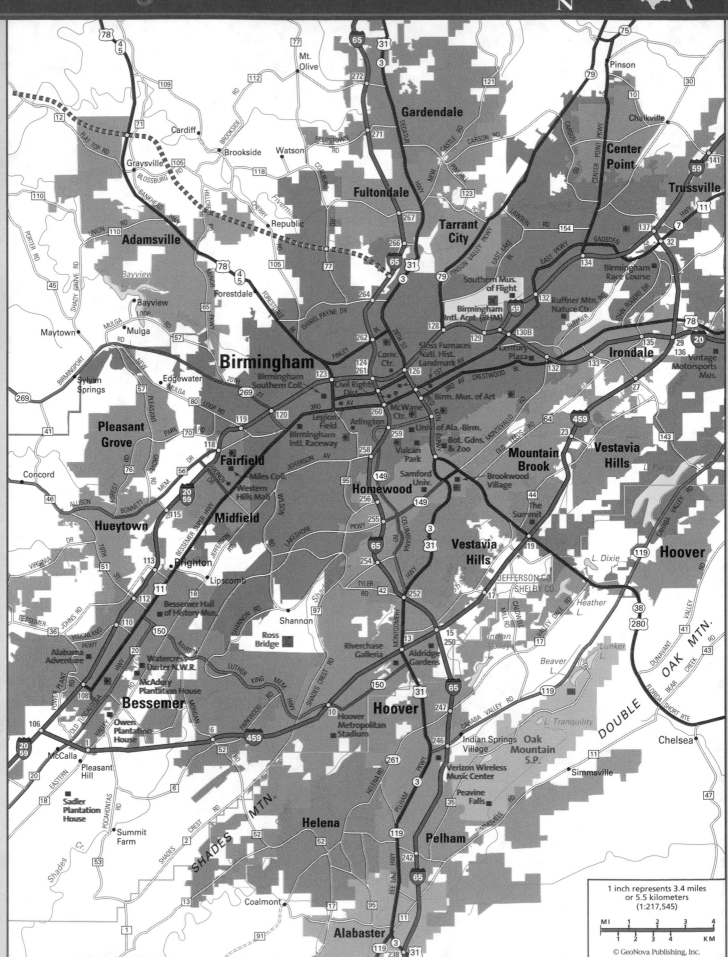

N

Birmingham

1 inch represents 3.4 miles
or 5.5 kilometers
(1:217,545)

MI 1 2 3 4
KM 1 2 3 4 5 6

© GeoNova Publishing, Inc.

1 inch represents 2.5 miles
or 4.0 kilometers
(1:156,252)

MI
0 1 2

KM
0 1 2

© GeoNova Publishing, Inc.

1 inch represents 3.0 miles
or 4.8 kilometers
(1:187,179)

MI 1 2 3
KM 1 2 3

© GeoNova Publishing, Inc.

Charlotte

1 inch represents 2.3 miles
or 3.7 kilometers
(1:147,007)

© GeoNova Publishing, Inc.

P 40
North Carolina

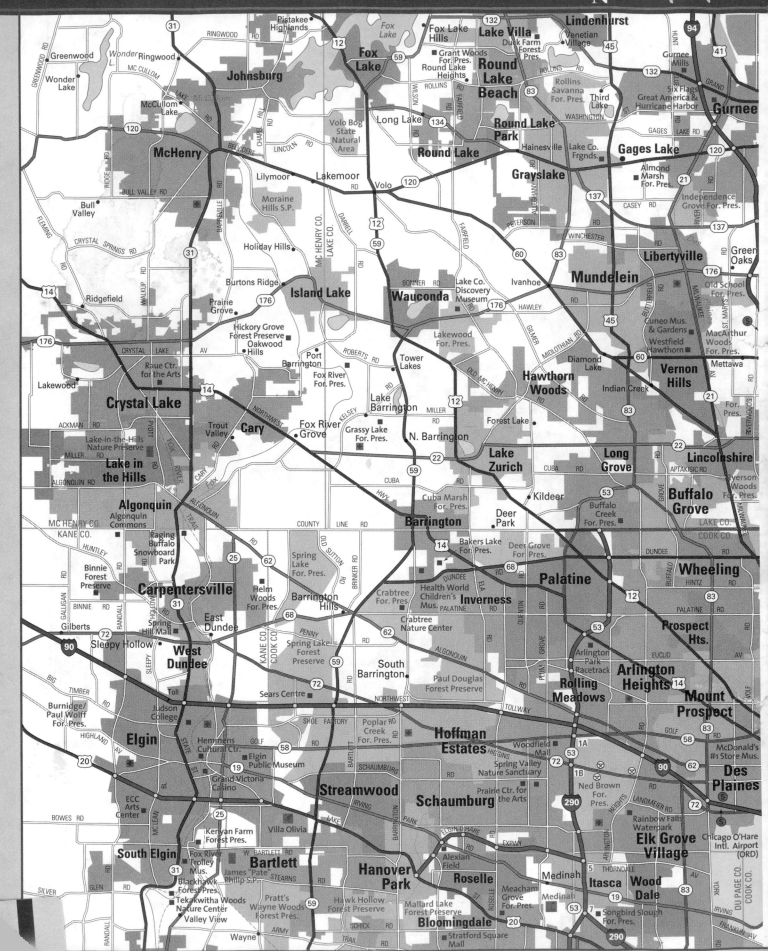

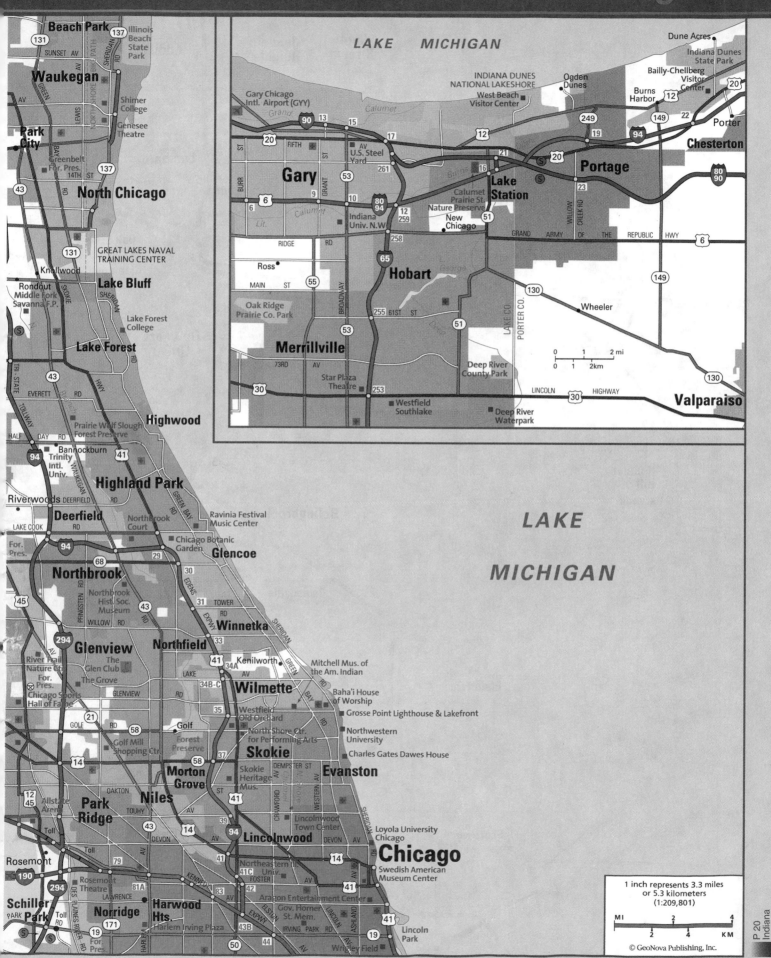

Inset Map

LAKE MICHIGAN

Dune Acres
Indiana Dunes State Park
INDIANA DUNES NATIONAL LAKESHORE
Ogden Dunes
Bailly-Chellberg Visitor Center
West Beach Visitor Center
Burns Harbor
Gary Chicago Intl. Airport (GYY)
Grand
Calumet
90 13
15
20
FIFTH
ST
17
12
21
16
20
Porter
Chesterton
249
19
149
22
94
12
80 90
U.S. Steel Yard
AV
BURR ST
GRANT ST
53
9
ST
261
Gary
6
10
80 94
12 259
Calumet Prairie St. Nature Preserve
New Chicago
Lake Station
51
S
23
Portage
WILLOW CREEK RD
GRAND ARMY OF THE REPUBLIC HWY
6
80 90
Calumet
Lit.
Indiana Univ. N.W.
258
RIDGE RD
65
Hobart
51
LAKE CO.
PORTER CO.
130
149
Ross
MAIN ST
55
Oak Ridge Prairie Co. Park
BROADWAY
255 61ST ST
Lk. George
Wheeler
1   2 mi
0 1 2km
53
Deep River County Park
Merrillville
73RD AV
Star Plaza Theatre
253
30
Westfield Southlake
Deep River Waterpark
LINCOLN
30 HIGHWAY
Valparaiso

Main Map

Beach Park
131 137
SUNSET AV
Illinois Beach State Park
GREEN BAY
NORTHSHORE BIKE PATH
SHERIDAN RD
Waukegan
AV
Shimer College
Park City
Genesee Theatre
Greenbelt For. Pres.
14TH ST
137
North Chicago
43
131
GREAT LAKES NAVAL TRAINING CENTER
Knollwood
SKOKIE
SHERIDAN
Rondout Middle Fork Savanna F.P.
Lake Bluff
S
Lake Forest College
Lake Forest
RD
Tri-State Tollway
43
EVERETT RD
41
Highwood
HALF DAY RD
Prairie Wolf Slough Forest Preserve
94
Bannockburn
Trinity Intl. Univ.
41
Highland Park
GREEN BAY RD
Riverwoods
DEERFIELD RD
Deerfield
LAKE COOK RD
Northbrook Court
Ravinia Festival Music Center
For. Pres.
94
29
Chicago Botanic Garden
Glencoe
68
Northbrook
Northbrook Hist. Soc. Museum
30
EDENS EXPWY
PFINGSTEN RD
WILLOW RD
43
31
TOWER RD
Winnetka
SHERIDAN
294
45
Glenview
The Glen Club
The Grove
Northfield
33
41
34A
Kenilworth
GREEN BAY RD
Mitchell Mus. of the Am. Indian
LAKE AV
GLENVIEW RD
34B-C
Wilmette
Baha'i House of Worship
Grosse Point Lighthouse & Lakefront
21
35
Westfield Old Orchard
North Shore Ctr. for Performing Arts
Northwestern University
GOLF RD
Golf
58
Golf Mill Shopping Ctr.
Forest Preserve
37
Skokie
DEMPSTER ST
Charles Gates Dawes House
14
Morton Grove
58
Skokie Heritage Mus.
Evanston
OAKTON ST
CRAWFORD AV
WESTERN AV
Niles
TOUHY AV
41
12 45
Park Ridge
Allstate Arena
43
14
39
DEVON AV
94
Lincolnwood
Lincolnwood Town Center
DEVON AV
Loyola University Chicago
41
Rosemont
Northeastern Univ.
41C
FOSTER AV
42
Chicago
Swedish American Museum Center
190
294
Rosemont Theatre
LAWRENCE
81A
Harwood Hts.
Aragon Entertainment Center
Gov. Horner St. Mem.
43B
Schiller Park
Toll
19 171
Norridge
HARLEM
DES PLAINES RIVER RD
For. Pres.
Harlem Irving Plaza
50
44
IRVING PARK RD
ELSTON AV
ASHLAND AV
LINCOLN AV
41
19
Lincoln Park
Wrigley Field

LAKE

MICHIGAN

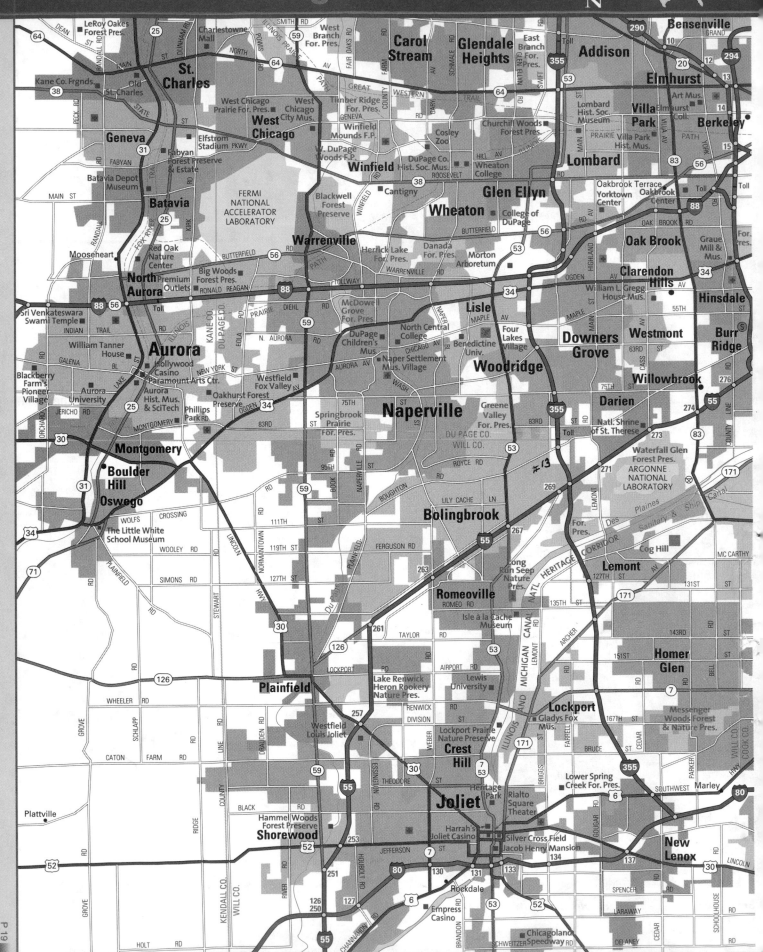

1 inch represents 3.3 miles
or 5.3 kilometers
(1:209,801)

MI   2   4

2   4   KM

© GeoNova Publishing, Inc.

LAKE

MICHIGAN

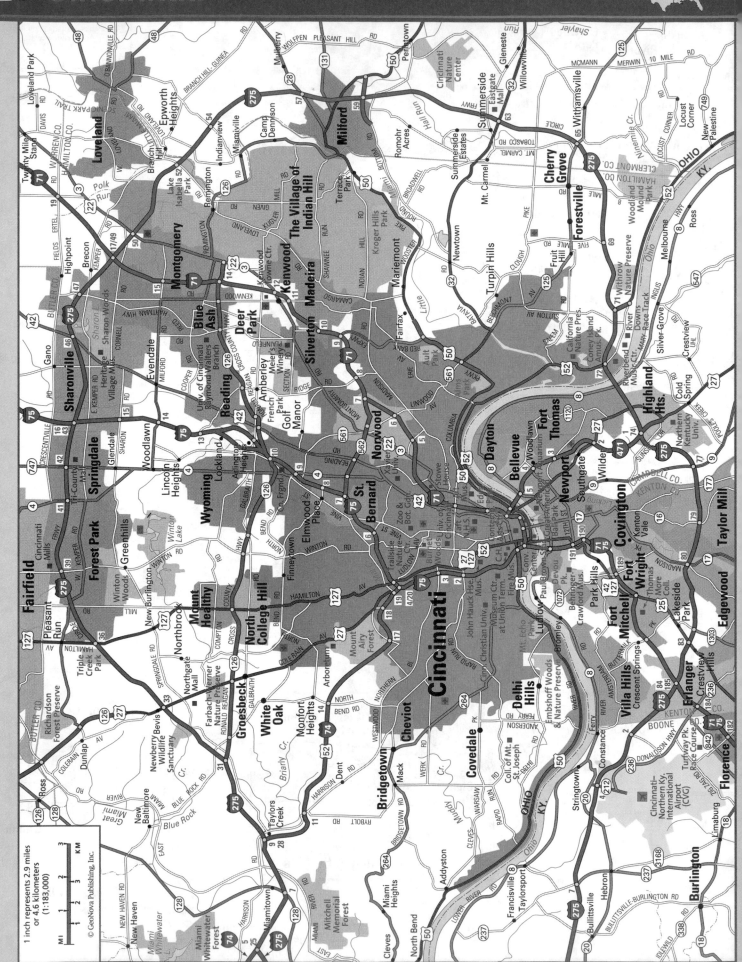

Cleveland

N

LAKE ERIE

1 inch represents 3.3 miles
or 5.3 kilometers
(1:207,000)

© GeoNova Publishing, Inc.

KM
MI

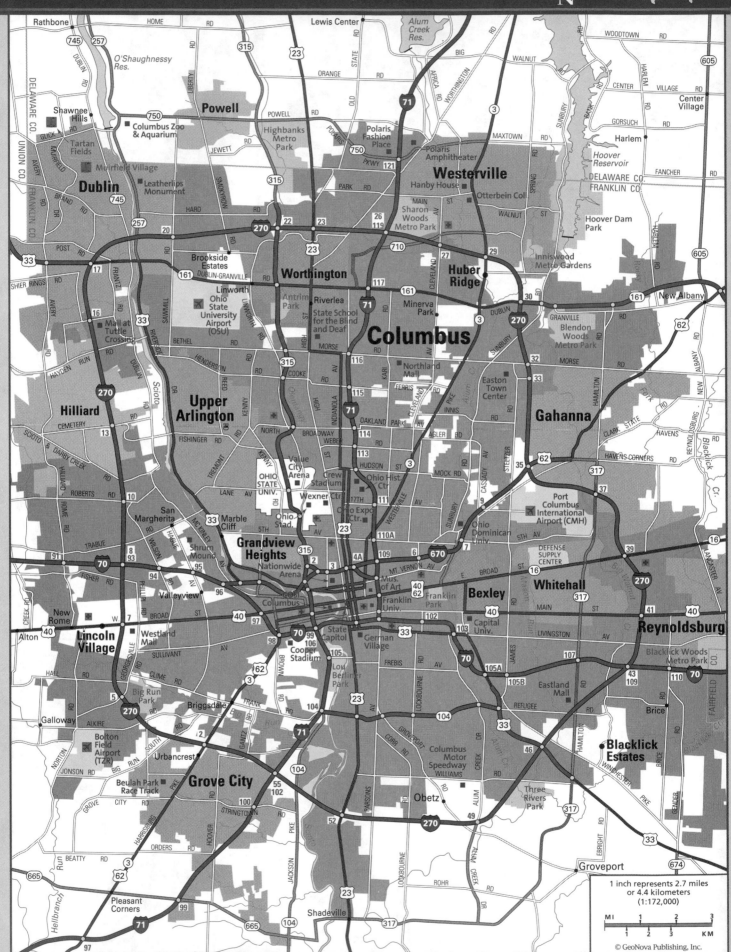

Columbus

1 inch represents 2.7 miles
or 4.4 kilometers
(1:172,000)

MI | 1 | 2 | 3
KM | 1 | 2 | 3

© GeoNova Publishing, Inc.

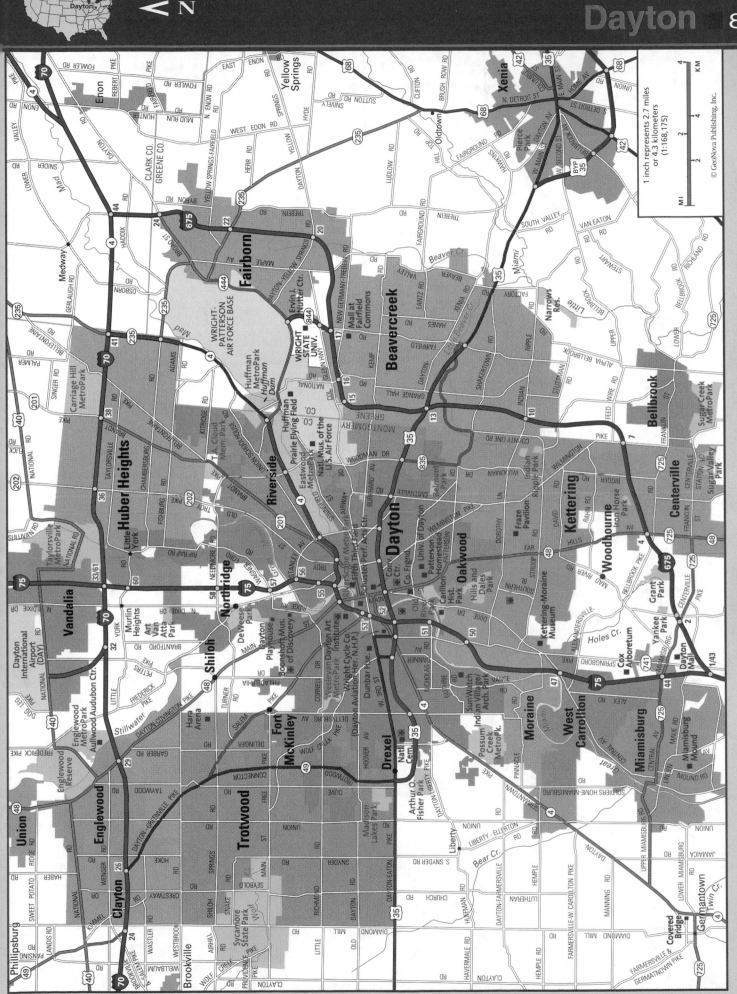

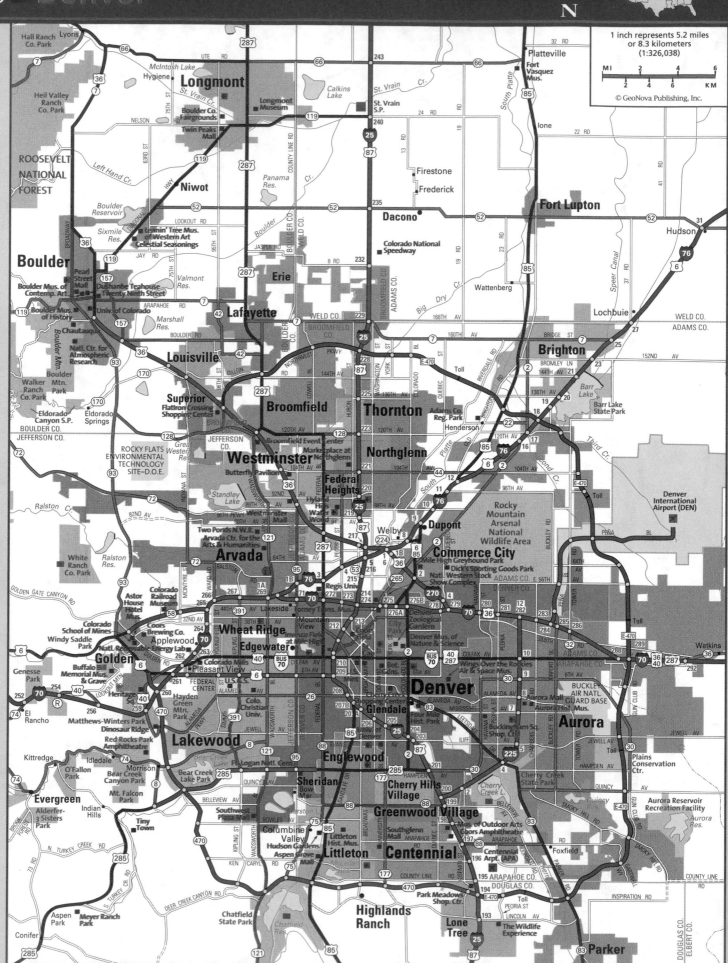

N

1 inch represents 5.2 miles
or 8.3 kilometers
(1:326,038)

© GeoNova Publishing, Inc.

ROOSEVELT NATIONAL FOREST

Longmont

Boulder

Niwot

Erie

Lafayette

Louisville

Superior

Broomfield

Thornton

Westminster

Northglenn

Federal Heights

Arvada

Commerce City

Wheat Ridge

Edgewater

Golden

Denver

Lakewood

Glendale

Aurora

Englewood

Sheridan

Cherry Hills Village

Greenwood Village

Littleton

Centennial

Evergreen

Highlands Ranch

Lone Tree

Parker

Fort Lupton

Brighton

Dacono

Hudson

Lochbuie

Platteville

Firestone

Frederick

Denver International Airport (DEN)

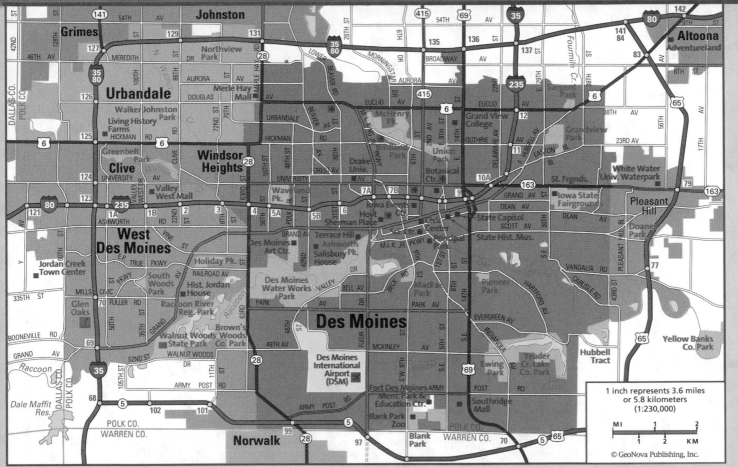

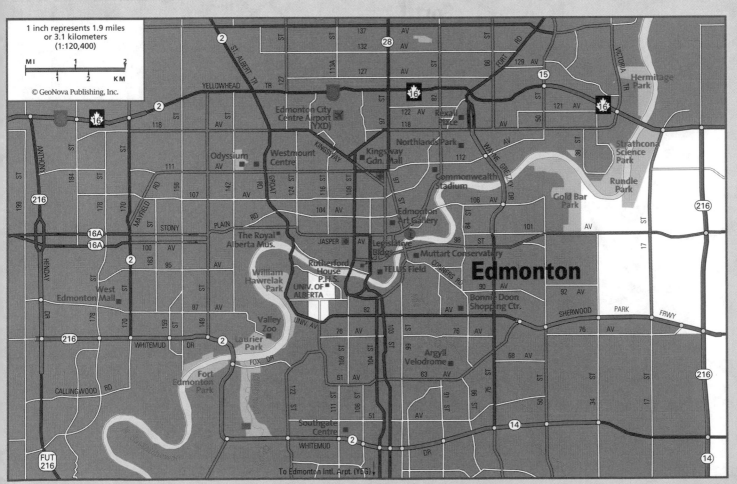

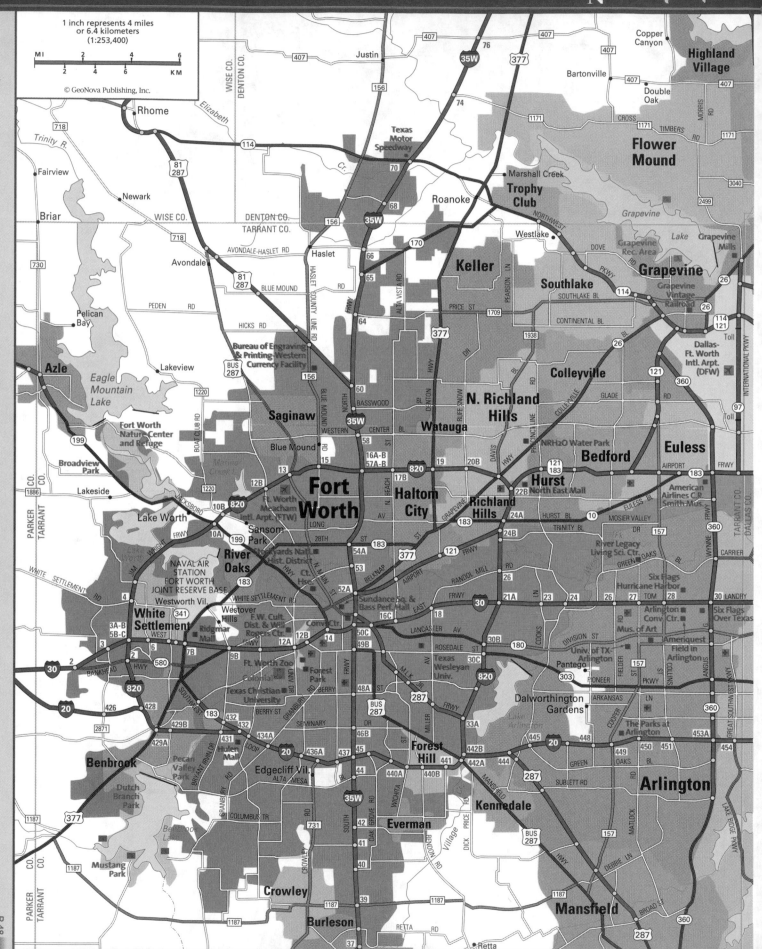

1 inch represents 4 miles
or 6.4 kilometers
(1:253,400)

MI
2 4 6

2 4 6
KM

© GeoNova Publishing, Inc.

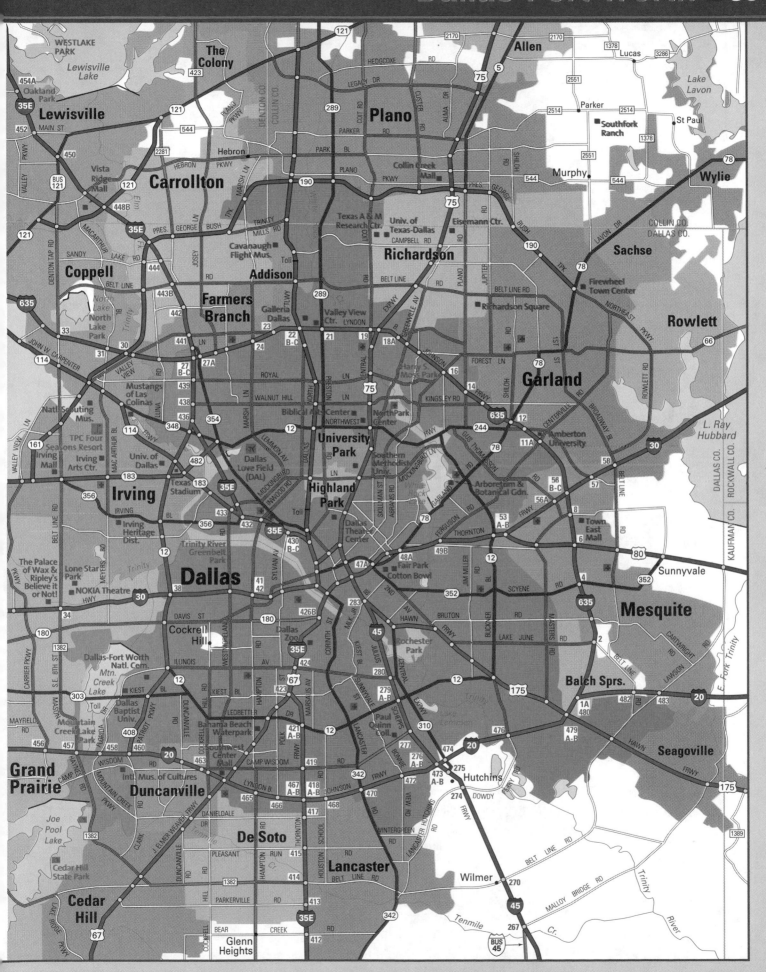

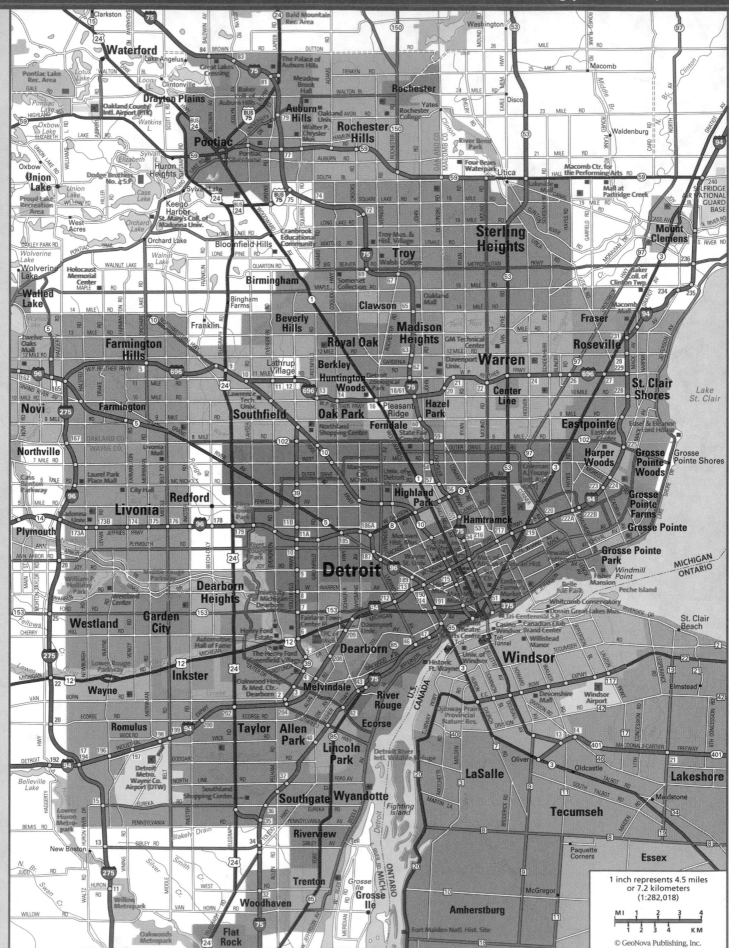

N

1 inch represents 4.5 miles
or 7.2 kilometers
(1:282,018)

MI 0   1   2   3   4

0 1 2 3 4 KM

© GeoNova Publishing, Inc.

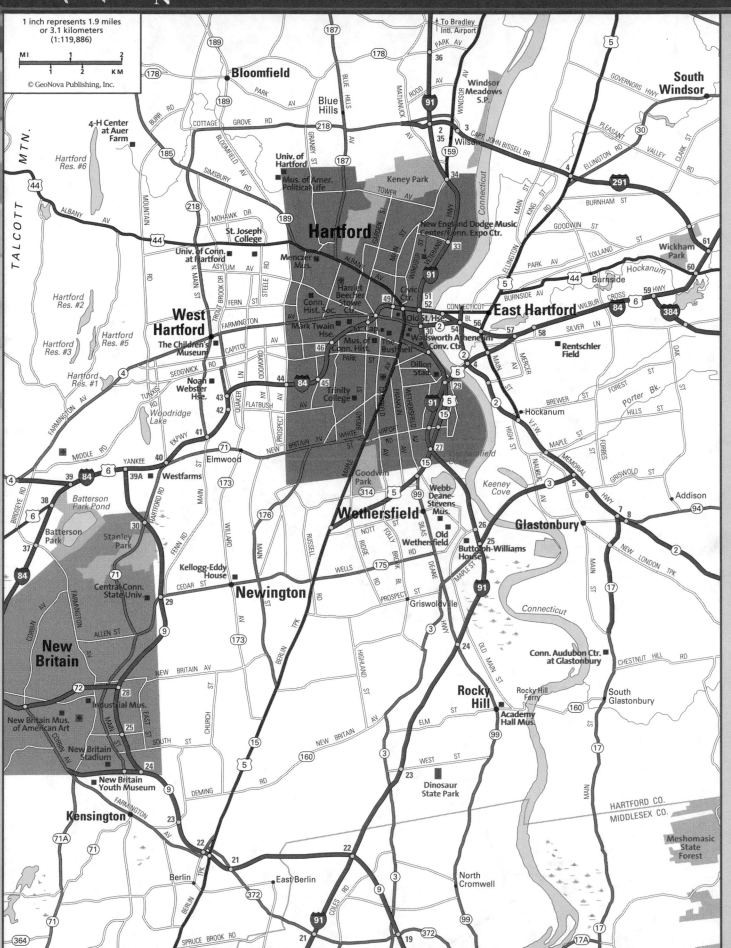

1 inch represents 1.9 miles
or 3.1 kilometers
(1:119,886)

MI 1 2

1 2 KM

© GeoNova Publishing, Inc.

Hartford

To Bradley
Intl. Airport

PARK AV

Bloomfield

187

189

178

36

178

91

South
Windsor

GOVERNORS HWY

5

189

178

Blue Hills

BLUE HILLS AV

MATIANUCK AV

WINDSOR AV

Windsor
Meadows
S.P.

Connecticut

30

PLEASANT ST

185

BURR RD

COTTAGE GROVE RD

PARK AV

218

GRANBY ST

TOWER AV

Keney Park

2
35

3
Wilson

CAPT. JOHN BISSELL BR.

ELLINGTON RD

VALLEY RD

CLARK ST

4-H Center
at Auer
Farm

Hartford
Res. #6

44

ALBANY AV

SIMSBURY RD

BLOOMFIELD AV

MOHAWK DR

St. Joseph
College

Univ. of
Hartford

Mus. of Amer.
Political Life

187

34

159

4

291

MAIN ST

KING ST

BURNHAM ST

44

MOUNTAIN RD

218

Univ. of Conn.
at Hartford

ASYLUM AV

N. MAIN ST

FERN ST

STEELE RD

Menczer
Mus.

ALBANY AV

GARDEN ST

WINDSOR ST

New England Dodge Music
Center/Conn. Expo Ctr.

33

ELLINGTON

PARK AV

TOLLAND ST

GOODWIN ST

61

Wickham
Park

60

Hockanum

TALCOTT MTN.

Hartford
Res. #2

44

TROUT BROOK DR

FARMINGTON AV

Conn.
Hist. Soc.
Ctr.

Harriet
Beecher
Stowe
Ctr.

MAIN ST

91

Civic
Ctr.

49

51
52

Old St. Hse.

CONNECTICUT BL 56

54

BURNSIDE AV

Burnside

5

44

East Hartford

84

59 HWY

6

384

West
Hartford

CAPITOL AV

SEDGWICK RD

OAKWOOD AV

The Children's
Museum

Mark Twain
Hse.

46

Mus. of
Conn. Hist.

St. Cap.

The
Bushnell

Wadsworth Atheneum

Conn. Ctr.

30

2

57

58

MERCER

SILVER LN

OAK ST

FOREST ST

PORTER

BREWER ST

Rentschler
Field

Hartford
Res. #5

Hartford
Res. #3

Noah
Webster
Hse.

43

QUAKER LN

FLATBUSH AV

84

45

Trinity
College

PARK ST

BROAD ST

WETHERSFIELD AV

FRANKLIN AV

Dillon
Stad.

2

4

5

29

91

5

15

Hockanum

HIGH ST

MAPLE ST

V.F.W.

Porter Bk.

HILLS

Hartford
Res. #1

TUNXIS RD

Woodridge
Lake

42

41

NEW BRITAIN AV

PROSPECT AV

WHITE ST

AIRPORT RD

27

MAPLE AV

Goodwin
Park

15

NALRUC AV

MEMORIAL

Keeney
Cove

5

6

GRISWOLD ST

FORBES ST

Addison

94

MIDDLE RD

4

39

84

6

40

YANKEE EXPWY

71

Elmwood

39A

Westfarms

HARTFORD RD

MAIN ST

173

176

314

5

99

Webb-
Deane-
Stevens
Mus.

Wethersfield

Old
Wethersfield

26

25

Buttolph-Williams
House

Glastonbury

MAIN ST

7
8

NEW LONDON TPK

2

17

Batterson
Park Pond

Batterson
Park

BIRDSEYE RD

6

38

37

84

Stanley
Park

30

71

Central Conn.
State Univ.

29

FENN RD

WILLARD AV

MAIN ST

CEDAR ST

Kellogg-Eddy
House

Newington

9

RUSSELL RD

NOTT ST

FOLLY BROOK BL

SILAS DEANE HWY

WELLS RD

175

PROSPECT ST

Griswoldville

3

91

24

Connecticut

Conn. Audubon Ctr.
at Glastonbury

CHESTNUT HILL RD

South
Glastonbury

New
Britain

CORBIN AV

FARMINGTON AV

ALLEN ST

173

BERLIN TPK

HIGHLAND ST

NEW BRITAIN AV

MAPLE ST

OLD MAIN ST

Rocky Hill
Ferry

160

Rocky
Hill

ST

ELM ST

99

Academy
Hall Mus.

72

28

Industrial Mus.

New Britain Mus.
of American Art

EAST ST

MAIN ST

25

SOUTH ST

New Britain
Stadium

24

CHURCH ST

NEW BRITAIN RD

WEST ST

3

23

Dinosaur
State Park

17

New Britain
Youth Museum

9

DEMING RD

FARMINGTON AV

15

5

160

HARTFORD CO.
MIDDLESEX CO.

Meshomasic
State
Forest

Kensington

23

22

21

Berlin

BERLIN TPK

East Berlin

372

91

COLES RD

SPRUCE BROOK RD

22

3

North
Cromwell

99

19

372

17A

71A

71

364

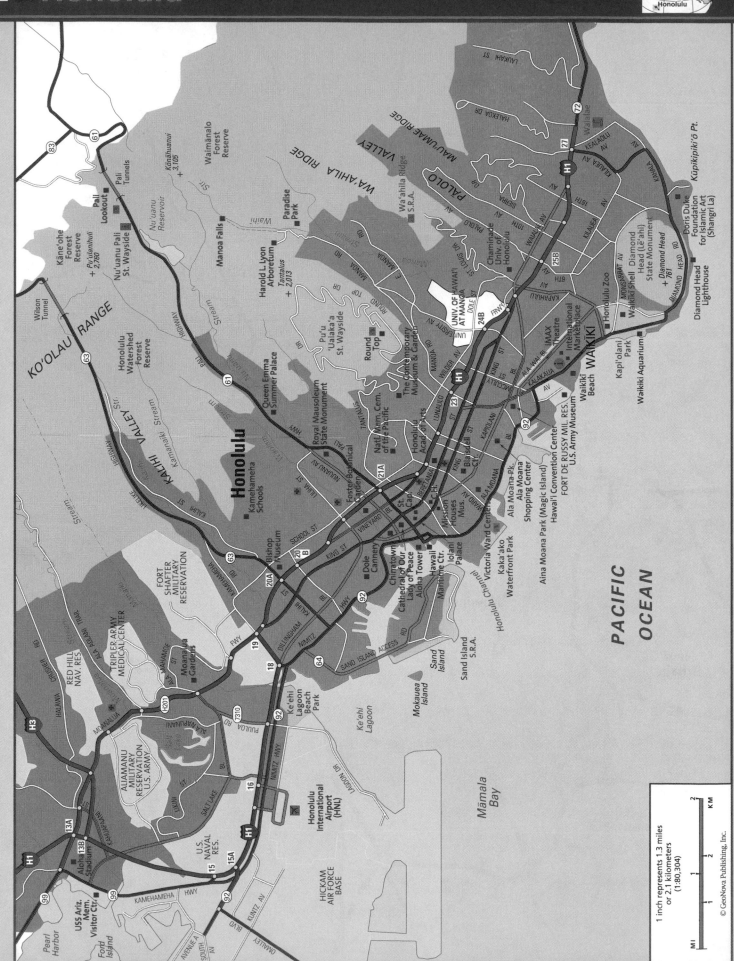

N

Honolulu

LAUKAHI ST

72

WAHAKOA DR

Wailalae

KO'OLAU RANGE

Pali Lookout

Wilson Tunnel

63

Honolulu Watershed Forest Reserve

83

61

Kāne'ohe Forest Reserve

Pali Tunnels

Nu'uanu Pali St. Wayside

Pu'ulanihuli + 2,760

Nu'uanu Reservoir

Kōnāhuanui + 3,105

Waimanalo Forest Reserve

Waihi

Manoa Falls

Paradise Park

WA'AHILA RIDGE

Wa'ahila Ridge S.R.A.

MAU'UMAE RIDGE

HALEKOA DR

KEALAOLU AV

KILAUEA AV

KAHALA AV

KALA

H1

27

KILAUEA AV

15TH AV

18TH AV

Doris Duke Foundation for Islamic Art (Shangri La)

Kūpikipiki'ō Pt.

PALOLO VALLEY

PALOLO

ST. LOUIS DR

PALOLO AV

SIERRA DR

10TH AV

25B

6TH AV

Diamond Head (Lē'ahi) State Monument + 761

Diamond Head RD

Diamond Head Lighthouse

Harold L. Lyon Arboretum

Tantalus + 2,013

MAKIKI HEIGHTS DR

ROUND TOP DR

MANOA RD

E MANOA RD

DOLE ST

Chaminade Univ. of Honolulu

UNIV. OF HAWAI'I AT MANOA

24B

FRWY

WAIALAE AV

MONSARRAT AV

KAPAHULU AV

Waikīkī Shell

Honolulu Zoo

DIAMOND HEAD RD

Kapi'olani Park

Waikīkī Aquarium

Pu'u 'Ualaka'a St. Wayside

Round Top

Queen Emma Summer Palace

Royal Mausoleum State Monument

Nat'l Mem. Cem. of the Pacific

The Contemporary Museum & Garden

Honolulu Acad. of Arts

UNIVERSITY AV

WILDER AV

LUNALILO ST

H1

23

KING ST

MCCULLY ST

92

KAPAHULU AV

KALAKAUA AV

ALA WAI BL

IMAX Theatre

International Marketplace

WAIKĪKĪ

Waikīkī Beach

Pali Hwy

61

PALI HWY

NUUANU AV

LIKELIKE HWY

Honolulu

KO'OLAU RANGE

63

KALIHI VALLEY

Kamanaiki Stream

Kalihi Stream

Likelike Hwy

Kamehameha Schools

Bishop Museum

ILIHA ST

SCHOOL ST

20

B

KING ST

20A

B

Foster Botanical Garden

St. Cath

VINEYARD BL

21A

LUNALILO

BERETANIA

Blaisdell Ctr.

KAPIOLANI BL

KING ST

WARD AV

ALA MOANA

Mission Houses Mus.

Iolani Palace

Victoria Ward Center

Hawaii Maritime Ctr.

Chinatown

Cathedral of Our Lady of Peace

Aloha Tower

Dole Cannery

Kaka'ako Waterfront Park

Ala Moana Pk. (Magic Island)

Ala Moana Shopping Center

Hawai'i Convention Center

FORT DE RUSSY MIL. RES.

U.S. Army Museum

Aina Moana Park

FORT SHAFTER MILITARY RESERVATION

KAMEHAMEHA HWY

KALIHI ST

19

18

DILLINGHAM

NIMITZ

92

HWY

KALIHI ST

64

SAND ISLAND ACCESS RD

Sand Island

Mokauea Island

Sand Island S.R.A.

Ke'ehi Lagoon

Honolulu Channel

PACIFIC OCEAN

TRIPLER ARMY MEDICAL CENTER

RED HILL NAV. RES.

MOANALUA RD

ALA AOLANI TRAIL

CRUSHER RD

Moanalua Gardens

ALA MAHAMOE

H201

7310

92

Ke'ehi Lagoon Beach Park

PUULOA RD

MOANALUA

H3

HALAWA

ALA NANUANU

AIAMANU MILITARY RESERVATION U.S. ARMY

LIKONI ST

SALT LAKE BL

16

NIMITZ HWY

LAGOON DR

Honolulu International Airport (HNL)

Māmala Bay

H1

13A

Aloha Stadium

13B

KAHANAUI

INA

99

15

U.S. NAVAL RES.

15A

HICKAM AIR FORCE BASE

KAMEHAMEHA HWY

92

KUNTZ AV

OMALLEY BLVD

AVENUE A

SOUTH AV

99

USS Ariz. Mem. Visitor Ctr.

Pearl Harbor

Ford Island

1 inch represents 1.3 miles or 2.1 kilometers (1:80,304)

MI

KM

© GeoNova Publishing, Inc.

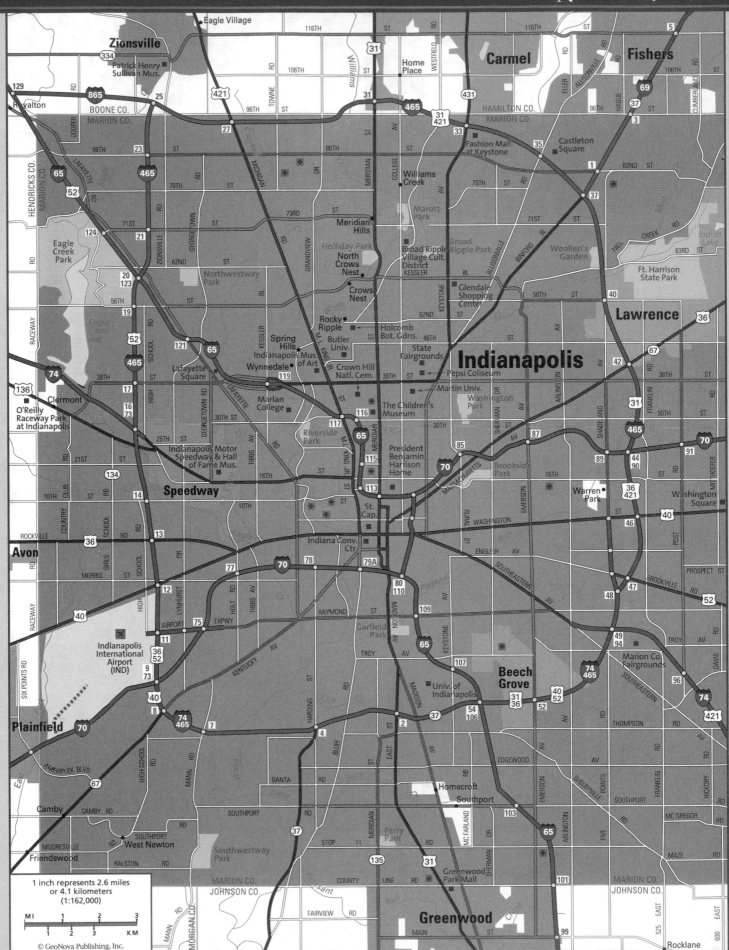

N

Indianapolis

Eagle Village
Zionsville
334
Patrick Henry
Sullivan Mus.
BOONE CO.
MARION CO.
129
Royalton
865
25
27
Carmel
Fishers
116TH ST
116TH ST
5
31
106TH
WESTFIELD RD
Home Place
431
465
31
421
HAMILTON CO.
MARION CO.
31
421
33
ELLER RD
ALLISONVILLE RD
69
37
3
106TH
96TH
HAGUE RD
CUMBERLAND RD

65
52
421
23
79TH ST
Fashion Mall
at Keystone
35
Castleton
Square
1
82ND ST
37

124
71ST ST
21
Meridian
Hills
Williams
Creek
79TH
71ST
63RD
Woollen's
Garden
CREEK
FALL
Indian
Lake
Ft. Harrison
State Park

20
123
Northwestway
Park
Holliday Park
North
Crows
Nest
Broad Ripple
Village Cult.
District
KESSLER
Broad Ripple
Park
ALLISONVILLE RD
BINFORD BL
56TH
40

19
56TH ST
Crows
Nest
Rocky
Ripple
Holcomb
Bot. Gdns.
52ND
Glendale
Shopping
Center
KEYSTONE
Lawrence
67
36

74
52
465
121
65
38TH ST
Spring
Hills
Indianapolis Mus.
of Art
Wynnedale
119
Butler
Univ.
M.L. KING JR. ST
46TH
State
Fairgrounds
Crown Hill
Natl. Cem.
38TH
Pepsi Coliseum
INDIANAPOLIS
42
31
30TH
465
91
70

136
17
16
73
Clermont
O'Reilly
Raceway Park
at Indianapolis
Lafayette
Square
Marian
College
117
116
65
The Children's
Museum
Martin Univ.
Washington
Park
SHERMAN DR
87
89
44
90
36
421
Washington
Square

134
14
Speedway
Indianapolis Motor
Speedway & Hall
of Fame Mus.
Riverside
Park
115
113
President
Benjamin
Harrison
Home
85
70
30TH
16TH
MASSACHUSETTS
Brookside
Park
16TH
Warren
Park
70

13
ROCKVILLE RD
St.
Cap.
WASHINGTON
46

36
Avon
Indiana Conv.
Ctr.
79A
ENGLISH AV
SOUTHEASTERN
47
BROOKVILLE RD
PROSPECT ST
52

77
70
78
80
110
109
RURAL ST
48

12
75
EXPWY
RAYMOND ST
Garfield
Park
MADISON AV
107
65
49
94
Marion Co.
Fairgrounds
74
465
SOUTHEASTERN

11
Indianapolis
International
Airport (IND)
36
52
9
73
40
8
74
465
7
TROY
Univ. of
Indianapolis
Beech
Grove
31
36
40
52
74
421

SIX POINTS RD
AMERIPLEX BLVD
67
Plainfield
70
Camby
CAMBY RD
West Newton
Friendswood
MOORESVILLE RD
RALSTON RD
Southwestway
Park
MARION CO.
JOHNSON CO.
FAIRVIEW RD
37
STOP 11
135
MERIDIAN ST
Perry
Park
31
Homecroft
Southport
103
Greenwood
Park Mall
99
SHELBYVILLE RD
EMERSON AV
ARLINGTON AV
SHERMAN DR
FIVE
MAZE
MARION CO.
JOHNSON CO.
Greenwood
101
525
600
Rocklane

1 inch represents 2.6 miles
or 4.1 kilometers
(1:162,000)

MI   1   2   3
KM 1 2 3 4 5

© GeoNova Publishing, Inc.

P 20
Indiana

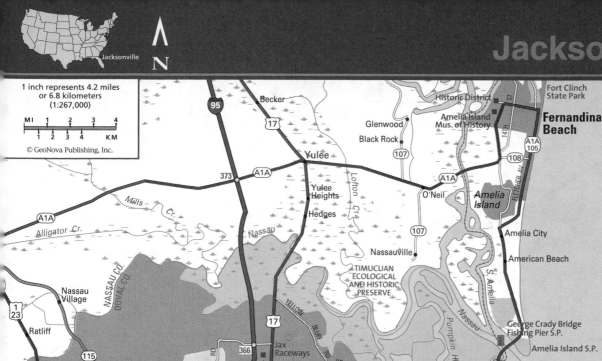

N

1 inch represents 3.8 miles
or 6.1 kilometers
(1:238,644)

© GeoNova Publishing, Inc.

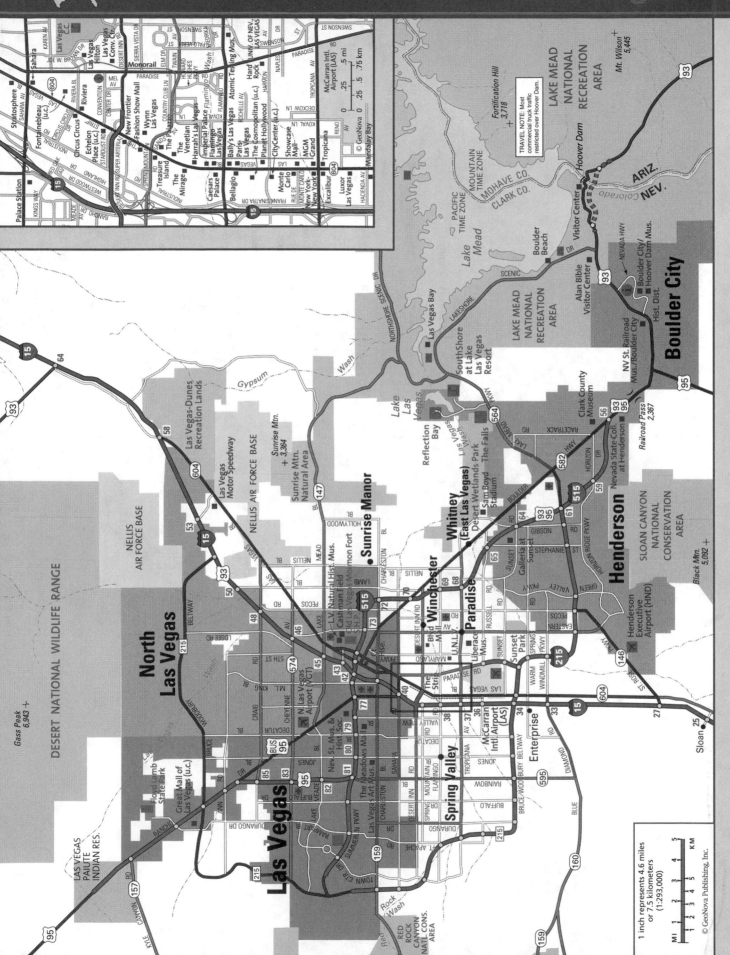

N

Las Vegas

TRAVEL NOTE: Most commercial truck traffic restricted over Hoover Dam.

LAKE MEAD NATIONAL RECREATION AREA

Mt. Wilson 5,445 +

Fortification Hill 3,718 +

PACIFIC TIME ZONE
MOUNTAIN TIME ZONE

MOHAVE CO.
CLARK CO.

ARIZ.
NEV.

Hoover Dam
Visitor Center

Lake Mead

Boulder Beach

SCENIC

LAKESHORE

LAKE MEAD NATIONAL RECREATION AREA

Alan Bible Visitor Center

Boulder City/ Hoover Dam Mus.

Hist. Dist.

Boulder City

NV St. Railroad Mus./Boulder City

Clark County Museum

Railroad Pass 2,367

Nevada State Coll. at Henderson

SLOAN CANYON NATIONAL CONSERVATION AREA

Black Mtn. 5,092 +

Henderson

Henderson Executive Airport (HND)

Las Vegas Bay

SouthShore at Lake Las Vegas Resort

Lake Las Vegas

Reflection Bay

The Falls

Sam Boyd Stadium

Desert Wetlands Park

Whitney (East Las Vegas)

NORTHSHORE SCENIC DR

Wash

Gypsum

Las Vegas-Dunes Recreation Lands

Sunrise Mtn. 3,364 +

Sunrise Mtn. Natural Area

Sunrise Manor

L.V. Natural Hist. Mus.

Cashman Field

Old Las Vegas Mormon Fort

N.H.P.

Winchester

Paradise

U.N.L.V.

Liberace Mus.

The Strip

Sunset Park

McCarran Intl. Airport (LAS)

Enterprise

Spring Valley

The Meadows Mall

The Las Vegas Art Mus.

New. St. Mus. & Hist. Soc.

N. Las Vegas Airport (VGT)

North Las Vegas

NELLIS AIR FORCE BASE

Las Vegas Motor Speedway

DESERT NATIONAL WILDLIFE RANGE

Gass Peak 6,943 +

Floyd Lamb State Park

Great Mall of Las Vegas (u.c.)

LAS VEGAS PAIUTE INDIAN RES.

Las Vegas

RED ROCK CANYON NATL. CONS. AREA

Sloan

1 inch represents 4.6 miles or 7.5 kilometers (1:293,000)

© GeoNova Publishing, Inc.

P 34 Nevada

Inset map (upper left):

Stratosphere

Fontainebleau (u.c.)

Palace Station

Sahara

Las Vegas Hilton

Circus Circus

Riviera

New Frontier

Fashion Show Mall

Wynn Las Vegas

Echelon Place (u.c.)

Treasure Island

The Palazzo

The Venetian

The Mirage

Caesars Palace

Bellagio

Monte Carlo

New York-New York

Excalibur

Luxor Las Vegas

Mandalay Bay

Imperial Palace

Harrah's Las Vegas

Flamingo Las Vegas

Bally's Las Vegas

Paris Las Vegas

Planet Hollywood

The Cosmopolitan (u.c.)

CityCenter (u.c.)

Showcase Mall

MGM Grand

Tropicana

UNIV. OF NEV., LAS VEGAS

Atomic Testing Mus.

Hard Rock

Monorail

McCarran Intl. Airport (LAS)

© GeoNova

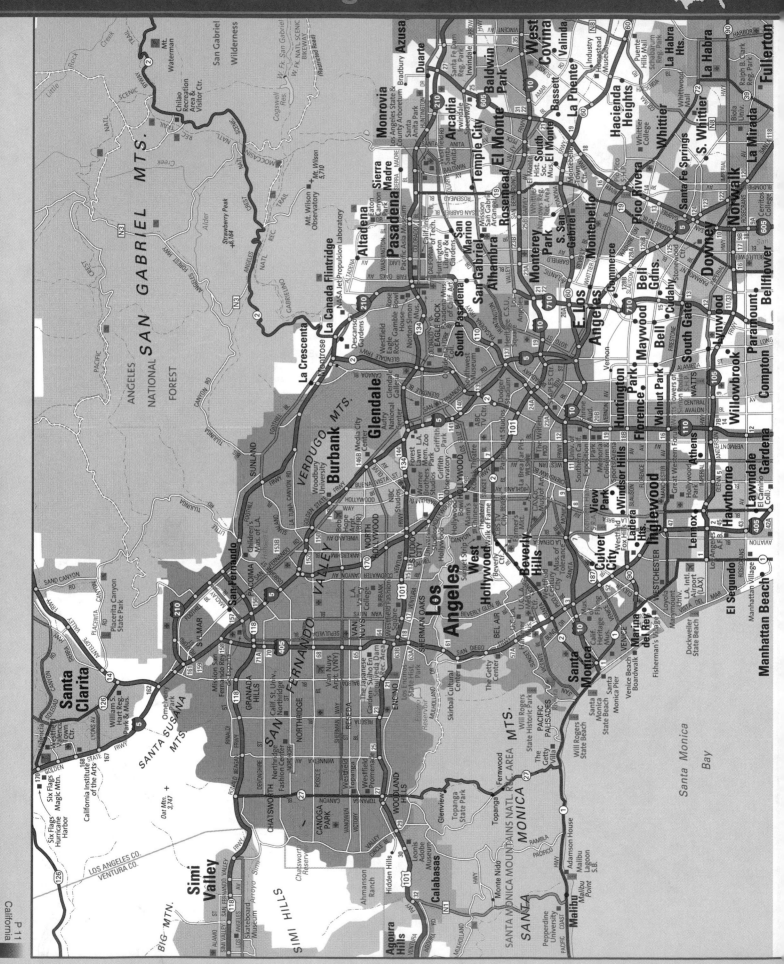

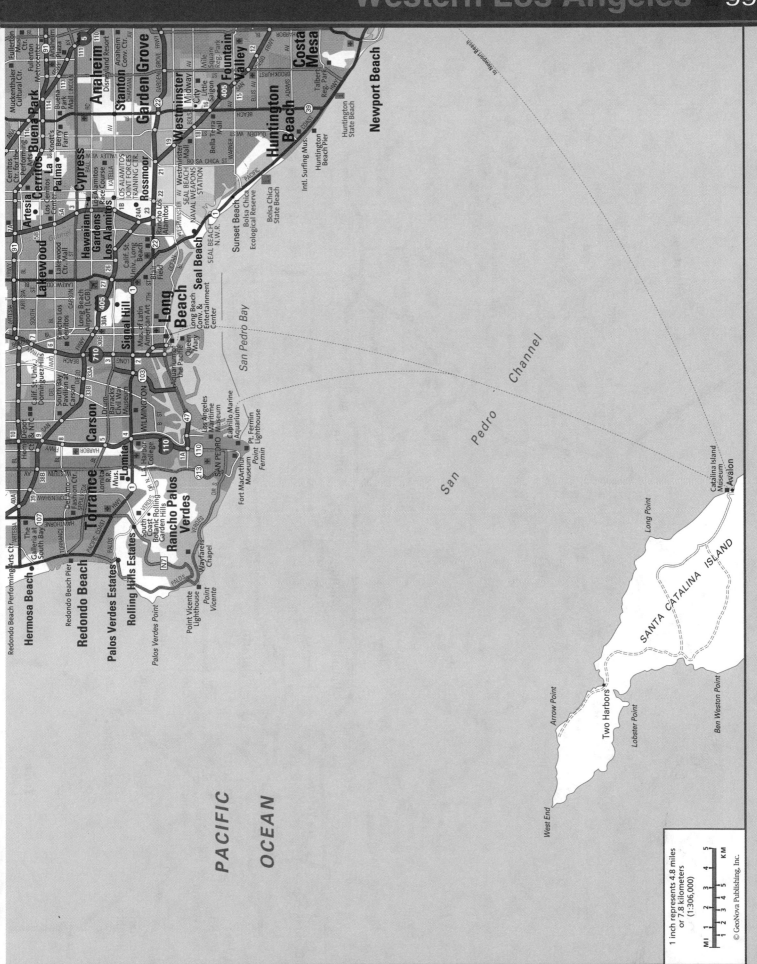

PACIFIC

OCEAN

San Pedro Bay

San Pedro Channel

SANTA CATALINA ISLAND

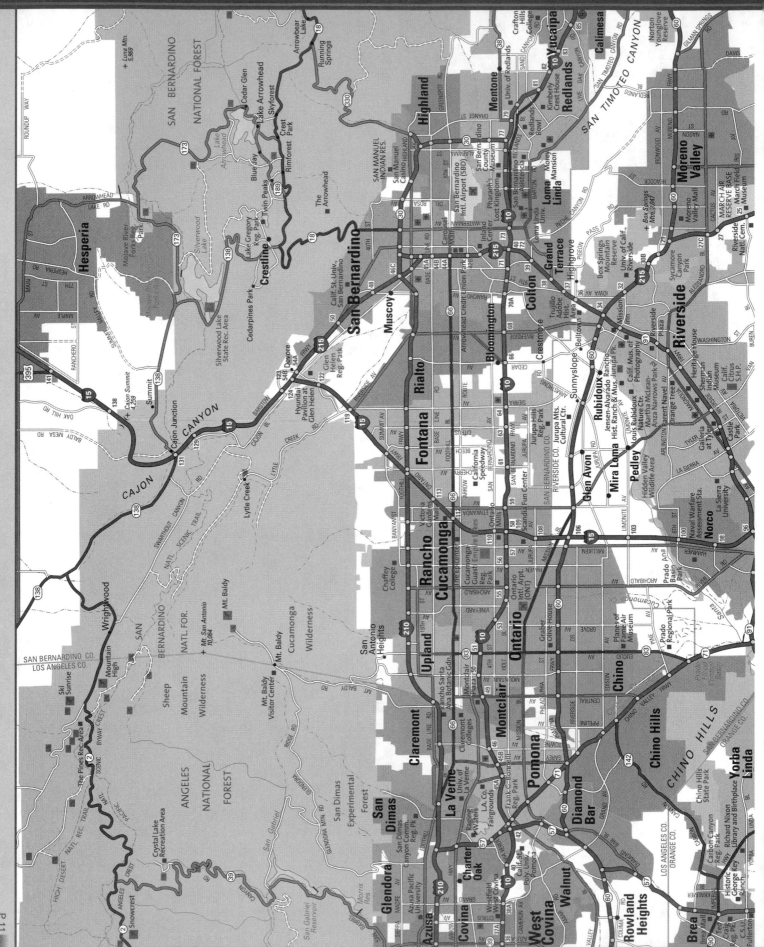

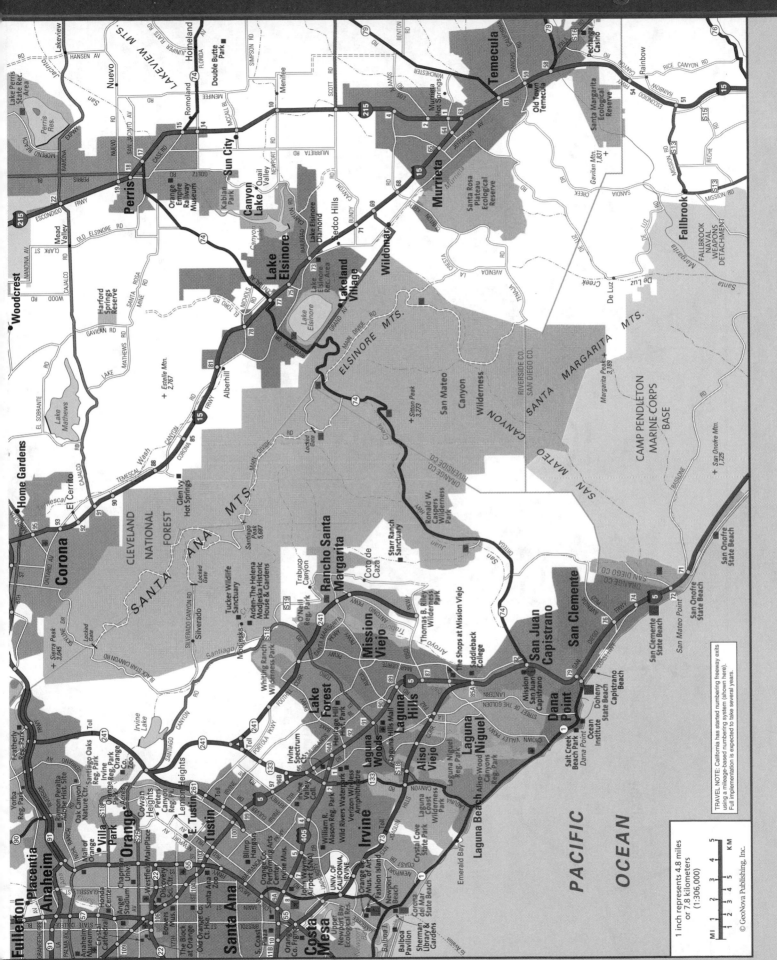

1 inch represents 4.8 miles
or 7.8 kilometers
(1:306,000)

MI 1 2 3 4 5

KM 1 2 3 4 5

© GeoNova Publishing, Inc.

PACIFIC

OCEAN

LAKE MICHIGAN

Milwaukee Bay

to Muskegon, Mich.

© GeoNova Publishing, Inc.

1 inch represents 2.5 miles or 3.9 kilometers (1:155,167)

Mexico
City

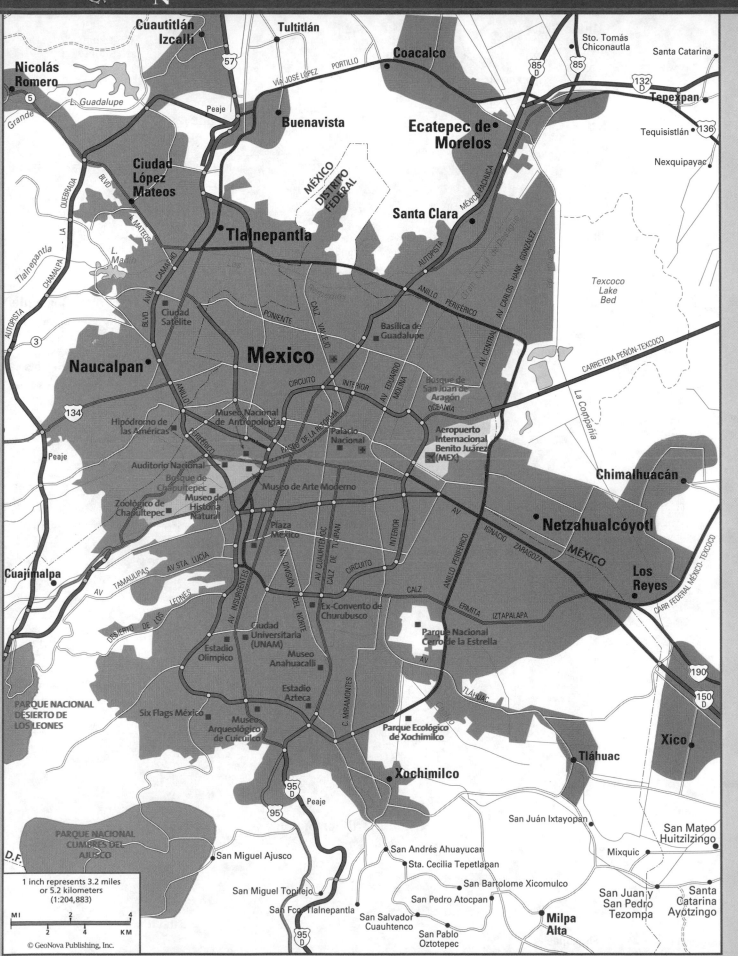

Cuautitlán
Izcalli

Tultitlán

Sto. Tomás
Chiconautla

Santa Catarina

57

Coacalco

85
D

85

132
D

Nicolás
Romero

5

L. Guadalupe

Peaje

Buenavista

Ecatepec de
Morelos

Tepexpan

136

Tequisistlán

Grande

VÍA JOSÉ LÓPEZ   PORTILLO

Ciudad
López
Mateos

QUEBRADA

BLVD

MÉXICO
DISTRITO
FEDERAL

Nexquipayac

Santa Clara

L. MATEOS

LA

Tlalnepantla

Tlalnepantla

CHAMALPA

L. Madin

AUTOPISTA

AUTOPISTA

Texcoco
Lake
Bed

3

BLVD AVILA CAMACHO

Ciudad
Satélite

Los

PONIENTE

CALZ VALLEJO

ANILLO   PERIFÉRICO

AV CENTRAL

MÉXICO-PACHUCA

MÉXICO-PACHUCA

AV CARLOS HANK GONZÁLEZ

Gran Canal del Desagüe

Basílica de
Guadalupe

CARRETERA PEÑÓN-TEXCOCO

Naucalpan

Mexico

La Compañía

134

ANILLO

Hipódromo de
las Américas

CIRCUITO   INTERIOR

AV EDUARDO MOLINA

Museo Nacional
de Antropología

PERIFÉRICO

PASEO DE LA REFORMA

Palacio
Nacional

Bosque de
San Juan de
Aragón

OCEANIA

Peaje

Auditorio Nacional

Aeropuerto
Internacional
Benito Juárez
(MEX)

Chimalhuacán

Bosque de
Chapultepec

Museo de Arte Moderno

Zoológico de
Chapultepec

Museo de
Historia
Natural

Netzahualcóyotl

Plaza
México

AV DIVISIÓN DEL NORTE

AV CUAUHTÉMOC

CALZ DE TLALPAN

INTERIOR

CIRCUITO

MÉXICO

AV STA. LUCÍA

IGNACIO ZARAGOZA

Los
Reyes

Cuajimalpa

AV TAMAULIPAS

DESIERTO DE LOS LEONES

AV INSURGENTES

CALZ

ANILLO PERIFÉRICO

CARR FEDERAL MÉXICO-TEXCOCO

Ex-Convento de
Churubusco

ERMITA   IZTAPALAPA

190

Ciudad
Universitaria
(UNAM)

Museo
Anahuacalli

Parque Nacional
Cerro de la Estrella

AV

Estadio
Olímpico

C. MIRAMONTES

TLÁHUAC

PARQUE NACIONAL
DESIERTO DE
LOS LEONES

Six Flags México

Estadio
Azteca

150
D

Museo
Arqueológico
de Cuicuilco

Parque Ecológico
de Xochimilco

Xico

Tláhuac

Xochimilco

95
D

Peaje

San Mateo
Huitzilzingo

95

San Juán Ixtayopan

Mixquic

PARQUE NACIONAL
CUMBRES DEL
AJUSCO

San Andrés Ahuayucan

D.F.

Sta. Cecilia Tepetlapan

San Miguel Ajusco

San Juan y
San Pedro
Tezompa

Santa
Catarina
Ayótzingo

San Bartolome Xicomulco

San Miguel Topilejo

San Pedro Atocpan

1 inch represents 3.2 miles
or 5.2 kilometers
(1:204,883)

San Fco. Tlalnepantla

San Salvador
Cuauhtenco

Milpa
Alta

MI   2   4

San Pablo
Oztotepec

2   4   KM

95
D

© GeoNova Publishing, Inc.

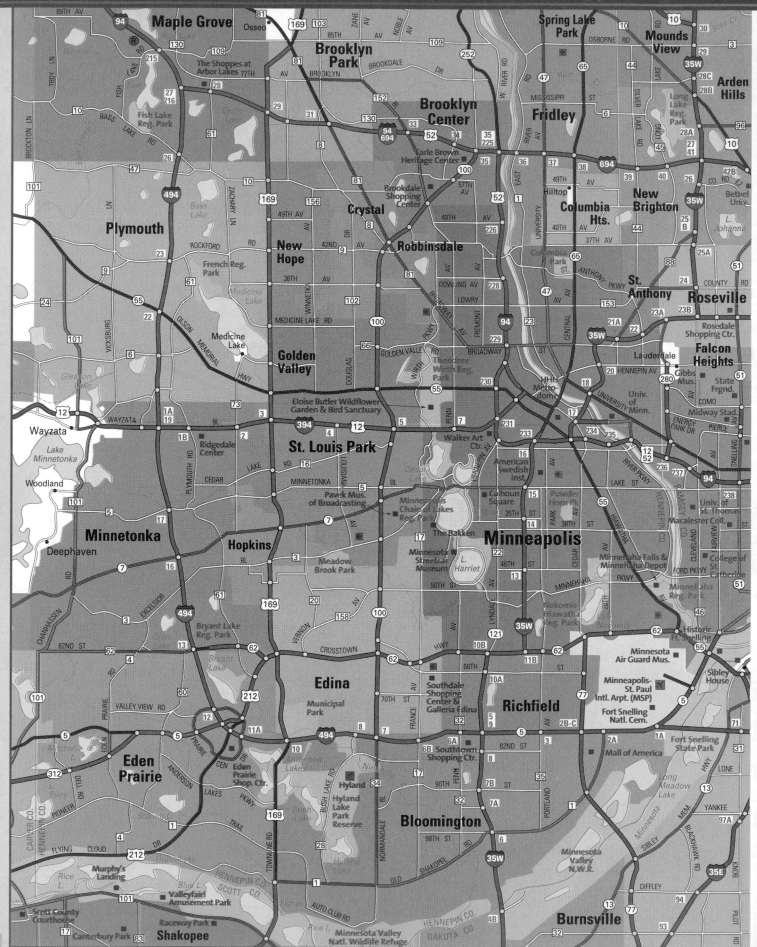

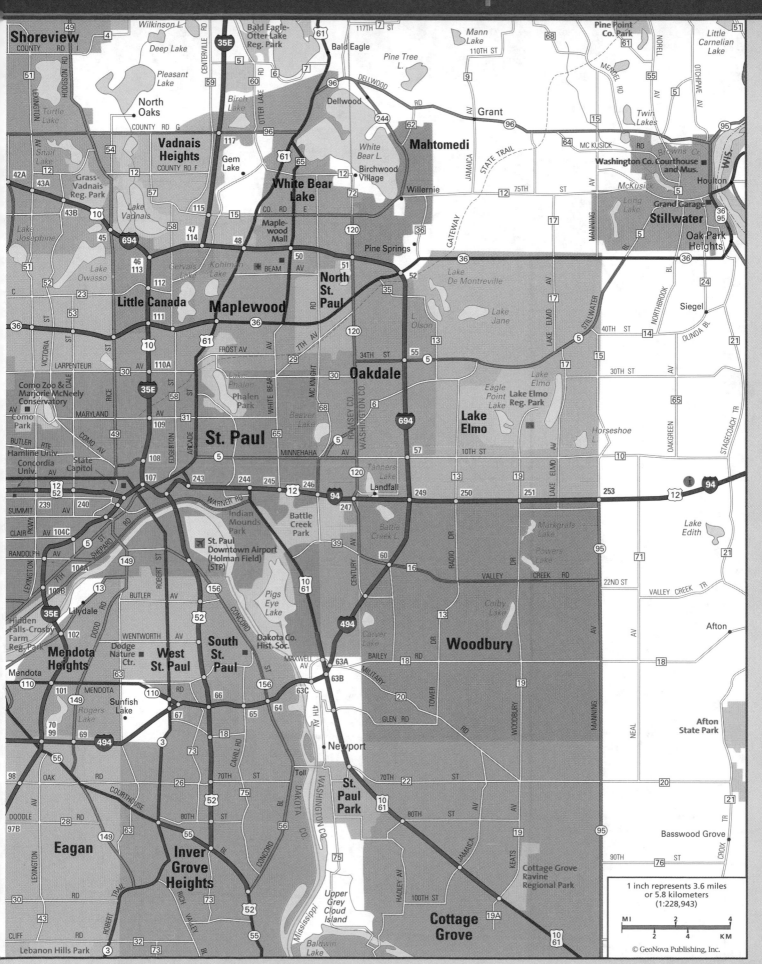

1 inch represents 3.6 miles
or 5.8 kilometers
(1:228,943)

MI   2   4

2   4   KM

© GeoNova Publishing, Inc.

N
Miami

1 inch represents 6.8 miles
or 10.9 kilometers
(1:431,020)

MI
0 2 4 6
KM
0 2 4 6
© GeoNova Publishing, Inc.

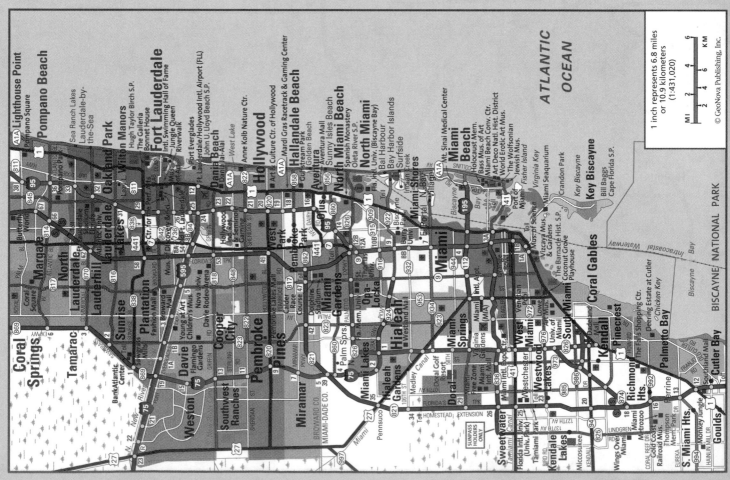

1 inch represents 6.8 miles
or 10.9 kilometers
(1:431,020)

MI
0 2 4 6
KM
0 2 4 6
© GeoNova Publishing, Inc.

1 inch represents 2.0 miles
or 3.2 kilometers
(1:125,094)

MI 1 2
KM 1 2

© GeoNova Publishing, Inc.

N

ST-FRANÇOIS

ST-MARIE

25

125

16

POINTE-
AUX-
TREMBLES

AV DES PERRON

138

87

RG DU BAS-
ST-FRANÇOIS

25

Montréal-Est

40

138

Îles-de-
Boucherville

BD STE-ROSE

335

ST-VINCENT-
DE-PAUL

12

11

125

25

10

ANJOU

82

MONTRÉAL-
NORD

25

Parc
des Îles-de-
Boucherville

VIMONT

19

148

7

8

9

Les Galeries
d'Anjou

25

Place
Versailles

Boucherville

To Montréal
Intl. Arpt.-
Mirabel (YMX)

440

335

ST-LÉONARD

77

78

4

PONT-
VIAU

125

1

15
90

20

Laval

Carrefour Laval
Cosmodôme

9

335

Jardin
Botanique

132

11

148

8

7

LAVAL-DES-
RAPIDES

19

Parc
Olympique
Biodôme de Montréal
Stade Olympique

20

117

73

74

75

40

125

Château
Dufresne

138

Longueuil

7

335

St-Laurent

4/5

15

3

Centre
Rockland

Parc
Jarry

Montréal

335

Parc
Hélène-de-
Champlain

20

Six Flags
La Ronde

Musée des Maîtres
et Artisans du Québec

2

1
70

OUTREMONT

8

13

ST-LAURENT

117

66

Mont-Royal

Univ. de
Montréal

Musée d'Art
Contemporain

Île Ste-
Hélène

Saint-
Lambert

LEMOYNE

6
60

40

15

65

Parc Mont-
Royal

Univ.
McGill

Musée
McCord

Hôtel
de Ville

Vieux-
Montréal
Vieux-Port

116
134

62

Place
Côte-Vertu

Musée
des Beaux-Arts
de Montréal

Gare Centrale

Casino

112
116

Oratoire
St-Joseph

CÔTE-DES-NEIGES

Le Centre
Bell

Basilique
Notre-
Dame

Île
Notre-
Dame

ST-
HUBERT

Aéroport
International
Pierre-Elliott-
Trudeau de
Montréal
(YUL)

520

Hampstead

Centre
Canadien
d'Architecture

Planétarium
de Montréal

3

112

GREENFIELD
PARK

13

Côte-St-Luc

138

64

Westmount

720

61

Marché Public
Atwater

Maison
St-Gabriel

10

132

2

54

20

58

60

Montréal-
Ouest

ST-PIERRE

63

20

62

53

15
20

PONT
VICTORIA

6
53

10

8

9

Dorval

56

LACHINE

VERDUN

10

15

20

PONT CHAMPLAIN

52

Les
Jardins
Dorval

Musée
de Lachine

Parc
Angrignon

LASALLE

Île des
Soeur
(Nuns I.)

15

132

Brossard

L'Île-Dorval

Île
Dorval

Commerce de la
Fourrure à Lachine

Bassin de
La Prairie

50

134

Lac
St-Louis

Île aux Herons

47

La Prairie

Kahnawake

207

138

132

RÉS. AMÉRINDIENNE DE KAHNAWAKE

Sainte-Catherine

Candiac

46

104

134

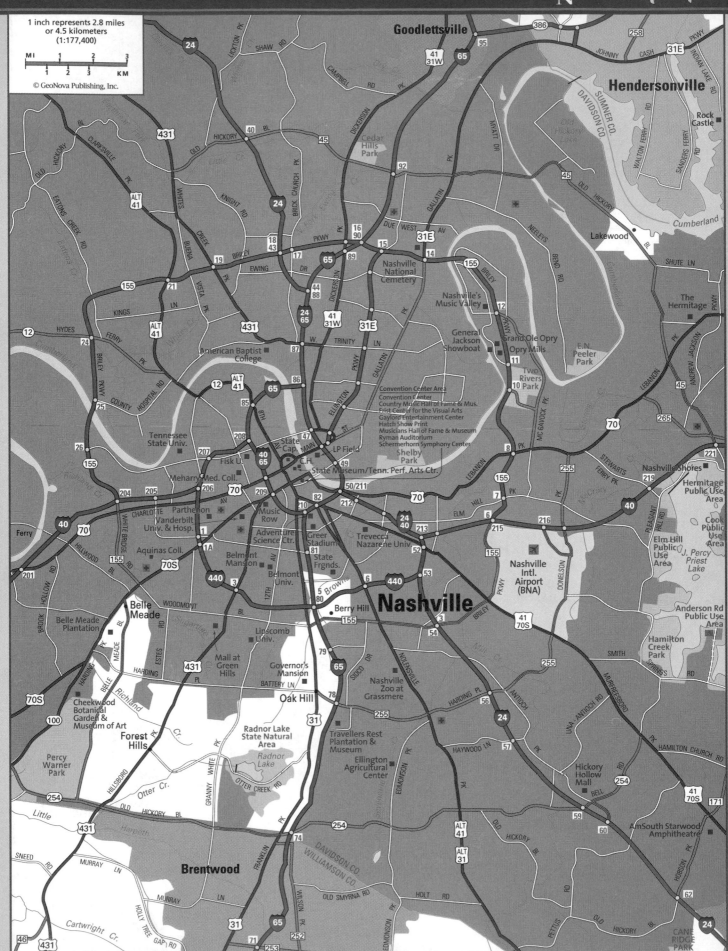

Nashville

1 inch represents 2.8 miles
or 4.5 kilometers
(1:177,400)

MI
KM
© GeoNova Publishing, Inc.

Goodlettsville

Hendersonville

Rock Castle

Davidson Co

Sumner Co

Cumberland

Lakewood

The Hermitage

Cedar Hills Park

Nashville National Cemetery

Nashville's Music Valley

General Jackson Showboat

Grand Ole Opry
Opry Mills

E.N. Peeler Park

Two Rivers Park

American Baptist College

Convention Center Area
Convention Center
Country Music Hall of Fame & Mus.
Frist Center for the Visual Arts
Gaylord Entertainment Center
Hatch Show Print
Musicians Hall of Fame & Museum
Ryman Auditorium
Schermerhorn Symphony Center

Shelby Park

Nashville Shores

Hermitage Public Use Area

Cool Public Use Area

Tennessee State Univ.

Fisk U.
Meharry Med. Coll.

State Cap.
D.C.H.
State Museum/Tenn. Perf. Arts Ctr.
LP Field

J. Percy Priest Lake

Elm Hill Public Use Area

Parthenon
Vanderbilt Univ. & Hosp.

Music Row

Adventure Science Ctr.

Greer Stadium

Trevecca Nazarene Univ.

Nashville Intl. Airport (BNA)

Aquinas Coll.

Belmont Mansion

State Frgnds.

Belmont Univ.

Browns

Nashville

Berry Hill

Anderson Rd Public Use Area

Hamilton Creek Park

Belle Meade

Belle Meade Plantation

Lipscomb Univ.

Governor's Mansion

Nashville Zoo at Grassmere

Mall at Green Hills

Oak Hill

Cheekwood Botanical Garden & Museum of Art

Forest Hills

Radnor Lake State Natural Area

Radnor Lake

Travellers Rest Plantation & Museum

Ellington Agricultural Center

Hickory Hollow Mall

Percy Warner Park

AmSouth Starwood Amphitheatre

Brentwood

Davidson Co.
Williamson Co.

Cane Ridge Park

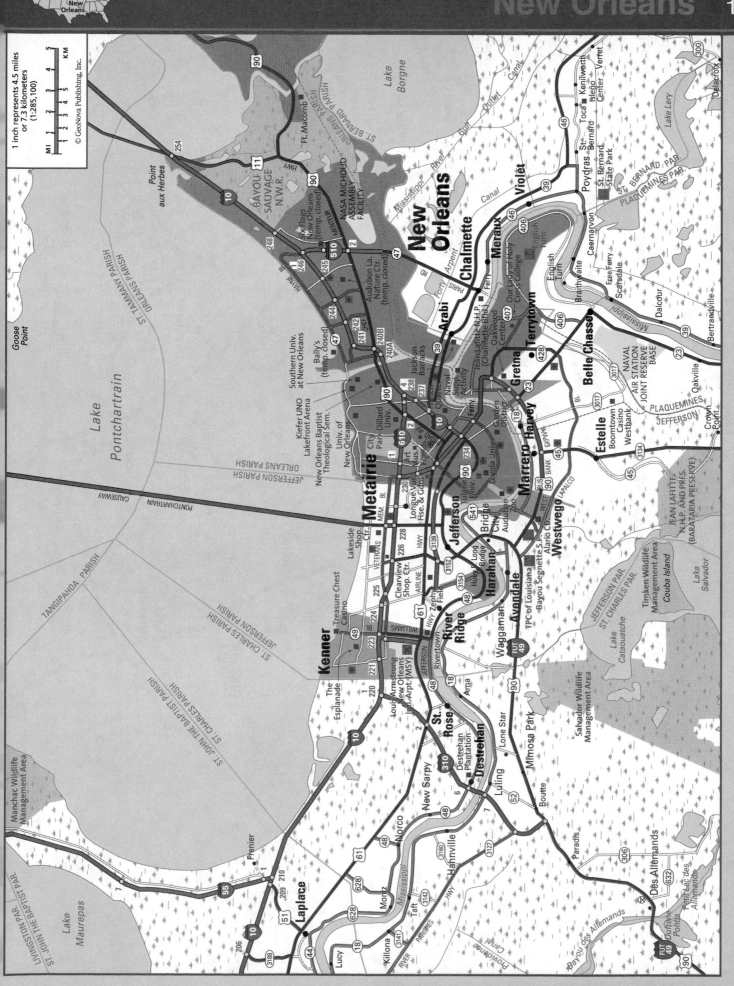

1 inch represents 4.5 miles or 7.3 kilometers (1:285,100)

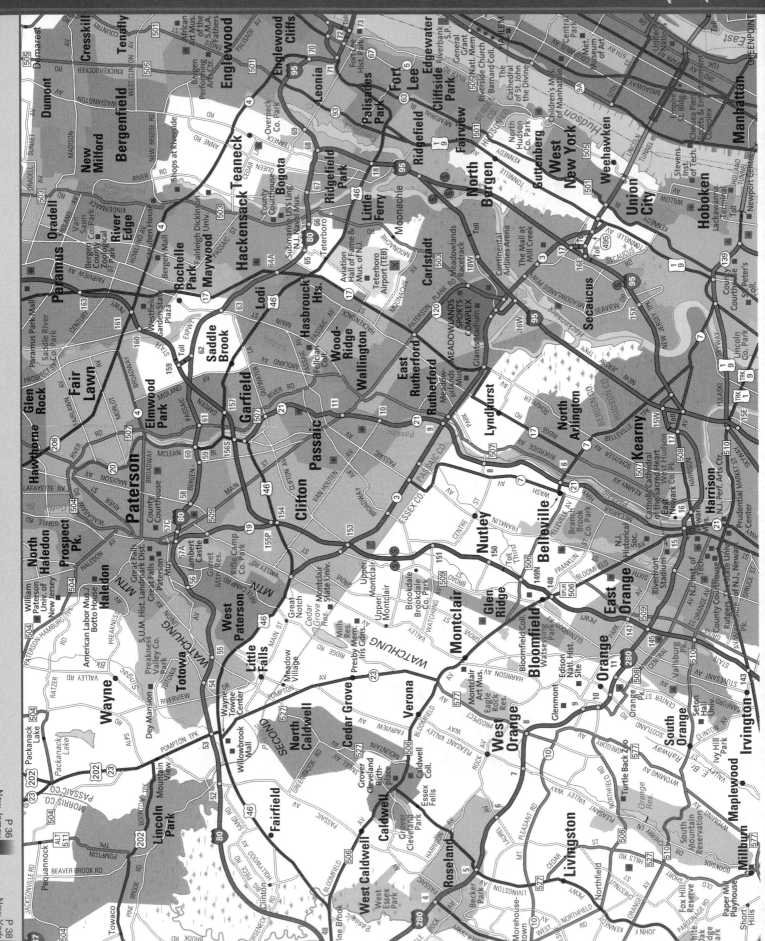

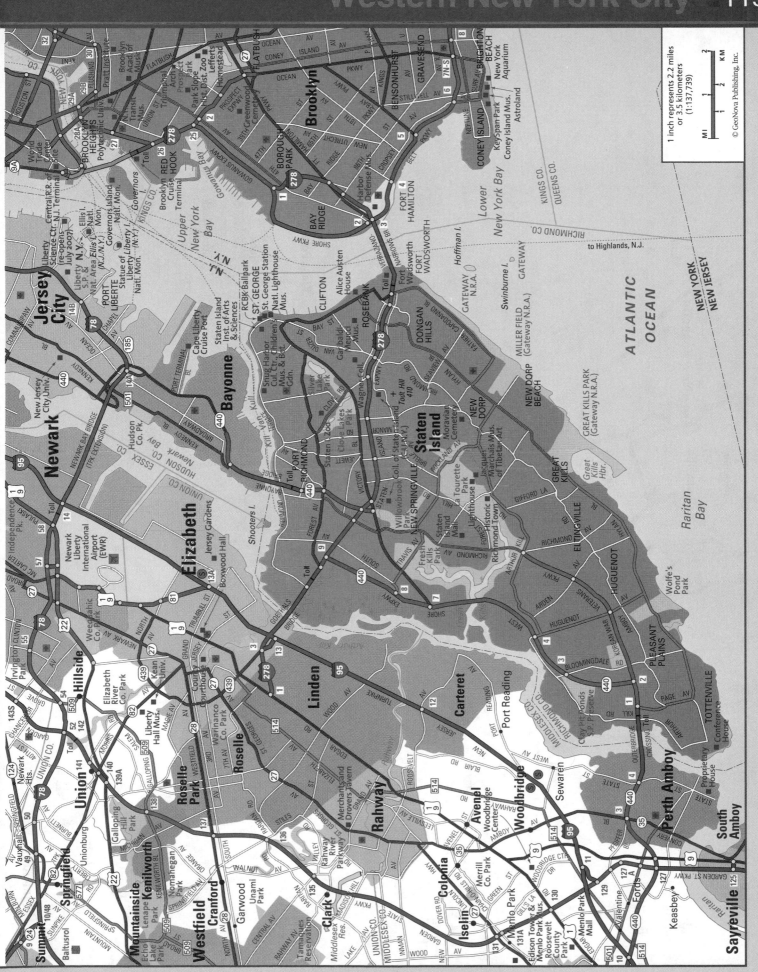

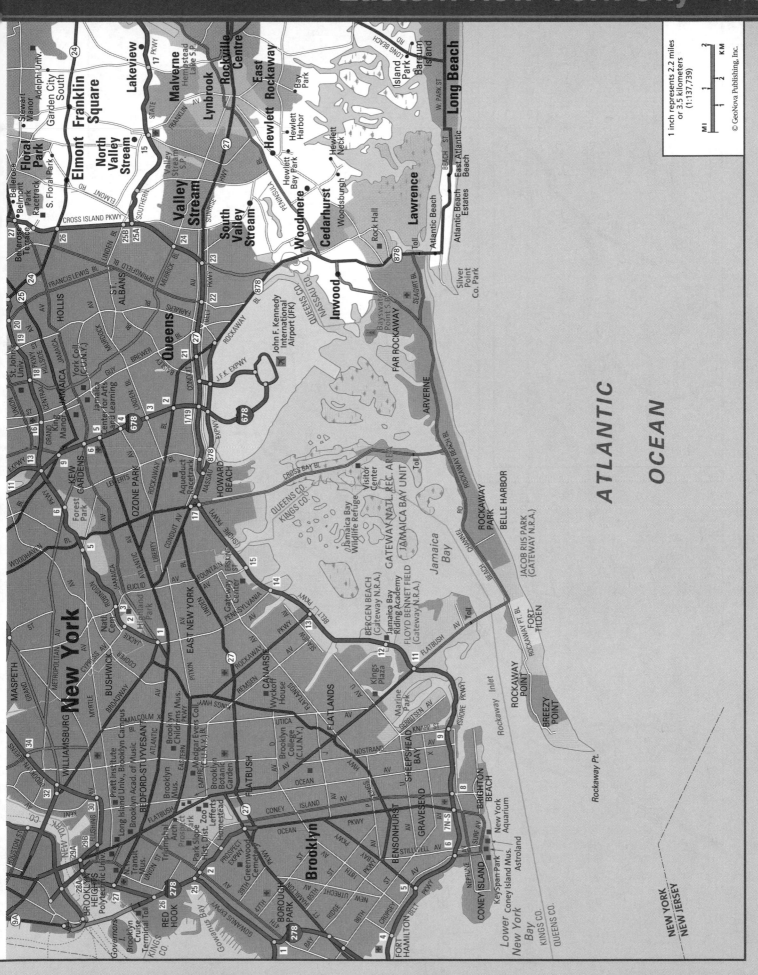

1 inch represents 2.2 miles
or 3.5 kilometers
(1:137,739)

© GeoNova Publishing, Inc.

ATLANTIC

OCEAN

New York

Queens

Brooklyn

Long Beach

Lakeview

Franklin Square

Malverne

Rockville Centre

East Rockaway

Hewlett

Lynbrook

Valley Stream

South Valley Stream

Woodmere

Cedarhurst

Lawrence

Inwood

FAR ROCKAWAY

ARVERNE

Jamaica Bay

GATEWAY NATL. REC. AREA

JAMAICA BAY UNIT

ROCKAWAY PARK

BELLE HARBOR

BREEZY POINT

ROCKAWAY POINT

FORT TILDEN

JACOB RIIS PARK (GATEWAY N.R.A.)

CONEY ISLAND

BRIGHTON BEACH

SHEEPSHEAD BAY

GRAVESEND

BENSONHURST

FLATLANDS

FLATBUSH

BUSHWICK

WILLIAMSBURG

BROOKLYN HEIGHTS

RED HOOK

BOROUGH PARK

CANARSIE

EAST NEW YORK

BEDFORD-STUYVESANT

ST. ALBANS

HOLLIS

JAMAICA

KEW GARDENS

OZONE PARK

HOWARD BEACH

MASPETH

WOODHAVEN

John F. Kennedy International Airport (JFK)

NEW YORK
NEW JERSEY

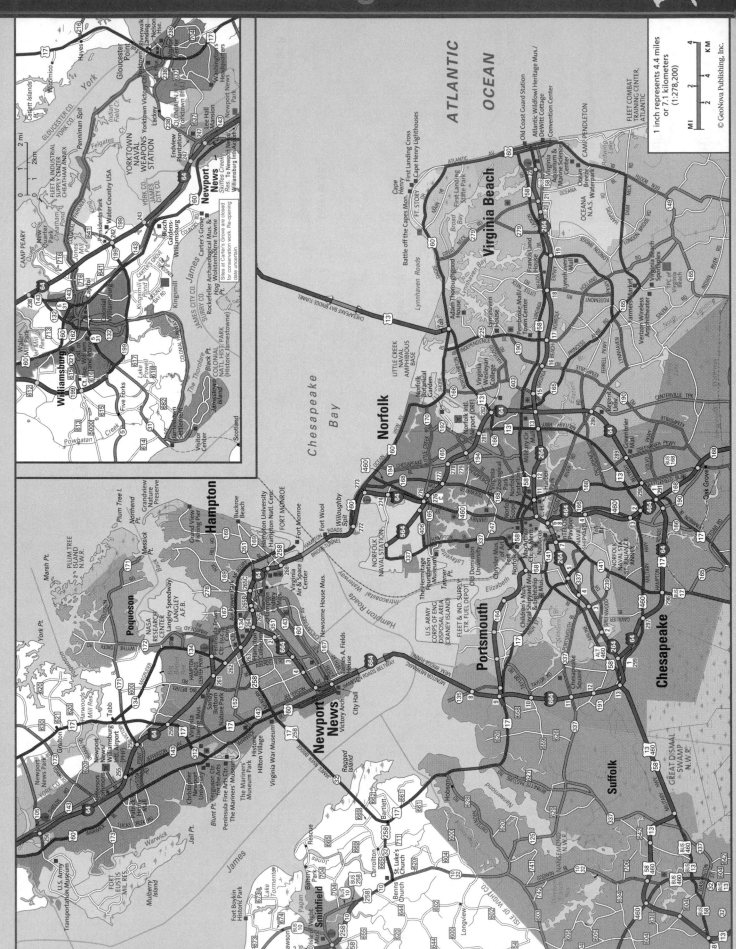

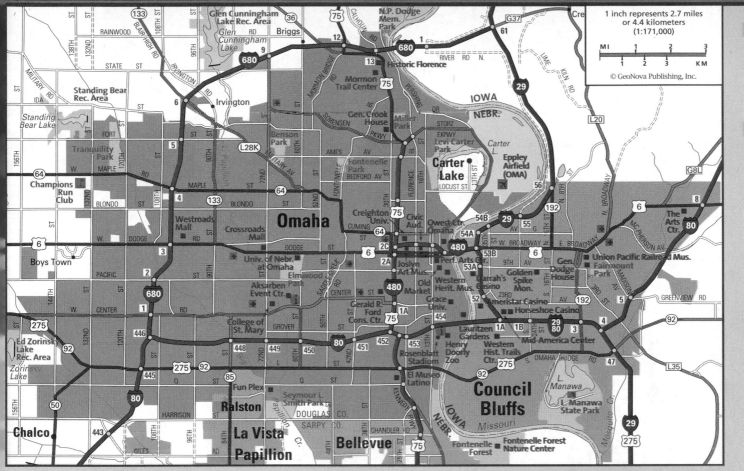

1 inch represents 2.7 miles
or 4.4 kilometers
(1:171,000)

© GeoNova Publishing, Inc.

P 33 Nebraska

P 21 Iowa

Omaha

- Standing Bear Rec. Area
- Standing Bear Lake
- Glen Cunningham Lake Rec. Area
- Glen Cunningham Lake
- Briggs
- Historic Florence
- N.P. Dodge Mem. Park
- Mormon Trail Center
- Gen. Crook House
- Miller Park
- IOWA / NEBR.
- Levi Carter Park
- Carter L.
- Carter Lake
- Eppley Airfield (OMA)
- Tranquility Park
- Champions Run Club
- Boys Town
- Westroads Mall
- Crossroads Mall
- Benson Park
- Fontenelle Park
- Creighton Univ.
- Civic Aud.
- Qwest Ctr. Omaha
- Univ. of Nebr. at Omaha
- Joslyn Art Mus.
- Elmwood Park
- Perf. Arts Ctr.
- Old Market
- Western Herit. Mus.
- Harrah's Casino
- Golden Spike Mon.
- Gen. Dodge House
- Union Pacific Railroad Mus.
- Fairmount Park
- The Arts Ctr.
- Aksarben Event Ctr.
- Grace Univ.
- Ameristar Casino
- Horseshoe Casino
- College of St. Mary
- Gerald R. Ford Cons. Ctr.
- Lauritzen Gardens
- Henry Doorly Zoo
- Western Hist. Trails Ctr.
- Mid-America Center
- Ed Zorinsky Lake Rec. Area
- Zorinsky Lake
- Rosenblatt Stadium
- El Museo Latino
- Council Bluffs
- Fun Plex
- Seymour L. Smith Park
- DOUGLAS CO. / SARPY CO.
- Ralston
- Chalco
- La Vista
- Papillion
- Bellevue
- Fontenelle Forest
- Fontenelle Forest Nature Center
- L. Manawa
- L. Manawa State Park
- Missouri

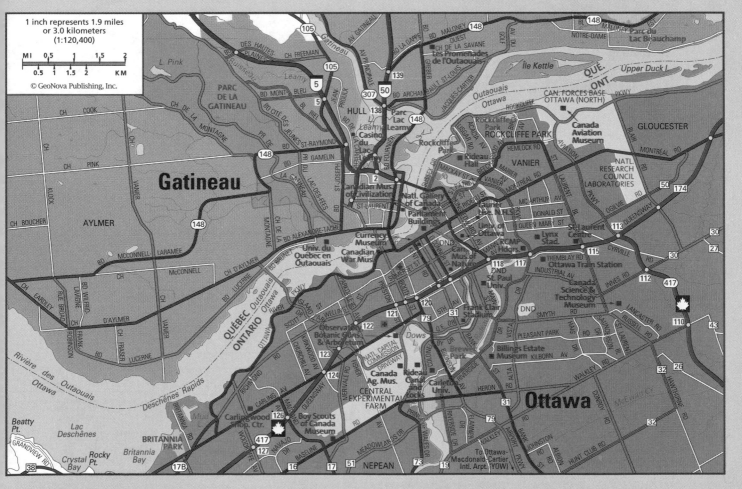

1 inch represents 1.9 miles
or 3.0 kilometers
(1:120,400)

© GeoNova Publishing, Inc.

P 64 Québec

P 62 Ontario

Gatineau / Ottawa

- PARC DE LA GATINEAU
- L. Pink
- Leamy
- Parc du Lac Beauchamp
- Île Kettle
- Upper Duck I.
- QUÉ. / ONT.
- Les Promenades de l'Outaouais
- HULL
- Casino du Lac Leamy
- Parc Lac Leamy
- CAN. FORCES BASE OTTAWA (NORTH)
- Canada Aviation Museum
- GLOUCESTER
- AYLMER
- ROCKCLIFFE PARK
- Rockcliffe Park
- Rideau Hall
- VANIER
- NATL. RESEARCH COUNCIL LABORATORIES
- Gatineau
- Canadian Museum of Civilization
- Natl. Gallery of Canada
- Parliament Buildings
- Univ. of Ottawa
- Lynx Stad.
- St-Laurent Centre
- Currency Museum
- Univ. du Québec en Outaouais
- Canadian War Mus.
- DND
- RCMP Hdqrs.
- Ottawa Train Station
- QUÉBEC / ONTARIO
- Earl Mus. of Nature
- St. Paul Univ.
- Canada Science & Technology Museum
- Observatory
- Frank Clair Stadium
- Botanic Gdns. & Arboretum
- Dows L.
- Brewer Park
- Billings Estate Museum
- Rivière des Outaouais
- Deschênes Rapids
- CENTRAL EXPERIMENTAL FARM
- Canada Ag. Mus.
- Rideau Canal and Locks
- Carleton Univ.
- Ottawa
- Beatty Pt.
- Lac Deschênes
- Carlingwood Shop. Ctr.
- Boy Scouts of Canada Museum
- BRITANNIA PARK
- Britannia Bay
- Crystal Bay
- Rocky Pt.
- NEPEAN
- To Ottawa-Macdonald-Cartier Intl. Arpt. (YOW)

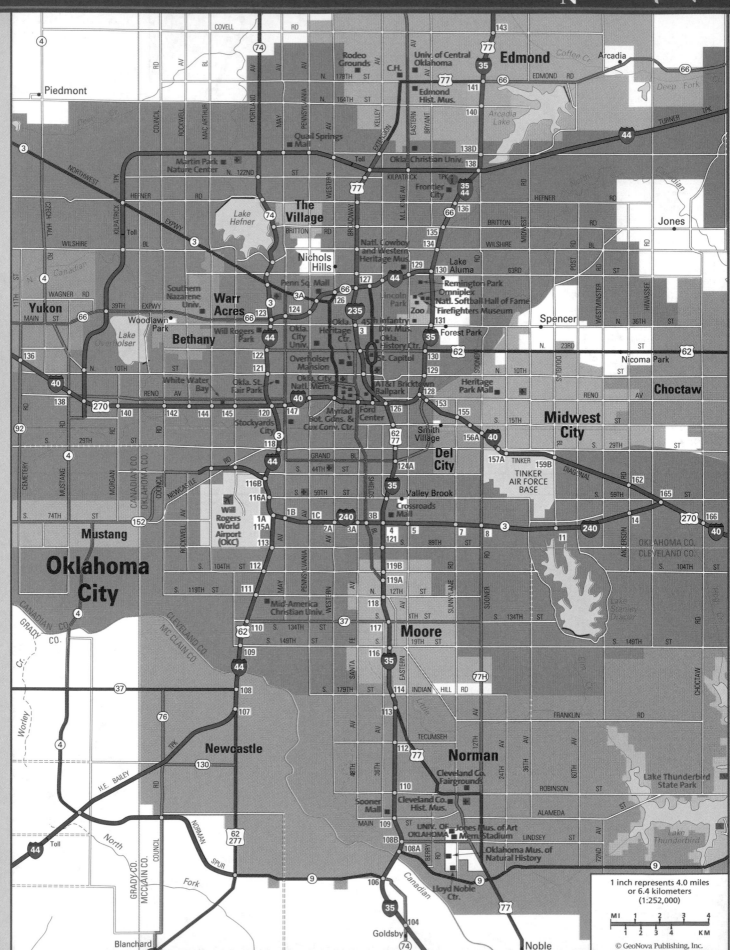

Piedmont

COVELL RD

74

143

77

Edmond

Arcadia

35

66

Rodeo Grounds

C.H.

N. 178TH ST

Univ. of Central Oklahoma

EDMOND RD

77

141

66

Edmond Hist. Mus.

140

N. 164TH ST

KELLEY

Arcadia Lake

Deep Fork

TURNER TPK

44

Quail Springs Mall

138D

Okla. Christian Univ.

138

4

Martin Park Nature Center

N. 122ND ST

Toll

KILPATRICK

TPK

35 44

Frontier City

Jones

The Village

74

Lake Hefner

BRITTON RD

BROADWAY

77

66 136

135

134

BRITTON RD

WILSHIRE

MIDWEST

HEFNER RD

POST RD

Nichols Hills

Natl. Cowboy and Western Heritage Mus.

129

130

Lake Aluma

63RD

Spencer

N. 36TH ST

Penn Sq. Mall

127

44

Remington Park Omniplex

Natl. Softball Hall of Fame

131

N. 23RD

62

Nicoma Park

62

Warr Acres

123

66

3A

124

66

126

235

Lincoln Park

Zoo

Firefighters Museum

Forest Park

35

Choctaw

Yukon

66

39TH EXPWY

Southern Nazarene Univ.

3

Woodlawn Park

Will Rogers Park

44

122

Okla. City Univ.

Okla. Heritage Ctr.

45th Infantry Div. Mus.

130

Okla. History Ctr.

129

Bethany

121

Overholser Mansion

St. Capitol

Lake Overholser

10TH

White Water Bay

Okla. St. Fair Park

Okla. City Natl. Mem.

AT&T Bricktown Ballpark

128

Heritage Park Mall

RENO AV

270

138

140

142

144

145

120

Stockyards City

147

Myriad Bot. Gdns. & Cox Conv. Ctr.

Ford Center

126

153

155

156A

40

Midwest City

92

40

3

118

44

GRAND BL

S. 44TH ST

124A

Smith Village

62 77

Del City

157A Tinker

159B

TINKER AIR FORCE BASE

162

DIAGONAL RD

165

Mustang

116B

116A

S. 59TH ST

SHIELDS

35

Valley Brook

S. 15TH

S. 29TH

S. 59TH

14

270

166

40

Oklahoma City

1B

1C

240

3B

Crossroads Mall

3

11

240

1A 115A

113

2A 3A

4 121

5

89TH ST

7

8

ANDERSON RD

OKLAHOMA CO. CLEVELAND CO.

S. 104TH ST

112

119B

S. 104TH ST

4

111

119A

12TH ST

Lake Stanley Draper

Mid-America Christian Univ.

118

Moore

4

110

37

117

19TH ST

Cleveland Co. Fairgrounds

ROBINSON ST

Lake Thunderbird State Park

62

109

116

35

114

INDIAN HILL RD

77H

Newcastle

108

13

TECUMSEH

FRANKLIN RD

37

76

130

112 77

Norman

H.E. BAILEY

4

110

Cleveland Co. Hist. Mus.

ALAMEDA

44 Toll

North Canadian

Fork

62 277

NORMAN

Sooner Mall

MAIN ST

109

UNIV. OF OKLAHOMA

Jones Mus. of Art

Mem. Stadium

LINDSEY ST

Lake Thunderbird

108B

108A

BERRY RD

Oklahoma Mus. of Natural History

9

GRADY CO.

McCLAIN CO.

9

106

Canadian

Lloyd Noble Ctr.

77

9

Blanchard

35

104

Goldsby

74

Noble

1 inch represents 4.0 miles or 6.4 kilometers (1:252,000)

© GeoNova Publishing, Inc.

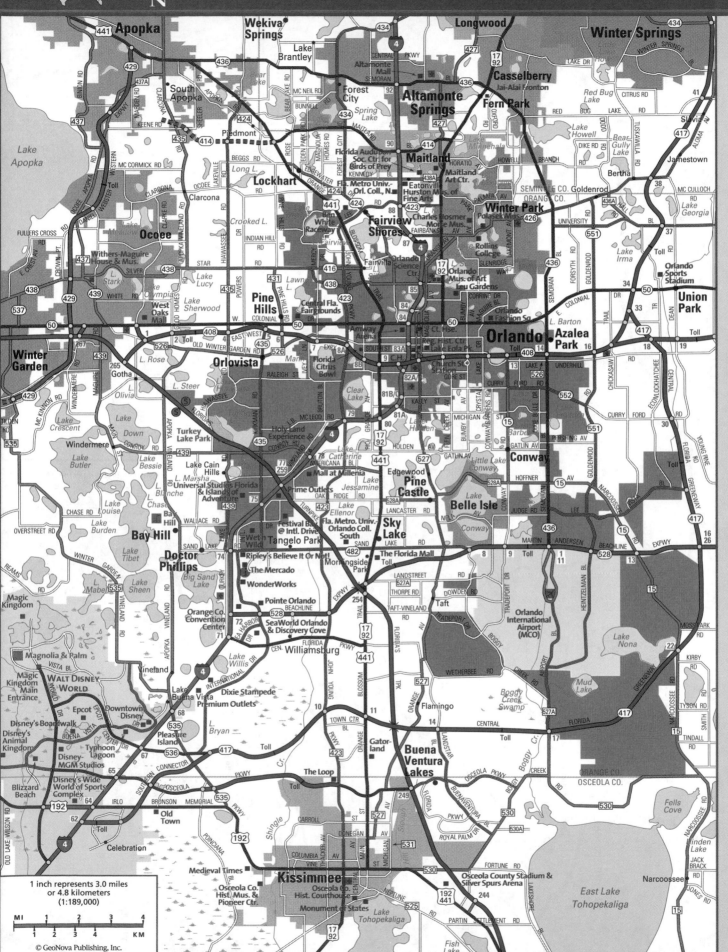

1 inch represents 3.0 miles
or 4.8 kilometers
(1:189,000)

MI 0 1 2 3 4

KM 0 1 2 3 4

© GeoNova Publishing, Inc.

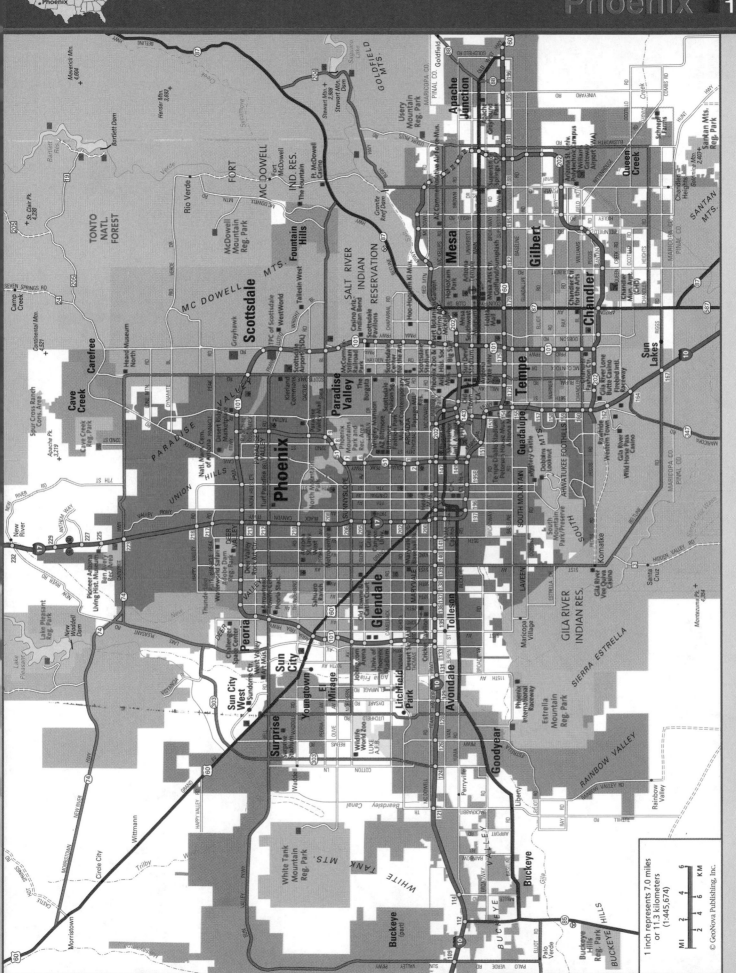

N

Phoenix

1 inch represents 7.0 miles
or 11.3 kilometers
(1:445,674)

© GeoNova Publishing, Inc.

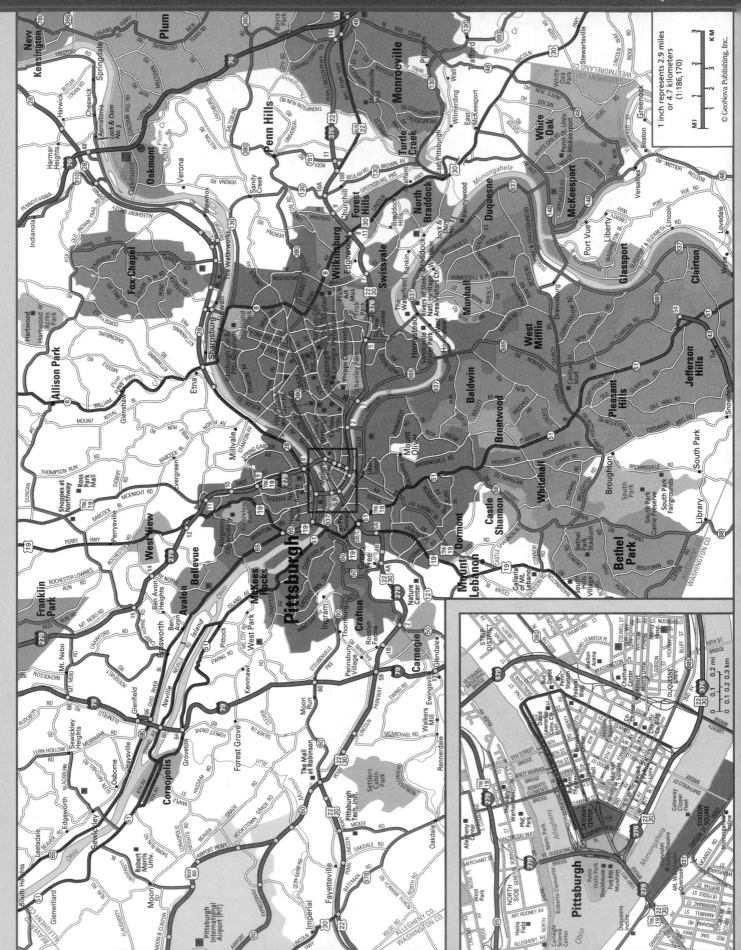

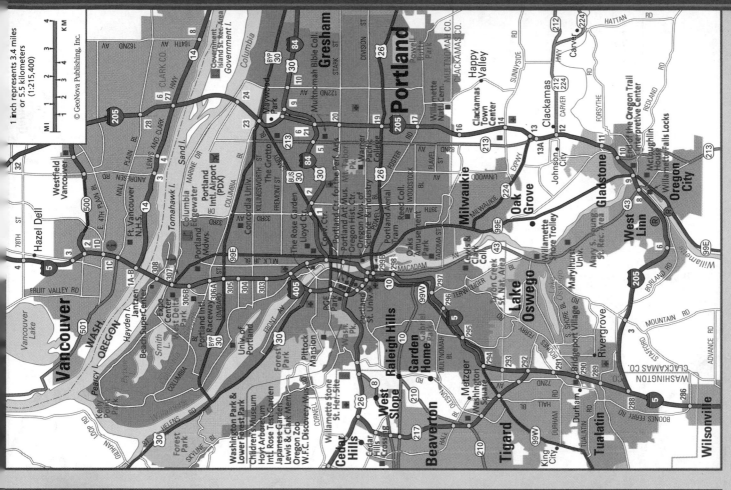

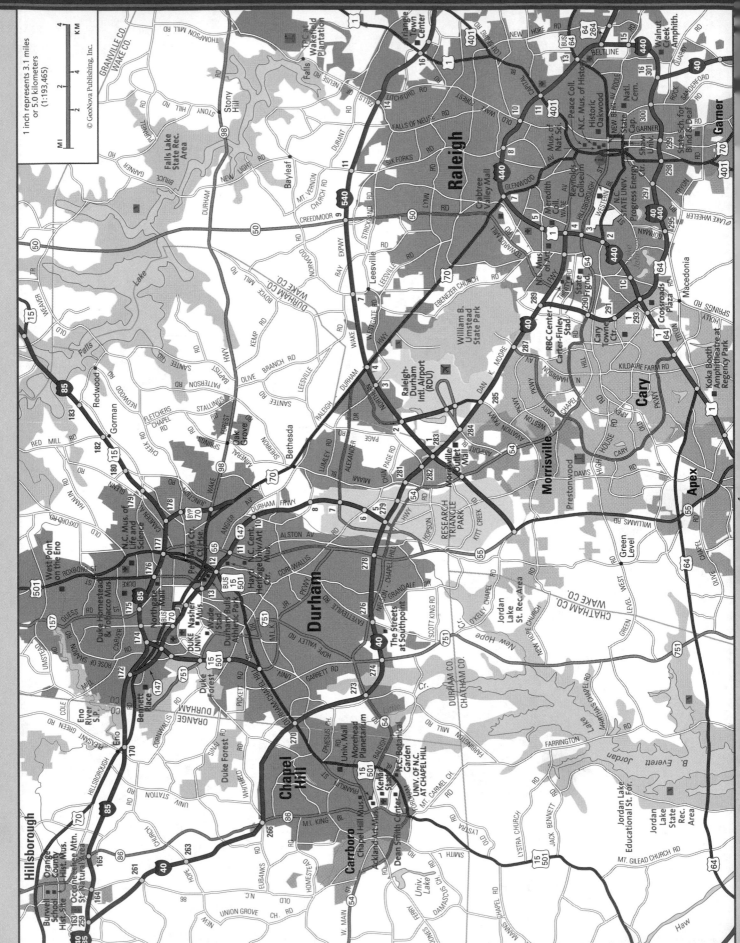

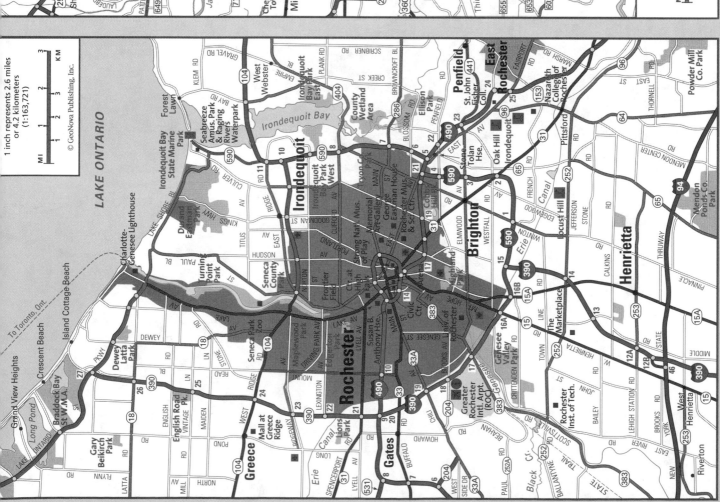

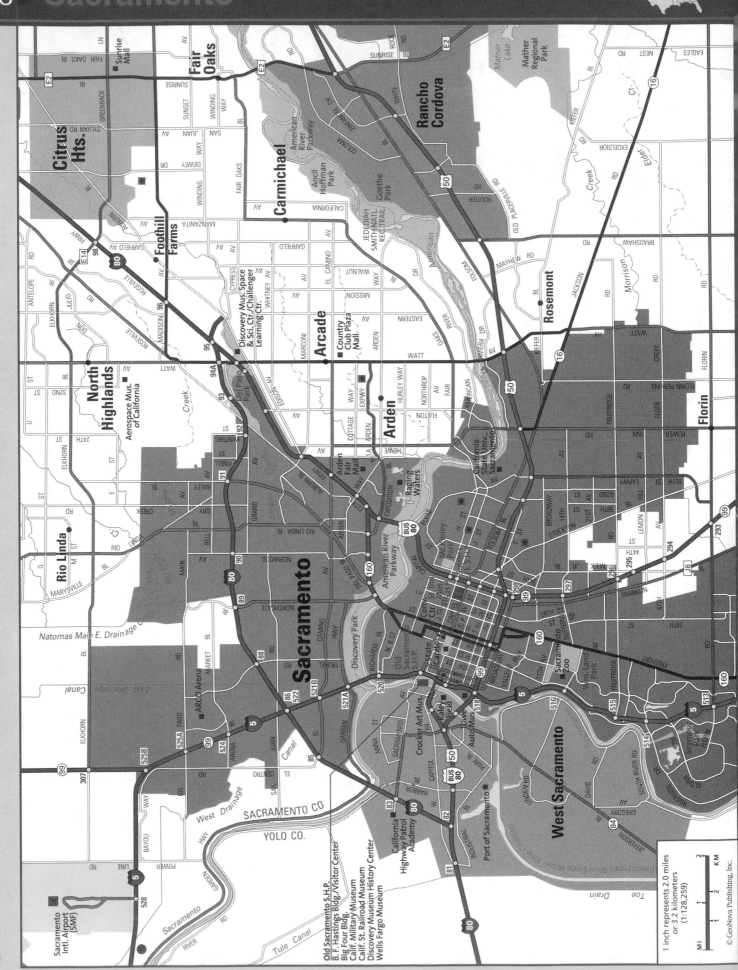

Sacramento

N

Sacramento

Citrus Hts.

Fair Oaks

Carmichael

Rancho Cordova

Foothill Farms

Arcade

Rosemont

North Highlands

Aerospace Mus. of California

Arden

Florin

Rio Linda

Sacramento

West Sacramento

Discovery Mus. Space & Sci. Ctr./Challenger Learning Ctr.

Country Club Plaza Mall

Arden Fair Mall

Raging Waters

California State Univ., Sacramento

ARCO Arena

Discovery Park

Old Sacramento S.H.P.

State Capitol

Crocker Art Mus.

Raley Field

Towe Auto Mus.

Sacramento Zoo

Wm. Land Park

Port of Sacramento

California Highway Patrol Academy

SACRAMENTO CO.
YOLO CO.

Natomas Main E. Drainage Canal

West Drainage

Old Sacramento S.H.P.
B. F. Hastings Bldg./Visitor Center
Big Four Bldg.
Calif. Military Museum
Calif. St. Railroad Museum
Discovery Museum History Center
Wells Fargo Museum

Sacramento Intl. Airport (SMF)

1 inch represents 2.0 miles
or 3.2 kilometers
(1:128,259)

© GeoNova Publishing, Inc.

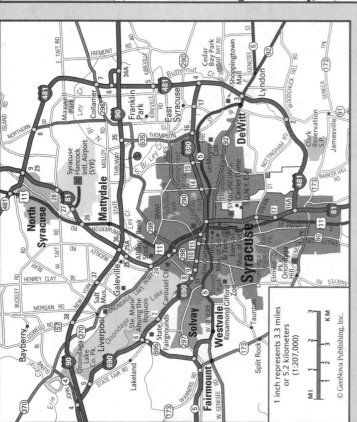

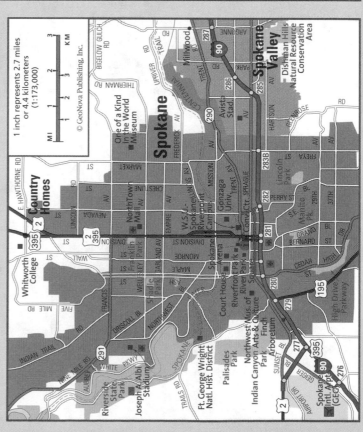

P 50
Utah

P 38
New York

P 51
Washington

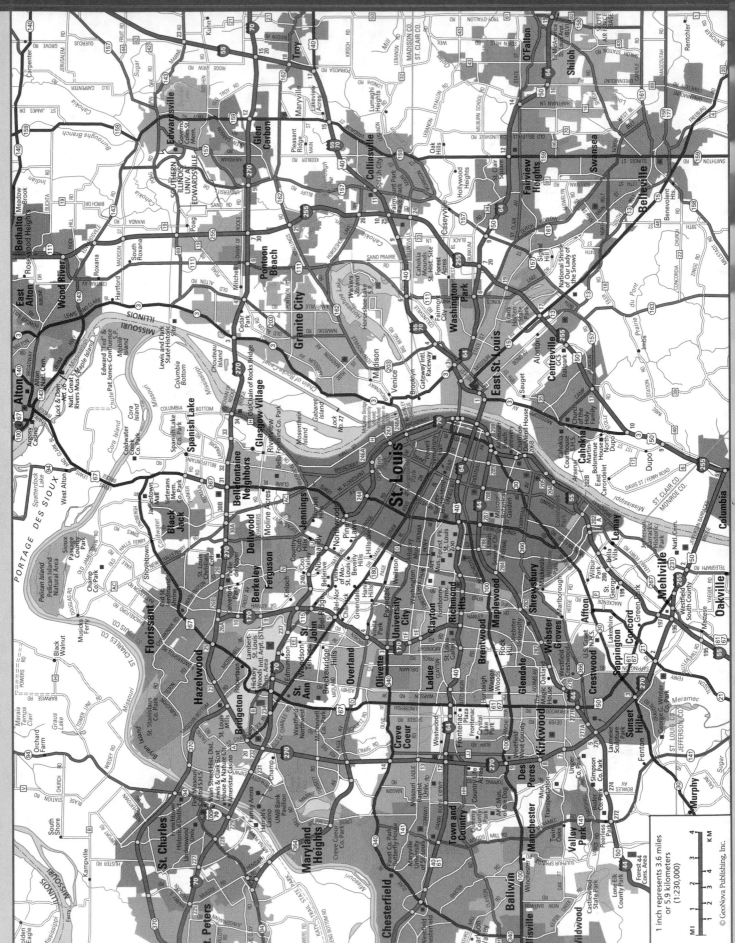

1 inch represents 3.6 miles
or 5.9 kilometers
(1:230,000)

© GeoNova Publishing, Inc.

1 inch represents 3.1 miles
or 5.0 kilometers
(1:195,000)

© GeoNova Publishing, Inc.

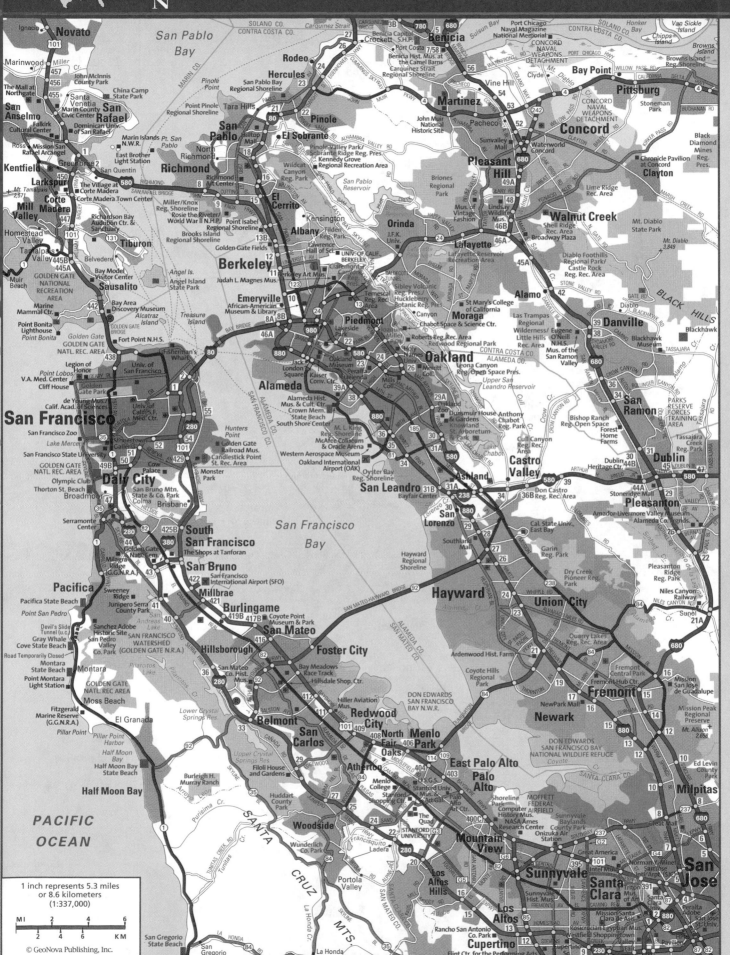

N

Seattle

1 inch represents 5.1 miles
or 8.3 kilometers
(1:325,000)

MI 0 1 2 3 4 5
KM 0 1 2 3 4 5

© GeoNova Publishing, Inc.

Port Ludlow
Foulweather Bluff Preserve
Maxwelton
Glendale
Boeing Tour Center
Everett
Snohomish
19
526
189
Hansville
Whidbey Island
Snohomish Co. Arpt. (PAE)
Mukilteo
Everett Mall
Pioneer Village
Monroe
2
104
Shine
ISLAND CO.
SNOHOMISH CO.
525
5
186
99
96
9
203
JEFFERSON CO.
KITSAP CO.
527
Mill Creek
525
Cathcart
Shine Tidelands S.P.
Port Gamble IND. RES.
182
183
Martha Lake
Lynnwood
Alderwood Mall
522
High Bridge Rd
Port Gamble
Port Gamble Hist. Mus.
Kitsap Mem. S.P.
104
Edmonds
181
Alderwood Manor
9
Maltby
524
Lofall
524
Edmonds Hist. Mus.
26
307
Kingston
104
Mountlake Terrace
Brier
527
Bothell
522
SNOHOMISH CO.
KING CO.
Woodway
177
Kenmore
Woodinville
Port Madison Indian Res.
Indianola
104
Woodinville-Duvall
Duvall
Poulsbo
Shoreline
176
Lake Forest Park
522
23
405
305
Suquamish
175
523
St. Edward State Park
202
KITSAP NAVAL BASE
Old Man House
The Bloedel Reserve
174
20
West Snoqualmie Valley Rd
Novelty Hill Rd
203
Fay Bainbridge S.P.
173
Northgate Mall
Kirkland
908
Redmond
Keyport
Suquamish Mus. & Clearwater Casino
Nordic Heritage Mus.
172
522
Redmond Town Ctr.
305
Naval Undersea Warfare Ctr. & Museum
Woodland Park Zoo
171
Univ. of Wash.
513
Northwest Univ.
Bridal Trails S.P.
Snoqualmie
Brownsville
Chittenden Locks
99
Lake Washington
Marymoor Co. Pk.
305
Rollingbay
Discovery Park
169
Mus. of Hist. Hunts & Ind. Point
Yarrow Point
520
City Univ.
Silverdale
Bainbridge Island
168
Seattle
14
Clyde Hill
Sammamish
303
Wash. Park Arboretum
Medina
13
Tracyton
Bainbridge Island
Seattle Center
Bellevue Square
Bellevue
U.S. NAVAL RES.
Illahee State Park
Elliott Bay
Beaux Arts
Sammamish
310
Bremerton
Puget Sound
90
8
Lake Sammamish State Park
Safeco Field
164
10/11
11
Eastgate
Bremerton Naval Mus.
Fort Ward S.P.
Mercer Island
13
15
Issaquah-Fall City Rd
PUGET SOUND NAVAL SHIPYARD
Manchester S.P.
163
99
Boeing Field/ King County Intl. Arpt. (BFI)
10
Cougar Mtn. Reg. Park
Issaquah
166
Retsil
Manchester Tillicum Village
Newcastle
900
17
90
Gorst
Colby
405
Preston
3
South Colby
Blake Island State Park
Fauntleroy
Westwood Town Ctr.
Museum of Flight
Skyway
22
Port Orchard
Southworth
White Center
509
Renton Hist. Mus.
Renton
TIGER MTN. STATE FOREST
Bethel
160
Vashon Heights
99
Skyway
900
2
4
May Valley Rd
Hobart Rd
18
Long Lake
16
599
Burien
156
Tukwila
518
167
169
Cedar
Vashon
Westfield Southcenter
SeaTac
Normandy Park
152
181
140th AV
Lake Youngs
Olalla
Vashon Island
509
Seattle-Tacoma Intl. Airport (SEA)
5
Tahoma Natl. Cem.
Burley
Ellisport
Kent
515
240th ST
132ND
Purdy
302
Portage
509
99
149
Covington
Maple Valley
Wauna
Burton
Des Moines
516
169
KITSAP CO.
PIERCE CO.
Maury Island
Saltwater State Park
147
167
18
516
Ravensdale
Dockton
Redondo
Lake Sawyer
Rosedale
Tahlequah
Dash Point State Park
Federal Way
Auburn
Emerald Downs
Pacific Raceways
Black Diamond
16
Gig Harbor
Point Defiance Zoo & Aquarium
509
143
181
White River Valley Mus.
Auburn-Black Diamond Rd
Kopachuck State Park
Dalco Passage
The Commons at Federal Way
18
SuperMall
Algona
Muckleshoot Casino
Cumberland
Arletta
Ruston
Rhododendron Species Botanical Garden
99
142
Wild Waves & Enchanted Village
White River Amphitheatre
Green River Gorge State Park
Nolte State Park
Henderson Bay
163
Tacoma
509
Pacific
MUCKLESHOOT INDIAN RES.
169
Wollochet
Fox Island
Tacoma Narrows Bridge
Toll (eastbound only)
Univ. of Puget Sound
Tacoma Dome
141
Milton
161
Sumner
Fox Island
705
167
136
137
Edgewood
Penrose Pt. State Park
Cheney Stadium
Broadway Ctr. Mus. Dist.
16
Fife
PUYALLUP INDIAN RES.
Lake Tapps
McNeil Island
University Place
Fircrest
132
167
Enumclaw

Carr Inlet

Puget Sound

Bainbridge Island

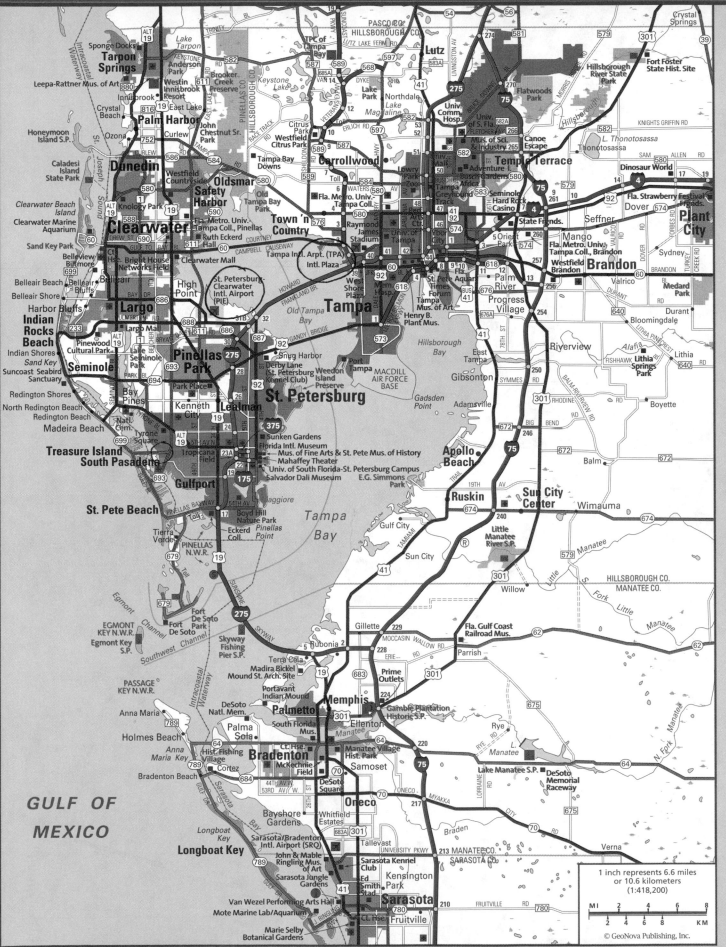

1 inch represents 6.6 miles
or 10.6 kilometers
(1:418,200)

GULF OF MEXICO

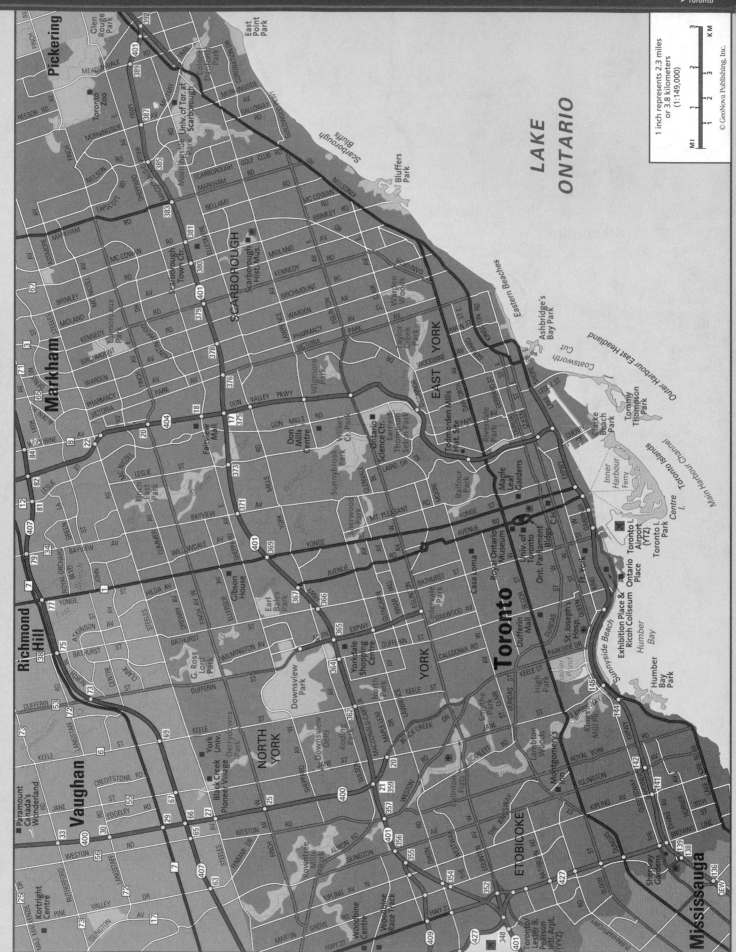

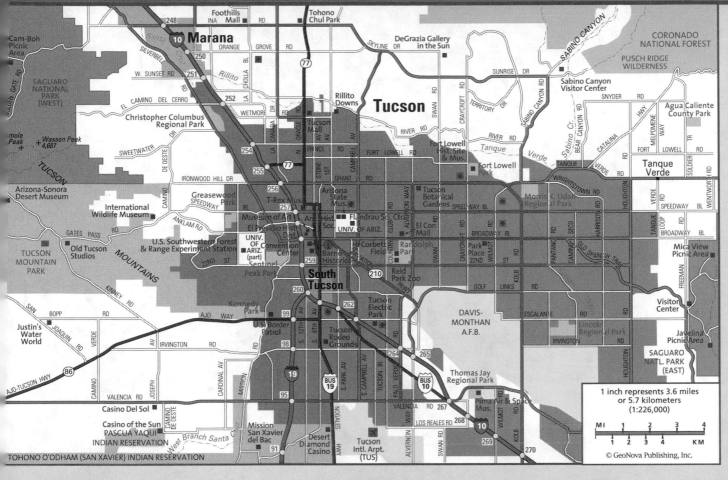

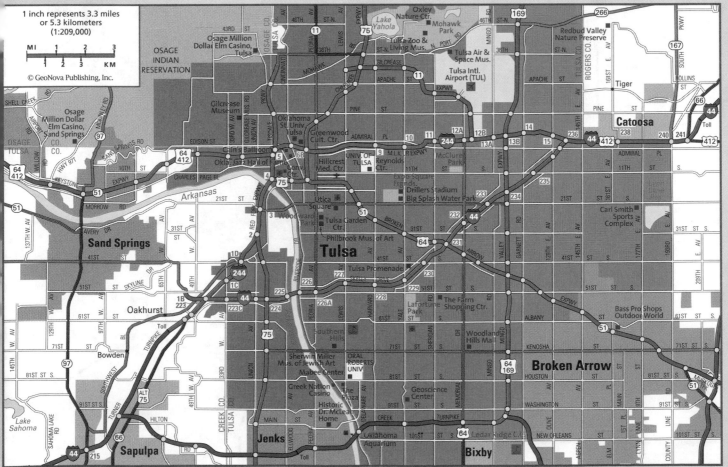

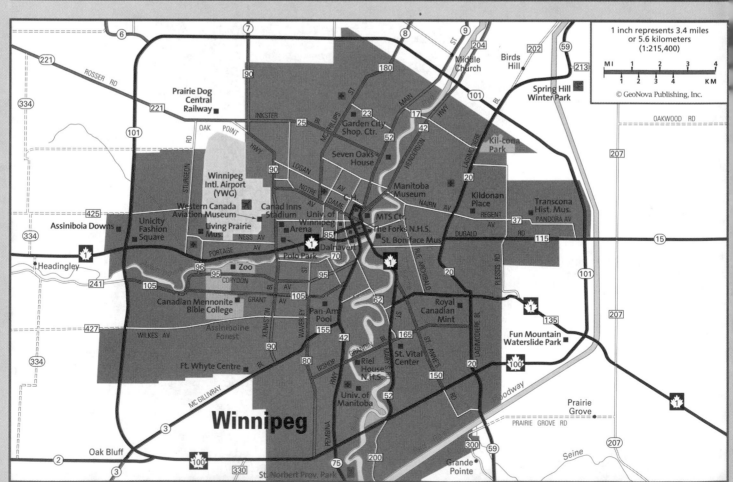

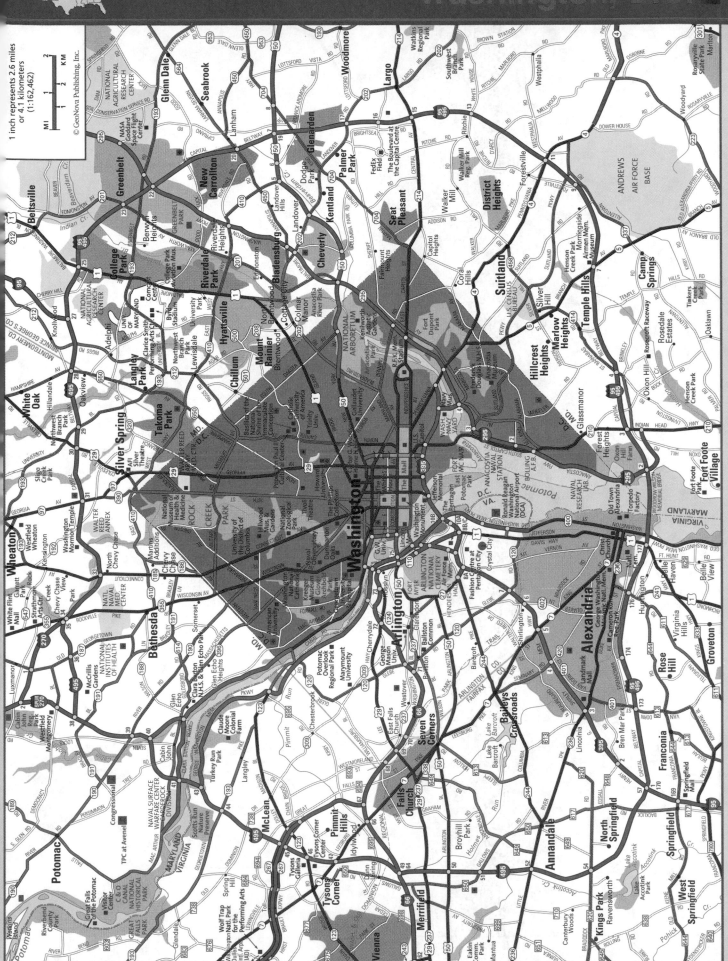

Washington, D.C.

1 inch represents 2.6 miles
or 4.1 kilometers
(1:162,462)

© GeoNova Publishing, Inc.

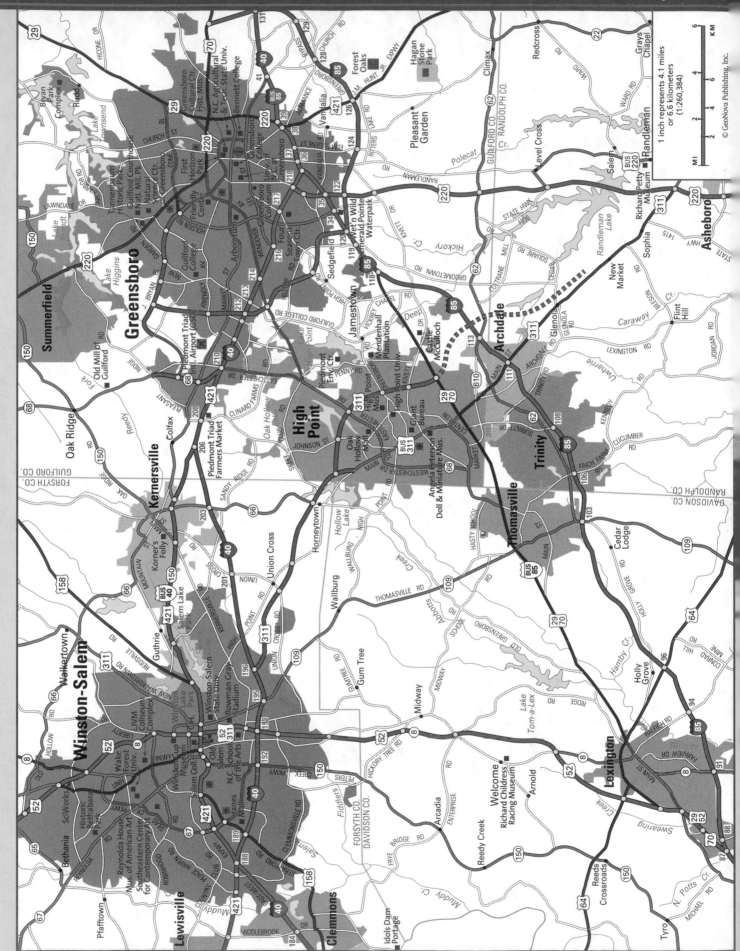

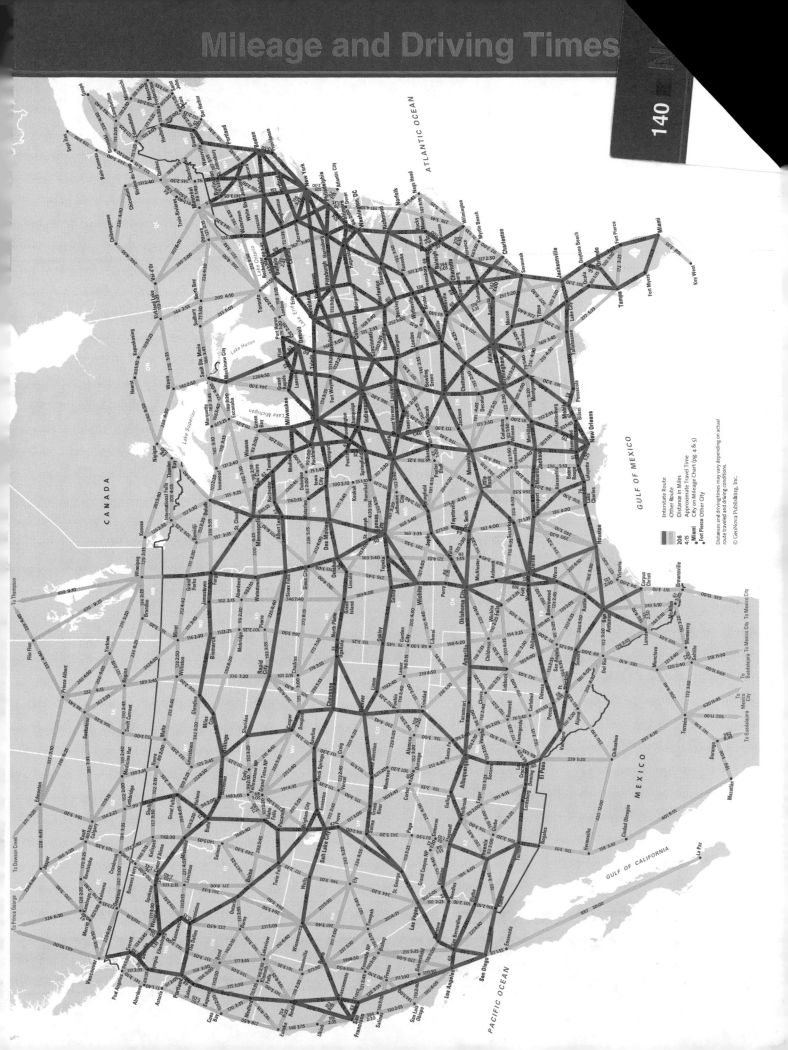

otes